BOBBY JEAN PERRY

M'Deah & Me

A Tale of Two Black Generations

SILVERSMITH
PRESS

Published by Silversmith Press—Houston, Texas
www.silversmithpress.com

Copyright © 2025 Bobby Jean Perry

All rights reserved.

This book, or parts thereof, may not be reproduced in any form or by any means without written permission from the publisher, except for brief passages for purposes of reviews. For more information, contact the publisher at office@publishandgo.com.

The views and opinions expressed herein belong to the author and do not necessarily represent those of the publisher.

ISBN 978-1-967386-06-2 (Softcover Book)
ISBN 978-1-967386-07-9 (eBook)

Dedication

I dedicate this book to our Lord and Savior, Jesus Christ. Through all our lives, He never left nor forsook M'Deah and me. He has been with us ALWAYS! We are forever thankful to Him. He truly is the Light of the world.

Only God gifted me with my beloved birth family—especially M'Deah and my brother Billy to be lights as well. I thank God for the wonderful blessing that these gifts of His brought into my life. He added even more gifts of light in the persons of my husband (Perry), our children (Todd, Scott, Dru), our grandchildren (Khelli, Chris, Bilon), and even our great-granddaughters (Madison, Kennedy). I am immeasurably blessed by the wonderful people that you are—that He has made you to be. Nobody could have a better family. Family are important. These are the people God chose for us to do life with. Whether their role and presence is large or small, they are always family. This can mean differenth things to different people—depending on what your family taught you as their values.

But He didn't stop there! I have been blessed greatly by wonderful in-laws and friends He gave me at every phase of my life—schools, jobs, neighborhoods, churches—to be lights as well. The list is so long that I won't name them. You know who you are, and I am grateful to God for you and for all you added to my life. Because I am so deeply loved by God, He gives me favor with all these and so many other people. All who made me who I am today and who will shape me in the future. Thank you ALL for your love and for your prayers! Thank You, Lord, for my journey Lights—the early and the latter! I'm sure I could say the same for M'Deah too.

Acknowledgment

Riley & Janie Mitchell:
A Proud & Lasting Legacy of /Family,
/Faith, & /Courage
By Eric A. Mitchell, Esq.
Copyright 2012

Table of Contents

Author's Note xi
Introduction xvii

Part 1
The Alabama Years

Chapter One: In the Beginning 1919 3
Chapter Two: Elementary Horrors 8
Chapter Three: The Family Grows 13
Chapter Four: A Church Apology, High School,
    and Big Drama 17
Chapter Five: My Arrival and Back to Chatom 20
Chapter Six: My Childhood in Chatom 25
Chapter Seven: A Father at Last (1945) 31

Part 2
The Minneapolis Years

Chapter Eight: A Brand New Life! 51
Chapter Nine: Why Divorce? 59
Chapter Ten: Harrison Elementary School
    (1947-1951) 67
Chapter Eleven: Buster: Who Is He? 94

Chapter Twelve: Recovery 105
Chapter Thirteen: Home at Last..121
Chapter Fourteen: The Good at Home 141
Chapter Fifteen: Changes and Puberty 160
Chapter Sixteen: More Teen Home Life..............................182
Chapter Seventeen: Cause and Effect.................................198
Chapter Eighteen: Other Changes.......................................218

Part 3
The Henry Years

Chapter Nineteen: My Happy Place 237
Chapter Twenty: Other Family Now....................................257
Chapter Twenty-One: The Big Questions 263
Chapter Twenty-Two: What Happened?............................273
Chapter Twenty-Three: The Big Life Change 292
Chapter Twenty-Four: The Trial.. 302
Chapter Twenty-Five: My View of M'Deah's Siblings 315
Chapter twenty-six: Afterwards 324
Chapter Twenty-Seven: Life After K.C................................ 331

Part 4
After Henry

Chapter Twenty-Eight: M'Deah's Growth 341
Chapter Twenty-Nine: Forms Of Help 343
Chapter Thirty: A New Guy 350
Chapter Thirty-One: A Wedding Comes 362

Part 5
The Denver Years

Chapter Thirty-Two: Now, The Marriage 377
Chapter Thirty-Three: Great Loss 387
Chapter Thirty-Four: My Life Goes On 401
Chapter Thirty-Five: Childbirth #1 407
Chapter Thirty-Six: Our Interim Life 414
Chapter Thirty-Seven: What's Going On
  With M'Deah? 418
Chapter Thirty-eight: Onward and Upward! 436

Author's Note

I'm in my early 80s at the writing of this book, which I do from memories mostly. That's a lot to unpack! From what perspective do I write this book? From the only perspective I have—that of MY collected memories. I remember what I remember, and I forgot what I forgot. That doesn't mean this is a tell-all, even of my known memories. There are some things that I choose to keep private and hidden, for myself and for others. We all know that every family has secrets inconsequential and consequential. Also, some memories make more imprint on the mind than others and are thus more memorable. May you find them interesting.

So, this book is by NO means an exhaustive look at our lives. Why not? Because I don't have exhaustive knowledge of all we have gone through in our family—externally or internally. I don't completely know my own thoughts, feelings, and motivations, and I do NOT know those of my mother (M'Deah) either. Why she made her decisions or how she regarded the decisions others made which impacted her is impossible to know. We didn't discuss them. That's also a sign of our times. M'Deah's generation didn't talk much about life in general nor their lives in particular, and I was taught it was inappropriate for children to ask questions. So, I didn't. Children did NOT get into "grown-folk's business."

"Little pitchers have big ears," was a common slogan as I grew up, so some of what I remember from my childhood are things I simply overheard adults say. That was my learning style, necessarily! We were taught to listen when adults talk—not to miss instructions, and to *really* listen when adults talk to each other. The memories of other friends and family members are not included—I don't know them! I didn't consult with any others. For example, I have no input from any of my family contemporaries—my first cousins. Why not? Some didn't know me that well when I was young. Some take their privacy so seriously that they're not available. Some wouldn't want to participate. None of them lived in the household I grew up in. All of that. Maybe their input will come later for another time. My cousins are sure to remember things in common differently than I do. They may also remember things I've forgotten. That's to be expected. We are not the same person. I appreciate any corrections or additional input they may have for me after this book is written and published. Maybe I'll use it in a future corrected addition. Or not. And I apologize for not consulting them beforehand. I intend no harm or neglect.

M'Deah's generation is no longer available for me to question. I'm sure some of them could have had valuable input or given a perspective I may have missed. But time marches on and they're now gone from the Earth. I waited too late. Later generations will know even less than I do! And for that, I do apologize.

So, dear reader, YOU may want to find out such information about your own family while you still can. I only have what I have, so I write about that. May it be entertaining and educational and add somewhat to your knowledge about our two generations and their times.

M'Deah's was the Greatest Generation, born 1901-1927. Mine was the Silent Generation, born 1928-1945. (It was decades before I learned the name of my own generation!) I encourage you to be a seeker of knowledge about your own family and its generations before it's too late. I do so now to provide a snapshot of our time on Earth—our two generations.

I've found that books generally fall into two categories—entertainment or information. In all cases, they seem to be complete or incomplete. As a writer, I tend to be someone who aims for the complete. I may be slow getting there, but that's my target! Ultimately, I can thus become victim to "paralysis by analysis." That didn't seem the appropriate way to go this time. So, I didn't allow myself to get trapped there—for better or for worse.

Who is M'Deah? It's a name similar to Tyler Perry's "Madea," which I had never heard pronounced that way before the character became so famous. M'Deah is pronounced with two syllables instead of three and with a soft rather than a hard "e" sound. It was a rare but not atypical Southern slave name for a slave mother or for a slave descendant mother. Madea and M'Deah are somewhat alike. They both possess a similar character in that they have hearts of gold and truly care about others. M'Deah is my mother. and learned my uncle Dan's children called their mother 'M'Deah'. I suppose that's where we got it from.

Herein are my CHOSEN collected memories of two redeemed 20th century lives. The memories are mine. The opinions are mine. Where I say anything positive about myself, they are merely reflections of lessons I thankfully learned from various experiences. I don't seek to pin any roses on myself, by any means! M'Deah and I were both women of the 20th century and of the 21st century—just in different parts of them.

This book includes periods when M'Deah and I didn't have a personal relationship with God through Jesus Christ and periods of time when, happily, we did! We lived our lives as best we knew how but had NO idea that we were on a journey to find God. But He did.

Late in life, I learned that every destination involves a journey. I'm forever grateful that our journey reached its rightful destination of LIFE in Christ Jesus—Abundant Life and Eternal Life. We were born free from the sin of slavery. We were born again free from the slavery of sin!

Note: I learned in school that someone's name is to be treated as a proper noun and thus capitalized. I don't regard our spiritual enemy as anyone proper at all and I do NOT capitalize his name: satan.

All scripture verse references are from the NKJV (New King James Version) translation unless indicated otherwise.

Introduction

"It was the best of times; it was the worst of times." Charles Dickens said it well as he opened his book, *A Tale of Two Cities*, about London and Paris around the time of the French Revolution. I use those same words to begin to tell of two black lives in the 20th century. The lives are those of my mother (M'Deah)—and me—in rural Alabama and in urban Minneapolis.

Each of our lives happily reveals that survival is still possible in the worst of times. I pray that gives you some measure of hope too—no matter what kind of times you may face or have faced.

In a visit to my mother in 2000, the Lord told me to write a book. What? It was to be about my mother's life! She'd just had surgery for a needed heart pacemaker, and I went there to assist in her recovery. The Lord showed me the value of the lives that I knew of her generation—her family and her friends. They weren't famous people, but He wanted them known. I was pleasantly and greatly surprised. I decided that I would go on to write the book and did so. Slowly. God had also widened the net to include others of M'Deah's generation—her friends and contemporaries. Unfortunately, the net closed as each departed this life. I had waited too long. As a born-again Christian who now has a relationship with the Living God, He and I do communicate with each other. On His giving side, it's perfect; on my receiving side, not so much. But He is Good! He works with me despite my many faults and defects.

My mother's and my life are not particularly extraordinary lives. They can be said to be as common as dirt. But in some ways, they are VERY extraordinary—like the unicorn! As the 3rd and 4th generations from slavery (I think!), we enjoy ALL the benefits of the Declaration of Independence, of the U.S. Constitution, of its Bill of Rights and other amendments. It's up to us as Americans how we use those benefits. It was many years later that I could understand these were God-given documents for how He wants us to live with one another well as His nation.

M'Deah and I had our share of problems in life. But we also had the gift of Christian values which strengthened and stabilized us. Sadly, I've seen that wasn't always true for later generations, reflected in their life instabilities and choices. Our parents had a strong sense of right and wrong and taught it to us. It was what their parents had taught them and what church and society expected.

Each of us was "born for such a time as this"—in the right time for God's best plan and purpose for us. We can survive AND thrive in our assigned time. We're well able to make the most of it! We have Jesus and His perfect gift of salvation. We get to be born again to rightly fit our time.

Where do our values come from? Whose view and beliefs count most to you? Is it how others view you? Or how YOU view you? The latter, of course! As YOU think, so are you. (Proverbs 23:7) The values of others can only affect you to the extent that you AGREE with them. NONE can compel you to do that. The choice is totally yours. The Bible asks the question in Amos 3:3, "Can two walk together except they be agreed?" "No" is the obvious answer. And we usually agree with the values of those who teach us their values. It begins at home. M'Deah and my values were not unique at all. They were the common fabric of American cultural society of our times. Some of our problems were common to many families as all families have problems; that is not unique. Their uniqueness is reflected in which problems they have or don't have. And how they handle them.

Hindsight is always 20/20. My viewpoint now is quite different than when we were traveling that journey. Perspective makes all the difference! I can appreciate things past which I certainly didn't at the time. Not only can I see more clearly now, but I know that our God was not being random but very purposeful regarding our destination which is salvation in Jesus Christ. And I'm grateful for the whole journey—not just for some parts. All parts served His divine purpose for our lives. And it happens, one step at a time.

PART ONE
The Alabama Years

CHAPTER ONE

In the Beginning 1919

Houston Lawrence and Euberta (Houston) Lawrence were my mother's parents. They were married in 1911. Their kids called them Papa and Mama. The grandkids called them Papa and Big Mama. Papa's family was small. The only sibling I knew he had was his sister, Mary. I knew nothing of their parents and doubt I ever met them at all. I do remember hearing that they were possibly slaves brought from the Caribbean. On the other hand, Big Mama, had nine siblings: Virginia, Arthur, Corinne, Irene, Daisy, Jerry, (Euberta), Lloyd, Susie, Eugene. For years, I only knew Daisy, and in my teen years I got to be acquainted with Jerry, Lloyd, and Eugene when they visited us sparingly and separately. I heard of the twins, Corine and Irene for reasons I'll mention later. I knew nothing of their parents either.

My mother was born at home on August 7, 1919, as Drussie Juanita Lawrence in Mt. Sterling, Alabama. Her mother was attended by a midwife, probably. I don't know who else may have been present other than Euberta's sister, Daisy. When she delivered that day, her baby girl seemed healthy at first, but she

CHAPTER ONE

did not live. The midwife realized there was a second baby inside her womb and worked quickly to get the baby out. The second was also a baby girl—my mother—but she was frail and didn't seem as healthy as the first baby. Surely, she would soon die too. So, to avoid any further grief for my grandmother, my mother was immediately given away! To whom? To Big Mama's childless sister, Daisy. She was to keep the baby until this baby died too.

I have no idea how this decision was made. My grandmother had NO child to show for her nine-month pregnancy. To me, that's certainly the worst kind of grief.

My mother was the fourth of six children. Born already were Carrie, Dan, and George. Arliece and Eloise would come later.

Rather than dying, my mother lived and thrived under Aunt Daisy's care! She said that she remembered being taken to visit her birth family occasionally so she would have other children to play with. After each visit, when it was time to go home, she would always cry. Finally, when my mother was age four or five, she begged to remain and was allowed to do so. My mother was so happy to join her family of origin! However, the upcoming years were not always easy for her. In many ways, her siblings regarded her as a perpetual outsider, different and a little wild or independent. Maybe that came from being raised at first as an only child by Aunt Daisy. She usually spoke her mind freely. This lasted for most of her life. I don't know where this trait came from. Except that my mother was never a conformist but thought for herself. At the same time, she was the most loving person I ever met. She loved deeply and wanted to be deeply loved in return. Her loving ways endeared her to MANY non-family members who appreciated and reciprocated that love. And maybe her birth family did too.

M'Deah's Formative Years

M'Deah's cultural formative years could not have been easy. My mother lived during the Jim Crow era in Alabama. It was a time of TRUE racial oppression in the South, the accepted and legal norm. *Systemic racism is legal racism?* Yes. If it's not legal racism, it's not systemic racism. And that's the life she knew. But, like many of and before her time, she was NOT a "victim" of her circumstances. With a strong positive attitude, her family made a GOOD life for themselves! Thanks to their belief in God, they had an essential called HOPE that carried them though many of life's storms. That generation took life's lemons and made lemonade by simply believing in themselves because they believed in GOD. That is the vital missing ingredient for many. Compare them to the more recent generations often filled with hopelessness because people give in to feelings and beliefs of helplessness, depression, suicide, and a lack of genuine care for

CHAPTER ONE

the value of life—their own and others. The default is PC, political correctness—blind agreement and consensus with political and popular culture. However, belief in God is ESSENTIAL in a moral, civil life! Our society was once TAUGHT belief in God at home, and it was reinforced in church and in both public and private schools. It was the societal NORM then.

It was even recognized as such by Alexis de Tocqueville—the French aristocrat, diplomat, political scientist, political philosopher, and historian who toured the new America and wrote the book, *"Democracy in America"* in 1835, which was one of the most influential books of the 19th century. One of his quotes is, "Despotism may be able to do without religion, but democracy cannot." Additionally, he is cited for this quote;

> "Not until I went into the churches of America and heard her pulpits flame with righteousness did, I understand the greatness and genius of America. America is great because America is good. If America ever ceases to be good America will cease to be great."

This quote's origin is attributed to having been written by Andrew Reed and James Matheson, English ministers who wrote about their travels to the U.S. in the 1830s. "America will be great if America is good. If not, her greatness will vanish away like a morning cloud," reads their account, published in 1835. Either way, both quotes ring true regarding our American existence and success.

Back then and later, if an American's culture did not include moral teaching and atmosphere in their homes, they got it in school. ALL knew the basics of John 3:16, the 23rd Psalm, the Lord's prayer, the Golden Rule, and the Ten Commandments. Or, at least, they knew ABOUT them. Society had a common moral culture. And it was of great benefit to ALL Today's culture stands in great contrast to this. Now, each does what is right in THEIR own eyes, believing in "MY" truth and maybe "YOUR" truth and not "THE" Truth. (John 17:17) We suffer greatly for it. Entire books could be written on this subject and probably have been. But not this one!

At one point in M'Deah's childhood in Mt. Sterling, some adverse racial circumstances required they leave to start all over again. They were actually ordered out of town, so her family packed up and moved to another small town—Chatom, Alabama.

CHAPTER TWO

Elementary Horrors

It was in the 1930's when M'Deah was elementary school age that there were a couple of instances that marked her life and shaped her perspective of the world.

The Accident

One night, there was a terrible auto accident on the highway leading into the rural town of Chatom, Alabama where they lived. Two buses and many cars were involved. All who heard the loud crash in the area immediately left their farms and went to the scene to help—black and white. One vehicle was a bus returning white passengers home from a church revival out of town. The other vehicle was a bus of slave descendants returning home from another church revival elsewhere. There was wreckage all over the highway and on nearby fields with many fatalities and injuries.

The injured white people were given medical care by those whites who arrived on the scene. Many whites were outraged that blacks were present in the other bus and blamed them for the wreck. "How dare the blacks have an accident that hurt white people?

Don't they know their 'place?'" The injured blacks were not treated. Some whites—accident survivors or nearby neighbors—made a collective decision to finish them off. Death by clubbing helpless, injured black people was the result. The fit black neighbor people present who were observing and aiding in rescue were helpless to do anything about what was going on.

My mother's family was part of the rescue efforts. They heard a white mother yell out for her missing baby. All who were able searched the area. Apparently, the baby had been tossed from the bus as it crashed. Now, the baby couldn't be found, and the mother was near hysteria. Everyone on the scene was asked to look for the baby. But it was Big Mama who found the baby and returned her safely to the mother. The white people were all thankful that the baby had been safely recovered. It never occurred to Big Mama to harm the baby or "punish" the white people for the wreck. That was unthinkable, even after the murder of the blacks they had just witnessed. Big Mama didn't blame the baby. She thought about how she would want HER baby to be treated.

I never forgot my mother's telling of this story. Her attitude was the same as that of Big Mama and the other black people present at the scene of the accident—of course you would do right by the baby! It was Godly to do so. It is what church taught and believed. It was a common American value to take

CHAPTER TWO

care of your neighbor back then—unless racism got in the way. I may not have all the details but one thing I do know, my family was not taught to hate.

My mother also never forgot the contrast. Whites had murdered the injured slave descendants. Yet her mother had rescued and returned the white baby unharmed. Slave descendants didn't generally see racial inequality as an excuse to do harm to others. Although it was told anecdotally, the lesson was NOT lost on me. Even when others do wrong, YOU do right. YOU are not the avenger of others' wrongs. Wow. I never forgot it. And that's just the way our family was raised. Anything else was quite unthinkable. All life was valuable—it came from God. I was never taught racism by anyone in my family, nor was it ever modeled before me. Never. Consequently, I never taught it to my children either. I learned in my later teen years that there were many we knew of as "reverse racists"—black racists against whites. MANY! They had been fed the poison of hate and it made them bitter. Did they have reasons to hate white people? Usually. But it didn't help anyone—at all and it still doesn't. One may have a REASON to hate; but you NEVER have the "right" to hate. What does hatred profit? Absolutely nothing good.

I often wondered about the courage of those living during slavery and Jim Crow. How did they hang on and retain any sense of humanity? They certainly did NOT live their lives as victims who had no hope! Far from it! They did marvelous, even miraculous, things although they began from slavery with absolutely nothing. After the Civil War, they were no longer slaves but were without any economic or other means for survival or thriving. Yet, they did. I know that's true from my own family history—maternal and paternal. It's easy to see how some may have stayed on the plantations and worked for meager salaries, if any. Most of them struck out to make their way in the world. And, if possible, to seek family members who had been sold away from them—usually unsuccessfully. Amazing.

It's mind-blowing to me how these emancipated slaves and their children had NOTHING yet were able to accomplish so much in such hostile social environments. They didn't cry "victim" but took personal responsibility to use what God gave them to improve and live their lives. So much was accomplished by using their brain and brawn. Did they have help? Yes, sometimes. Not all whites were evil, of course. Some whites who came from the North were carpetbaggers, taking advantage of the social disorder for their own benefit. Thank God for the many brave young white ladies who flooded the South after the Civil War to teach ex-slaves to read, write, and do 'rithmetic! It was a gift my people used well to better their lives. Others helped too. I'm glad I learned that in ALL people groups, the whole lot are not to be judged as good or evil. As Martin Luther King, Jr. said: it's about the content of one's character and not the color of their skin. (Or any other distinction.) And that applies to each individual. And not to their people group,

The Watermelon Incident

It was a real treat for farm children to break open and eat a watermelon on a hot summer day. One day, my mother and her siblings were doing so as she sat on a log in the field. She was wearing a typical farm outfit—a pair of overalls. Somehow a snake got underneath the overall straps and crawled across her shoulders. When she felt the slithering under her strap across her shoulders, she froze in absolute terror. One of her brothers saw and came to her rescue. He got rid of that snake, but the damage had been done. From that time on, my mother wanted no one to ever hug her or touch her shoulders because it brought back that terrible memory. Even though she loved deeply, for all the rest of her life she was just not a hugger.

CHAPTER THREE
The Family Grows

Big Mama's siblings included a set of twin girls: Irene and Corine. When one sister, Corine, died leaving behind six children, Papa and Big Mama took them in. Their own family of six children was suddenly a family of twelve children! I don't know M'Deah's age then, but "Big Mama" certainly had earned that title! Unthinkable? Not to them. It's just what family did during those times. What would happen to these motherless children today? Welfare? It didn't exist then for the descendants of slaves in the South. Homelessness? Unthinkable as long as they had family—or even good neighbors. Those who had been slaves knew the value of family and of helping one another.

Once when things were tight financially, Big Mama prayed for God's help. She had a dream one night with the answer. In it, her deceased sister told her of money she had left for her children's care under a pile of quilts that were stored away. When my grandmother looked there, she found money that was an on-time answer to prayer! My mother never forgot that. It was an invaluable lesson for her to trust

God in her hard times too—and she certainly got the opportunity to do so years later.

Large families were common then. Queen Victoria of the British Empire was the mother of nine children. Extra slave children enriched their masters and were valuable later in families as extra working hands. Where was birth control then? Pretty much non-existent. But how do you pay for the care of so many children after slavery? Just trust God. And work hard. That's all they knew to do. That's all that had worked for them for all their history in the USA and before. And it's still true today—one of the lessons our history can teach us. Trusting God and being responsible works!

The Great Depression (1929-1939)

Blessed were those who had their own farm and were able to grow their own food! During the Great Depression, there were no jobs to be had. My mother's parents were both working elementary teachers with little, deferred, or no salary. The state didn't provide money for higher education for "the coloreds"—a polite term used instead of the usual "nigger."

Papa later became a school principal—very rare for those times. It was a private black high school 12 miles away from Chatom.in Koenton, Alabama. Each of M'Deah's siblings graduated from this high school, I think. Back then, having a high school diploma was seen as the social and educational equivalent of a college education in later times. During segregation, the state of Alabama didn't provide high school education for "niggers." During the Great Depression, they didn't even PAY salaries to black schoolteachers at times, citing there was only enough money available to pay white teachers. The black teachers got partial pay or promises of being paid later.

My Papa valued education highly. He used to tell me, his elementary-school-aged granddaughter, that it was so valuable because once knowledge was in your head, it could never be taken from you. That is so true. He valued education more than he valued land, which could be taken from you.

So, how did M'Deah's family survive? Because they never saw themselves as victims, they were prepared through hard work and savings. They had already bought a small farm on a few acres to raise their children and their own vegetables and meats. They only had to go to the Chatom General Store for things like flour and sugar. As a community, parents would send to the school whatever they could spare from their farms for the teacher. Blessed are those who have means of providing for their own survival and have some left to help others less fortunate I never forgot that.

At one time, Papa had owned a much larger farm in Mt. Sterling. I don't remember all the details of what my mother said, but Jim Crow whites manipulated all that land away from him. She said that they

CHAPTER THREE

outright stole it from them. One of the ways they used to do this was by NOT sending these owners a bill for their property taxes. Then when the bill wasn't paid, their land would go up for sale for non-payment of taxes. Then it was available for auction and could be purchased by whites for pretty much the price of the overdue taxes alone. Not very nice. But it happened a lot. The history books of that era are filled with stories of all the ways this happened.

At one time, my paternal grandfather, Riley Mitchell in Koenton, Alabama, and his brother were among the largest black landowners in Alabama. But the land was stolen from them as well over the years. Riley Mitchell became a barber.

CHAPTER FOUR
A Church Apology, High School, and Big Drama

A Church Apology

My rambunctious independent-minded mother was not like her siblings. In rural Alabama, there was nothing social for slave descendants to do for entertainment. Nothing. M'Deah's Baptist church upbringing was very strict and legalistic. Members were not allowed to go to movies, play cards, and so much more. It was all seen as "frolicking" and forbidden. It was a sin to have fun—certainly not as the "world" did. But my teenage mother went to a "juke-joint" once to listen to the jukebox and dance to the popular music of the day. After all, it was the Big Band era! But that was a DEFINITE no-no for her as a strict Baptist congregation member. When it was discovered, she was required to stand before the church and apologize in repentance for her sinful behavior. Knowing the consequences, she still REFUSED to do so. Why? She said that children of the pastor and the church deacons had also been at the "juke-joint" with her and yet THEY were not required to apologize. So, why should SHE? It just wasn't fair or right. M'Deah was tough in her youth but usually not very self-assertive. She was not coarse or lewd either but always a lady. Her parents stood by her and agreed that if one had to apologize, then all had to apologize. Well, she was "put out" of the church—excommunicated. What was she to do? My mother got her parents' permission to join the C.M.E. church—the Colored Methodist Episcopal church. She never looked back.

High School

My parents met in high school. My paternal grandfather, Riley Mitchell, donated some of his land for a black high school in the county. It was necessarily private because the state of Alabama didn't provide for public high school for black students then. Papa was hired later to be the school principal. Papa highly valued education and wanted all his children to be able to get a high school education. I know M'Deah and her younger sister, Eloise, were students and graduates there. I don't know which other of their siblings attended. M'Deah graduated at age 16 and I have her diploma, signed by her father.

I have since learned that Chatom was founded in 1904 and has a current population of 1,200. It was certainly smaller in M'Deah's youth. It was 12 miles south from Koenton, too far to walk to and from school daily so they were somewhat boarded at school and also stayed with the Mitchell family. M'Deah met Riley Mitchell, Jr. there and Eloise met

Sears (Buster) Mitchell there. Two brothers ended up marrying two sisters. The Mitchells had 12 children, I thought, but later learned they had 14!

While boarding at the school, students were introduced to a new food called "corn flakes" that they liked. One evening, still feeling hungry, several students decided to sneak into the kitchen and eat some corn flakes. They found the opened box but didn't dare light a lantern or they'd surely be caught. So, they ate in the dark, however, the texture sometimes seemed strange from what they remembered. They found out why the next day. There was an uproar from staff about the nearly empty corn flakes box. Inside were a few corn flakes and several rat turds deposited in the opened box! I don't know about other students, but M'Deah was sickened at the thought of having eaten rat turds. She vowed then and there to never eat another corn flake. And she didn't!

Big Drama

When she was sixteen and graduated from high school, my mother made another daring move. She ran away and got married! I don't know why she did such a brazenly courageous thing. I don't even know who he was. Papa went after her to retrieve her and had the marriage annulled. That was marriage number one.

CHAPTER FIVE

My Arrival and Back to Chatom

My parents were married in Iowa. At that time, my father was in the Army as a heavy-duty equipment operator. He was stationed state-side. My mother had a schoolteacher's certificate and a beautician's license by then, but she did many other things as well.

My father was stationed in Joliet, Illinois where his sister, Mary Jane, lived with her husband, Frank Washington. Happily, my mother became pregnant with me then. Decades later, when I was in my sixties, I asked her more about my birth. She said she believed she became pregnant after buying and using a very popular ladies' scent of the time. She still had two bottles that she kept when she had moved later from Chatom to Minneapolis, a bottle of talcum powder and a bottle of cologne. She never used them completely and I now have them. The scent remains! Perhaps, they were souvenirs of happier times for her. The bottles are cobalt blue, and the product is named Evening In Paris. It's a beautiful flowery scent.

I was born on February 14, 1941, in the home of Aunt Mary Jane and Uncle Frank. I was a Valentine's Day present for my family. Back then, Valentine's

Day was nowhere near the celebratory occasion it became years later. I was the firstborn to my parents who were in their early 20s. Each of them was born and raised in rural Alabama, but I was born "up North." Decades later, when I asked my mother about my birth, I learned for the first time that she had NOT been attended by a doctor or a midwife. The next-door neighbors had a teenage daughter who had a baby the year before—at age 14. Now at 15, this teen-age girl was my mother's birth attendant! She was to be the source of expertise help for M'Deah. The doctor came to the home later to check me over and to get information for the birth certificate. Years later, I learned that M'Deah's intent was that the birth certificate list my name as "Bobby Gene Mitchell." She had wanted a boy so badly that this was the only name she had selected for the baby, and she stuck with it. But someone filled it out as "Bobby *Jean* Mitchell" for which I am grateful! And, no, it was not an easy experience for my mother. And, yes, home births were often still typical for that time. Thank God, all went well even though it was difficult. Of course, my childless Aunt Mary Jane was there as well. She and her husband became my Godparents.

    I don't know what M'Deah's early adult years were like. I'm sure there was joy. I'm also sure there was sorrow. Those happen in EVERY life! It was years before I even learned of some pieces of it. I do know

CHAPTER FIVE

that she was a very hard-working woman, interested in the continued progression of her family. That's how she was raised; it was just as her previous generations had been raised. Onward and upward! And you put your back and your mind to it.

Some ten months after I was born, World War II began with the bombing of Pearl Harbor on December 7, 1941. Previously, the U.S. tried NOT to get entangled by the war, but it was no longer possible. The Japanese monarchy had seen to that with their sneak attack. Numerous lives changed as a result—American lives, Japanese lives, and many others as well. That also included new-born lives—like mine.

At the time, President Franklin Delano Roosevelt and his wife, Eleanor, were popular with slave descendants and with most Americans of all demographics. Prior to his presidency, the descendants of slaves primarily voted Republican. They were grateful for the Republican president who brought about their freedom, Abraham Lincoln. At this time though, they began to mostly vote as Democrats because they were thankful for the Democrat president who had freed them from the Great Depression and his wife, Eleanor, who often fought on their behalf. This was to last for many decades. Democrats were always the party of slavery, the anti-black Ku Klux Klan and Jim Crow laws, etc. Now, blacks accepted them, even after Democrat politicians and policies continued to be clearly contrary to their welfare. They had also forgotten the history of the Democrat party and set themselves up for manipulation and deception that still exists today.

Back To Chatom

Before I was a year old, my mother returned to the little town where her parents lived, Chatom, Alabama. She had always been a hard worker and a woman with ambitious dreams and plans. There she worked hard enough to have her own beauty shop. She saved my father's monthly spousal allotment checks from the military and used them to buy a small farm. I remember we had cows, chickens, pigs, and crops. As a growing toddler, I dreamed of the day when I could finally milk the cows! One of my chores, which I relished, was to help gather eggs from the henhouse. It was a good life that I remember fondly.

Another favorite chore of mine was to pump the dasher on our wooden butter churn. I assisted in doing this chore and I loved it. I felt very responsible and important. It was like magic to watch cream turn into butter the whole family could use. I looked forward to doing it by myself when I got older. Years later as an adult, I bought myself a wooden butter churn at Cracker Barrel. But I never explored how to properly use it, so I didn't.

Before M'Deah bought the farm, we lived with Papa and Big Mama. It was a most happy life, a typical rural country life of that day. It was very much

CHAPTER FIVE

like the pioneer days I watched on TV years later. I was fascinated by the TV show, "Little House On the Prairie," because of its many similarities to the bucolic farm life that I experienced in Chatom.

CHAPTER SIX

My Childhood in Chatom

Big Mama was an elementary school teacher, and Papa was a teacher too, known as Professor Lawrence, a title often bestowed on principals of secondary education. As I said, he became the principal at the black high school built on the land donated by my paternal grandfather, Riley Mitchell. Both sets of grandparents valued education greatly and had a love for learning. From an early age Papa instilled in me the value and importance of books. (Papa was born in 1885 and passed in 1958, Big Mama was born in 1888 and passed in 1950.)

The Stove

I marveled at how Big Mama and M'Deah cooked so well on a wood-burning, cast iron stove. I still don't know how they did it! But I remember well the delicious smell of their tea cakes. It was a sugar cookie with lots of freshly-ground nutmeg. Indescribably delicious! Everything that was produced in those little farmhouse kitchens was delicious! And unknown to me at the time, it was very healthy. My grandmother and M'Deah were excellent cooks. I remember fondly

CHAPTER SIX

their beans and greens, cornbread and biscuits, fried chicken and fried pork chops, grits and bacon—and so much more! And they were excellent bakers: tea cakes, coconut cake, pecan pie, lemon meringue pie, etc. How they could bake their wonderful biscuits and my favorite tea cakes with no way to really regulate the fire's temperature, I'll never know or experience. But they did that and more! Big Mama taught all her girls to cook, of course.

The Washpot

My grandparents also had a big black cast-iron washpot for the laundry. I remember seeing it resting on the bed of a wood fire in the backyard. Clothes were pushed down and agitated with a big wooden paddle in a hot water bath of home-made soap. Afterwards, the washed clothes were hung on the clothesline where they flapped in the wind as they dried. This process was effective, and the whites stayed really bright too! Then the clothes would be ironed with hand irons heated on the stove or at the fireplace. The cleaned laundry was crisp and without wrinkles. The simple "technology" they had worked! Years later, M'Deah bought a small painting of such a scene. I always liked it because it brought back a pleasant childhood memory. I now have that painting today and two hand irons that belonged to M'Deah as well!

Going To Town

Trips to town were always memorable for one reason or another. One afternoon, as a toddler, I was walking down the highway with M'Deah and Big Mama. I was barefoot and crying because my bare feet were burning on the highway asphalt on this hot summer day. Big Mama relieved my misery, carrying me for a while and then requiring me to wear my shoes. M'Deah must have been pregnant then. I remember seeing a big yellow school bus full of white kids drive by. It was so intriguing to me. Black kids had no such school buses.

On another trip to town, I was the passenger in a pick-up truck. The driver was going a little too fast when he made a right turn from the highway into town, and somehow the truck accidentally turned over into the ditch! I was terrified! This was decades before the existence of car seatbelts. Thankfully I was okay physically, but that terror lasted into my teen years. I wasn't happy about car travel after that for a long time but accepted it as just a necessary part of life.

I don't remember why we were going to town that day. It was probably a usual trip to the general store for needed supplies like sugar and flour. I remember particularly that the flour and sugar came in big sacks with lovely prints which were used for clothing. M'Deah made my flour sack panties that I wore. She used the family's treadle sewing machine

CHAPTER SIX

which was operated by your foot and not by electricity. We could have been traveling to pick up the mail at the post office or maybe it was for a trip to the bank. Most of my family had a savings account there. I remember because they opened a new account and gave me a clear Chatom Bank glass savings bank to store my cash that I got for birthdays, etc. It was small—maybe six inches tall—and had a key. I added money to it as I could and was very proud of it. I kept it for over 25 years before it was stolen from me years later in D.C. I was sorry for its loss. That bank was my last link to a bucolic life in Chatom.

The Big Storm

Sometimes very bad storms would occur. On one such time, I was standing at the front door of the house with Papa. There was lots of thunder and lightning going on and I was fascinated. I had no fear because I was holding onto Papa's hand. That is, until a great bolt of lightning struck the big hickory nut tree in the yard! The tree split open and fell. And I went screaming in terror and hid under the kitchen table. Thankfully, Papa came and rescued me. He convinced me to come out, put his arm around me, and calmly walked me back to the front door with him. He spoke gentle words that settled my fears, telling me that the storm was all natural, would not hurt me, and that I was safe with him. Of course, I believed him and was never afraid of storms again.

It's amazingly powerful what a single moment like that can do for your fears for the rest of your life, when a loved one diminishes the danger. Amazing. I later encountered a few adults who were deathly terrified of storms. And I was grateful to have had this different experience. Thanks, Papa!

Barbed Wire

Like any other child, I too was naturally curious. In one of my explorations, on the farm I somehow got into close contact with a roll of barbed wire, which was necessary equipment for farm life. I was the worst for the encounter, and badly cut my left knee. Country home remedies were used to stop the bleeding and prevent infection. I remember fireplace soot and cobwebs. They were effective home remedies. I didn't have an infection, but I was left with a scar for decades afterwards. The good outcome of this adventure was that I never did that again! I was fully convinced that it was too dangerously painful! I remember that Papa was again right there for me at the time, being such a comfort.

The New Addition (1943)

My brother was born in August 1943 on M'Deah's birthday and named after his two grandfathers, Houston and Riley: Houston Riley Mitchell. Like me, he was born at home, but at the home of Papa and Big Mama. I do remember that Big Mama was on the

CHAPTER SIX

scene, but I don't remember who else, except the white doctor. How do I remember? I was present! Having no one else to babysit me, I was in the room sitting in my highchair, when he was born. It is one of my earliest memories. And no wonder! I recalled my mother screaming, her feet and legs were elevated on a trunk in the bed, and out came this little funny-looking red thing that cried, and I was told it was my baby brother. He was nicknamed later, "Billy, the Kid" by M'Deah's sister Arliece (our Auntie) and her husband (Uncle Robert). It was later shortened to "Billy." We were Bobby and Billy. I don't remember Billy as a baby, only as a toddler. Later, he became my dearly beloved brother in fact and in my eyes. I don't think I was a very good big sister in our early years. I mostly assumed Billy was my contemporary.

CHAPTER SEVEN
A Father at Last (1945)

When the war ended, M'Deah still had ration stamps left. But, happily, they were no longer needed. The war and rationing were over. I still have that ration book today.

After the war, it was time to rebuild our countries, lives, and families. The Greatest Generation had survived the Great Depression and WWII. Both were HORRIBLE, but most had survived. They knew HOW to survive. I would say they were a very tough group because they HAD to be. And they looked to God and to each other for help—that was their very valuable heritage and legacy.

I have no remembrance of my father coming to visit us in Chatom on his furloughs. Surely, he did, or my brother wouldn't have been conceived! But with the end of the war, my father returned home to the farm—I simply don't have any memories of him before that. I had heard of him spoken of in the third person only, "Your Father..." So that's how I thought of him. I knew he was my father, but I didn't think of him as "my" anything. We didn't have that kind of relationship yet. I don't think there had been enough time or contact for that.

CHAPTER SEVEN

The Jeep

My father had bought one of the Jeeps from the Army surplus that was sold to the discharged soldiers. It had attachments for plowing and other farm work. The Jeep was also great for trips on the horrible unpaved and sometimes muddy red rural roads. He used it for trips we took to visit his parents in Koenton, Alabama: Riley and Janie Mitchell. At some point, the roads we traveled became very rough—lots of potholes. In the rain, the potholes/ruts became worse, and the trip became very hazardous! Jeeps were known to sometimes topple over. But ours never did. These were scary but happy trips. When it rained, there was a top to attach but you still got wet! I don't remember my father ever mentioning anything of his Army experiences.

The Clay

I remember one such trip, although it probably occurred more than once. My other grandmother, Miss Janie, and I were at a beautiful little clearwater creek on their land. She was showing me how to gather something wet from the creek bottom with our bare hands. It was soft and very white. She called it 'clay', as she ate some before giving me some to eat. It was soft and neither pleasant nor unpleasant—just bland. But I liked it! I didn't know then, but read years later, that it was sometimes eaten as a survival food by slaves and then by freed slaves when necessary. It provided no nutrition but stopped the discomfort of hunger pangs when they lacked food. And their descendants ate it as a dainty—as Miss Janie and I did that day. Unable to get it "up North," their descendants sometimes used Argo corn starch as a substitute for it—especially women in pregnancy for whom it became a craving. Some traditions are strange! I remember my aunt Eloise sometimes ate it when she was pregnant. I never did. Eating clay for me was a once in a lifetime event. I still remember that the water of the little creek was crystal clear and maybe 2 feet deep. It was another new experience for me to look through the clear cold water and see the small stones on the creek bed. It wasn't muddy at all. I had my feet at the edge of the clear rushing creek. My grandmother didn't allow me to come in too far

Great-Grandma

Miss Janie's blind mother, "Miss Georgiana," also lived with them. She was my great-grandmother. Miss Georgiana was the child of a slave woman and her master. I learned decades later from an e-book written by my somewhat-cousin, Eric Mitchell, which Ruby discovered and told me about. Georgiana's slave mother was beaten after she gave birth. Why? The child's father was obviously a white man. Whose fault could that be? Why the slave's fault, of course. Georgiana, born in 1850, had sometimes been used as a companion/playmate for his legitimate white

CHAPTER SEVEN

children. When their typical home-schooling lessons were being done, she would be sitting in a corner of the room and, of course, NOT allowed to participate. It was actually illegal during slavery to teach slaves to read and write. But she paid very close attention. In this way, she surreptitiously learned to read and write. Later, she would teach this to her children. I have a few letters from her daughter, my grandmother—Miss Janie (1876-1975). They have NO punctuation or capitalization but are otherwise perfectly readable—her handwriting and spelling are fine. They truly "used what they had"—a very valuable lesson for us all! Blind in old age, Miss Georgiana lived well over 100 years—I remember her. She had arthritis but used a home remedy involving a bottle of alcohol in which sewing needles were dissolved. I was told that it was a real help to her when she rubbed the solution onto her hands. She had formerly been a trained midwife who smoked a pipe! (My paternal grandfather Riley lived 1874-1950.)

When Riley Mitchell died, he owned nearly 700 acres of land and it was published that 'He owned more land than any black man in Washington County, Alabama'. He bought his first acre for fifty cents and it was Miss Janie who always encouraged him to buy land. They produced their own food, clothing, and other goods. They produced syrup from their own sugarcane mill and had their own sawmill to cut timber. They owned approximately 30 milk cattle and 7 plow horses. They traded with other community families and outside Koenton. All tis enabled them to be self-sufficient and protected in a racially hostile environment. They also would give a calf to newlyweds to begin their life together. In 1929, they donated two acres of land for construction of the Koenton Rosenwald High School for grades 1-9. They donated another three acres in 1938 to expand the school. It then became the Koenton High School for grades 1-12. A school bus was purchased which was also used to transport people to church and elsewhere. They later built another school in a nearby community. In 1949 and 1950, they donated land in Koenton for a new church they organized and constructed: The New True Light Baptist Church. Adjacent land was set aside to provide and maintain a cemetery that was available to local residents without charge. The church motto was, 'God can do anything but fail'. That says a lot about how former slaves survived and thrived in a hostile society! And, like every family, it was a mixture of both and bad people!

Sibling Rivalry Begins

It took some getting used to having a father who lived at home; I don't remember what title I called him by—Daddy or Papa or the like—but the adjustment happened slowly. My parents bought a tricycle for Billy and me to share. Once, we were taking turns riding on the back porch, when my father told me

CHAPTER SEVEN

to get off and let Billy ride. I tried in vain to explain that it wasn't Billy's turn yet. He made me get off and pushed me when I tried to hold onto the trike. I fell off the porch and onto the pile of broken glass of a kerosene lamp chimney discarded there the day before. Thankfully, I didn't get hurt. I stood up before him in my most serious maybe 5-year-old stance and told him quite firmly and seriously, "I don't like you ANY MORE!" And I meant it. I think that was the day sibling rivalry took root in my mind. I don't think Billy ever had a problem with it though; it was all my problem.

More

My father helped me plant my own little garden patch. I don't remember what we planted except watermelon seeds, and I really looked forward to eating my very own watermelon. I waited eagerly for their ripening and harvest, but it was not to be.

My parents were having marital problems, but they didn't let it touch us. Again, in those days, children were excluded from "grown-folks business." And that's as it should be. Why burden children with things they are too young to handle or understand? I don't remember them ever quarrelling, although I'm sure they did. It was not done in front of the children.

Whatever a child's first memories are, they make an impact and effectively stamp them. I had a wonderful childhood in Chatom, full of many fond memories!

A FATHER AT LAST (1945)

My mother worked a lot, so she hired an older woman to look after my brother and me. Her name was Miss Luvenia and I heard later that she was a distant relative. We were happy and loved in a well-ordered and cozy home. Billy and I lived in a world of safe loving care with M'Deah, Papa and Big Mama, and Miss Luvenia. Everyone who came into our world was safe and kind. We were good. Really good.

(Speaking of distant relatives, M'Deah mentioned a couple of times that she had heard her family was some kin to gospel singer, Rosetta Tharpe. She didn't know how it was so and I guess she never asked anyone.)

One of my fondest memories was when Miss Luvenia or M'Deah would put a quilt astraddle the back of two wooden chairs in front of the fireplace. When the quilt got warm, it would be put onto the bed Billy, and I shared. We would run and jump into bed, be covered by the nicely warmed quilt, and snuggle under it in delight. It doesn't get any better than that! Sleepy time surely followed. I remember that warmth fondly.

While in Chatom, Billy and I had the normal childhood diseases of measles, whooping cough, and chickenpox. We never got mumps though. In fact, I have NO memories of any doctor visits there—either to or from! I guess we were given home remedies. We were all blessedly healthy. Vaccinations back then were not the norm for us in Chatom and would come into our lives later.

CHAPTER SEVEN

During my childhood, rural Alabama—like most of the South—was 50-75 years behind the rest of the country in so MANY ways—culturally, socially, economically, technologically. This gap increased as the North developed technology and by the end of WWII it had doubled. Living in the rural South was like living in pioneer days, VERY reminiscent of the TV show "Little House on The Prairie." We had NO electricity, NO running water or indoor plumbing, NO telephone, NO bathtub, and a one-room schoolhouse. But we didn't consider ourselves as "poor" victims. It was just the way it was—our normal life and it was a good time and a good life.

The Quilting Circle

Women sometimes in our home gathered around a frame suspended from the ceiling for a quilting session; I never heard it referred to as a "bee." Many hands made the toilsome work fun, and these farm women made beautiful patchwork quilts, a much-needed commodity. In my early teens, I wanted so badly to have one such quilt for my own home one day, but that day never came. I remember my Aunt Daisy's quilts. They were all burned by my Aunt Carrie because of a mistaken and feared diagnosis of tuberculosis. It turned out that Aunt Daisy had a respiratory problem that was slight asthma. I was very disappointed when I learned of this since those quilts were destroyed in vain; the loss of something

I regarded as invaluable. I can still see the quilting pattern in my mind after all these years, two bow ties in a square background.

The Beauty Shop

My mother was a hard-working entrepreneur. I remember her going into town in Chatom to her beauty shop. Many years later, maybe in my 50s, I learned that she had taken training at the Madam C. J. Walker School of hair care in Meridian, Mississippi, and graduated there after her teen-aged marriage. She bought her own tools (curling irons, straightening combs, etc. which I still have today) and learned to do all kinds of hair, for black folks and white folks. Still there was all the farm work to be done, and the housework which Miss Luvenia helped her with in addition to taking care of Billy and me. She saved her money as much as possible. I was in my 60s when M'Deah told me that my father was a reckless gambler. After his Army discharge, he eventually even bet and lost the farm she had worked so hard to get for the family. She was rightly devastated.

M'Deah's Dish Set

There were lots of farm chores to be done. I remember that the yard was dirt and not lawn. Instead of being mowed, it was diligently swept by broom to be kept neat and not be unkempt. I had

CHAPTER SEVEN

my own chores, of course, but my favorite one was maybe washing dishes.

When I was four or five years old, I loved helping out and I happily gathered eggs from the henhouse with my little basket. I was allowed to churn butter in the wooden churn, but, I really wanted to milk the cow and was told I was too young—"not yet." However, I was allowed to help with washing dishes. Papa's sister, Aunt Mary Chillis, and her husband had adopted a baby girl named after my mother and called "Little Juanita." She was now a teenager living with us temporarily and helping out my mother. One of them would use the hand-pump to put water in the dishpan and put a crate in front of the sink for me to stand on. They told me NOT to dry and put the dishes away but to only wash dishes. One day, I decided to surprise them by showing that I was capable of doing more: I would put the dishes away! They were to go into a stand-alone furniture cupboard that was on tall legs. My mother had struggled to save up ration stamps during WWII and saved money to buy a new set of dishes, probably from a Sears or Montgomery Wards catalog. Catalogs were a very necessary and welcome part of country living. In the days before online shopping, they were essential for access to shopping if you lived where there were no department stores—Chatom had none. Catalogs were your only access to participation in the cultural norm and to popular products of the times. You could even buy

A FATHER AT LAST (1945)

a house! (Sears sold them as kits to be assembled onsite and some of these houses still survive today.) Not being able to reach the upper shelves of the china hutch, I stood on the bottom shelf to put the dishes away. I didn't know that was a very bad idea. The cupboard tipped over forward and came crashing down on top of me. There was the loud sound of shattering glass and then my wails! Nearly all my mother's precious dishes were broken!

(Oh. Our generations were in the days of Sears and of Wards. Later generations were those of Walmart and Kmart. Penney's hung in there with us all. Until ALL ended—something we thought we'd never see.)

Later I was told that my mother was of course devastated, really devastated. Little Juanita visited us when I was in my teens, and we talked about that incident. She said that only two things saved me. One, she persuaded my mother to be thankful that I hadn't been badly hurt or killed. Two, she swept up all the broken pieces into a large, galvanized tub and buried them in the backyard out of my mother's sight! Whew! There were only two pieces left, a single cereal bowl and a saucer, which we had for many years afterwards. Eventually they each got broken too and all that was left of this large beautiful and preciously acquired set was our memories. I can still see the pattern of flowered edges. (Sigh. Sorry, M'Deah!) I never again saw that pattern for many years though, even in thrift stores.

CHAPTER SEVEN

After the "pandemic," I found the pattern on Etsy and I quickly ordered a vegetable serving dish that I didn't think was wildly overpriced. Then I saw a set of small plates reasonably priced and quickly ordered those too. They were the same pattern from my childhood! Were these purchases worth it? Maybe not to someone else who didn't have the same sentimental value for them. But I'm happy with them! It was a Noritake pattern, maybe Morimura or Vendome or Mystery Vendome, of fine bone china. That wasn't the end though. My daughter recently found and bought a small serving dish in this same pattern at Goodwill—very inexpensive! For decades, I saw NO dishes of this pattern and now it seems to be everywhere as older generations leave them behind.

Learning To Read

It was Papa and Big Mama who taught me to read. I can't remember ever not knowing how to read except maybe back when Billy was born. I attended the one-room schoolhouse where Big Mama taught grades 1-8. She taught me the alphabet. There was no such thing as kindergarten. I never heard of such a thing, until I was six years old, and in another world.

While it was Big Mama who taught me the alphabet, it was Papa whom I credit for teaching me to read. "Professor Lawrence" was an avid reader of the newspaper. Almost daily, he would have me point out in the newspaper any words I recognized. I began with the letter "a" and went on. I remember the exciting "eureka" day that I recognized "and" and "the"! I excitedly pointed out to him all appearances of these two words that I saw in the paper, and he was very patient in allowing me to do so. I would later add more words to my knowledge, as he continued to teach them to me. It was the beginning of a lifetime love for reading and for books. Books were highly valued in homes I grew up in and it was many years before I could conceive of marking up a book by writing in it in any way. Books were all seen as nearly sacred as the Bible!

At School

In class, seating was in the order of youngest to oldest child, in distance from the pot-bellied wood-burning stove in the center of the room, our only heat. Big Mama rang a school bell to mark the beginning of our day, a signal for children still enroute to hurry to school. There was a well in the schoolyard and we had a common water bucket and dipper for drinking, also individual glass canning jars for drinking water. There was an outhouse for our bathroom needs. Grade placement was based solely on merit. By age six, I was in the third grade, along with a girl who was the only other student in our grade. When my grandmother was working with other age groups, this classmate and I would quietly play. Our favorite activity was folding paper to make "pocketbooks" which we would decorate with our pencils. I don't

CHAPTER SEVEN

remember having coloring books or crayons in our school. I knew of no such things. The only pens were those you filled with liquid ink, but we younger kids didn't have those either. This was in the days of segregation, so our books were used textbooks discarded by the white schools. But I don't remember using any at all. A child's first impressions and experiences in school are essential. Mine were very positive, so I have always loved school. In fact, I have enjoyed learning all my life.

Billy At School

My brother, Billy, grew older and finally went to school too, but only on Fridays. Maybe it was Miss Luvenia's day off or a time when she could be free to focus on household tasks. The usual pattern was that Big Mama came to our house to get me for school and Billy accompanied us on Fridays as we went across the highway, through the woods, past the sawmill, over the creek, and across the railroad tracks to reach the school. How far? I don't know! Probably a couple miles or more. Sometimes, we would see yellow school buses go by, the white kids being taken to their schools. Other children would join us along the way, and we had a great time walking to school.

One day walking through the woods, we heard a horrible loud sound overhead and we screamed in fright. Was it the end of the world? We knew from church that the end would come one day, but Big

A FATHER AT LAST (1945)

Mama calmed us down and explained that it was an airplane. She had us look through the leaves on the trees and into the sky to see it. We had never known any such thing existed and I wasn't the only one who still didn't comprehend it. But after Big Mama calmly explained it to us and the plane moved on and disappeared, I was never afraid of that sound again.

I always believed that the reason Billy came to school on Fridays was for the lunch. That was the day Big Mama would cook home-made vegetable soup on the school's wood-burning pot-bellied cast iron stove. It would be smelling fragrantly throughout the room as we did our morning lessons. Usually, the vegetables were sent to school by parents if they could spare them. As I said, in depression days the teachers who were slave descendants were generally not paid, so, parents did what they could to help out. It was a community affair. It continued during the war and through all my school years there. At lunchtime, our pint-size mayonnaise or Mason jar that we normally used for drinking water, was now used for eating what I remember as the most delicious soup ever! At rare times we even had the luxury of cornbread with our soup. Incredibly unbeatable goodness.

Our Church

One year the school had a program at our church. All students in grades 1-8 were involved and a white sheet was hung for use as the stage curtain. Attending were the school's children, their parents and other family members, the church congregation, and Big Mama, of course. It was a very big deal indeed! I don't remember what the whole program was about, but I think the occasion was Christmas. I clearly remember that one of the numbers we performed was this:

> Three little children, lyin' in bed
> Two were sick and the other 'most dead
> Sent for the doctor and the doctor said,
> "Give those children some short'nin' bread."
>
> Mama's little baby loves short'nin', short'nin',
> Mama's little baby loves short'nin' bread,
> Mama's little baby loves short'nin', short'nin',
> Mama's little baby loves short'nin' bread.
>
> Put on the skillet, slip on the lid,
> Mama's gonna make a little short'nin' bread.
> That ain't all she's gonna do,
> Mama's gonna make a little coffee, too.[1]

---

[1] https://www.lyricsondemand.com/miscellaneouslyrics/childsongslyrics/shortninbreadlyrics.html
Wikipedia now says that it's "an African-American folk song dating back at least to the 1890s."
(1) Wade, Stephen. The Beautiful Music all Around Us: Field Recordings and the American Experience. Urbana: University of Illinois Press, 2012. p. 93.

A FATHER AT LAST (1945)

I knew nothing of the origin of the song—and I really didn't care. All I knew was that I was giving a public stage performance and that I was having so much fun! I participated heartily as we sang and danced this song and did so with all my childish gusto. I really poured myself into it! I doubt that any of us children thought it was racist. It was just fun to sing and dance to it, and to show off what we'd learned in school. We had our own little minstrel entertainment show. And we were proud of it. We didn't even know or care that this song was once well-known in American culture. But not so now—it's politically incorrect.

I'm sure I was taught Bible stories then. I just don't remember them. Or rather, I don't remember ever not knowing them. They were the familiar stories of Jesus, David, Daniel, Mary and Joseph, etc. These and more were always familiar to me. I grew to appreciate them much more later.

PART TWO

The Minneapolis Years

CHAPTER EIGHT
A Brand New Life!

The Train Ride

One summer day in 1947, Big Mama took Billy and me on our first train trip to visit M'Deah's brother, our Uncle George and his family in Minneapolis, Minnesota. He had met his wife Janie when he was stationed in the Army at Spartanburg, South Carolina. He had settled in Minneapolis with his own family after being stationed at Fort Snelling during the war. In 2010, I learned that it was Janie's decision that they move there, rather than return to the South or move to Chicago where she had two sisters; information I got from her obituary. George worked at some clerical position in the VA and Janie worked in the dietary department at the local Swedish Hospital. They later bought a 1920s era home at 1121 Glenwood Avenue North.

    The train trip was exciting. You wore your nice Sunday clothes on the train during those times, not your casual play clothes. But the best part was eating the shoebox lunch Big Mama had packed—her delicious fried chicken, biscuits, and tea cakes as being included. I didn't know then that this was the only

CHAPTER EIGHT

way slave descendants could eat in train travel from the South, where Jim Crow laws excluded us from the dining cars. I just knew how delicious this normal Sunday-only treat was to eat. I remember this being a happy trip—not grievous at all, unless for Big Mama! I was not too fond of our occasional crossing over large bodies of water, but it was never boring. There were always new places and people to see and while I didn't know it then, this trip marked a BIG change in life for Billy and me. And later, for M'Deah too; A LOT happened because of this trip.

I didn't know it then, but we were part of the Great Migration of blacks from the South to the North. The First Black Migration occurred from the 1920s and ended with the Great Depression. (Some date this period as 1910-1940.) It was occasioned by the opportunities for better housing and jobs. But it was also flight from the dangers of the brutal social conditions of the South for blacks at this time of Jim Crow segregation and lynchings in the South. The Second Great Migration that I was part of began with WWII and lasted until 1970. (Some list this period as 1940-1970.). The First involved 1.6 million blacks moving Northward. The Second involved 5 million blacks moving Northward. My family and I were part of that group. (See Wikipedia.)

My Culture Shock

When we arrived in Minneapolis, I experienced TOTAL culture shock. Uncle George, Aunt Janie, and their kids lived in a house that had things I had NEVER seen before! There was an indoor toilet, a bath tub, running water, electricity, a telephone, and a radio. Outside were streetlights, signal lights, drugstores, dime stores, movie theaters, a public library, and more! Chatom didn't have any of these things. It was all amazing! Billy and I had to learn to use this new-fangled technology, but I don't remember that it was difficult at all—it was a pleasure! One of my fondest memories was of a floor lamp in the living room. It featured a step-on switch for a night light, and it was both beautiful and magical. I have one now that is similar that M'Deah bought years later at a garage sale. Distance was measured in something called blocks, and school was nearby—about three blocks away.

Our Aunt Janie had two sisters, Polly and Ola Mae. Polly lived with them too and did so for decades—for the rest of her life. She was like another mother to my new-found cousins, Rose and Jimmy. She was also a cigarette-smoker all her life. It was not known then to be an unhealthy practice and was popularized by the wealthy tobacco companies as cool, glamorous, and sophisticated. They used Hollywood movie stars to persuade people—especially the young—that this was so. Later, TV commercials would tout smoking

CHAPTER EIGHT

as a healthy appetite-suppressant and featured "doctors" in their commercials. These ads were targeted to women. And to others. All lies. Her other sister Ola Mae lived with her family in Chicago, and they would sometimes come to Minneapolis for summer vacation visits.

Cousins Rose and Jimmy helped us a lot and I'm sure it wasn't always easy for THEM! They were our escorts into this strange new world of being "up North." I remember them taking us to the local Kresge dime store where they ordered "ice cream cones." When it was my turn, I loudly protested that I did NOT want an ice cream cone—I wanted "a cone of ice cream." Why? Because that's the way we ordered it down South. I don't remember that I had ever ordered it before. Adults did that in Chatom and I just enjoyed it. But I did remember how they ordered it. Who wants an empty "ice cream cone?" Not me! It took a while for Rose to explain to me that they meant the same thing and that I would actually have ice cream in my cone, but I wasn't convinced until I was served that very thing!

Billy and I had to learn that soda was now called "pop." We had to learn when to cross the street using a stop light. Very strange stuff indeed! I don't think Rose and Jimmy ever thought of us as anything but their backward country cousins! Jimmy was very friendly though and I happily used him years later as a groomsman in my wedding. Rose and Jimmy were our guides/mentors into this new life and I'm forever grateful for that smooth transition to a strange new life. I don't know how it came about; maybe they were instructed to help us, maybe they naturally assumed the roles. I was six and Billy was four; Rose was five and Jimmy was three.

I lost my Southern accent quickly. How? By listening to those around me—cousins and their parents, teachers, and other students. And the radio was a big help too. I don't remember any other kids in our new neighborhood. We just had our new cousins for playmates.

They served us well as our teachers about our new culture, although I don't know how they felt about this unsolicited role. But Billy and I learned quickly! And there was a LOT to learn! A lesson I took upon myself was to find out what lay behind the electric socket holes. I was curious. So, one day when no one else was around, I used a hairpin to insert into the holes. I didn't get any answers, but I did get a flash of sparks and a slight burn on my fingernails that held the hairpin! I realized the danger of what I had done and never did it again! If anyone asked about the spot on my finger, I decided to tell them it was dirt because I knew the truth would get me in trouble!

Billy and I didn't know then that this visit was to be an actual MOVE from Chatom, Alabama—the only home we had ever known. It slowly became evident that this "visit" had no mention of any plans for a return to Chatom; Minneapolis was now home.

CHAPTER EIGHT

I don't remember how or when I knew we were not going back to Chatom to live; it's likely that I asked some adult, and they answered me. My mind focused on my one big regret. I wouldn't be able to see my watermelon patch grow or be able to pick my watermelon and eat it! That regret overwhelmed me for a while. Plus, I wouldn't ever get to milk the cow! Oh, well.

We didn't know it then (nor for years), but my parents were planning to get a divorce. That was the reason for our move to Minneapolis. I was almost an adult before I knew of this fact. M'Deah, Billy, and I lived with George and Janie for maybe two years.

Familial Titles

M'Deah was different in another way too. What was not a big change for us was using titles for adults. M'Deah had never required Billy and me to use "Sir" and "Ma'am" when addressing adults. Maybe it was her response to the Jim Crow laws and she was determined that her children would not participate in that custom; or maybe she knew one day she too would live up North and it wouldn't be necessary. Either way, Billy and I did not have to change the way we addressed adults. We called them whatever M'Deah called them. Unless they asked us to do otherwise. For example, M'Deah called her mother "Mama" but we called her mother "Big Mama." Although we knew the relationships, we were not required to use

"Aunt" or "Uncle" either. For us, Uncle George was just George and Aunt Janie was just Janie. Of course, we were taught to show adult's appropriate respect. Adults were not our equals, but, unlike most families, we weren't required to use their titles. We just imitated M'Deah and it worked for us. There were a few exceptions, but we addressed and respected their requests and had no problem accommodating any adults who asked us to use titles. We did call Arliece "Auntie" and her husband "Uncle Robert," but they taught us to do that later. I really tried to avoid using titles as much as possible.

The Famous Lawrence Family Photo

I suppose when Big Mama took Billy and me to Minneapolis that we were told that my mother would join us later. She finally did come, but so did ALL of Big Mama's other children, one family at a time over the years. Before that though, they all appear in an early family photo taken in Uncle George's home—Big Mama and all her children—in 1947. All her children came up to Minneapolis where a professional photographer had come to the house for this event. Professional photos were a normal big deal in those days. In the photo, Big Mama had a very peaceful demeanor; maybe she was tired. There was some discussion as to who was to be included in the picture and I don't know who voiced the final ruling, but it was only to include Big Mama and her children.

CHAPTER EIGHT

Spouses were not included. I, for one, appreciate that decision. It's also the only photo I have of Big Mama. I have none of Papa. That's rare because blacks took a lot of photos in the "old days," both professional and from their personal cameras. It was the thing to do then for all in the civilized world culture at that time! And invaluable for those who came later to treasure these memorable photos. Big Mama left soon after the photo was done to begin the new school year in Chatom.

Each of Big Mama's children were given a copy of the photo. M'Deah gave me her copy years ago. I never saw her again—my dearly beloved "Big Mama." I regard the photograph as famous because the family of each sibling had a copy of this iconic photo which could never again be duplicated. When I saw it later, I realized what a beautiful woman M'Deah was.

CHAPTER NINE

Why Divorce?

I heard bits and pieces during my childhood, then years later (in my 60s), I learned that my father was a gambling addict and often lost much. He even used their farm deed in one of his gambling games and lost. But that wasn't all. The Mitchell boys were said to be womanizers, as their father was also. But not all the boys were like that. I learned (in my 70s) that my grandfather Riley had a mistress who lived down the road from his legal family. He would often ignore the dinner his wife, Miss Janie, cooked for him and go down the road to dine with his mistress instead. M'Deah reluctantly told me this many years later, after judging me sufficiently grown to know about it!

I always thought Riley and Janie had 12 children. I thought of that as a lot. But I learned after I retired years later that they actually had 14 children:

Willie
Mile "Preacher"
Julius
John "Tit"
Riley "Bo Leg"

CHAPTER NINE

Isaac
Eva
Lucy
Woodrow "Duster"
Sears "Buster"
Jonas
Georgia
Charlie
Mary Jane

What Were They Thinking?

I don't know what happened to my father's mind, but he chose to be in an adulterous relationship with another woman. She should have known better too because it was not just any woman, he had the affair with. It was a WHITE woman! That was a HUGE no-no in the South of that time. How much? It was to embrace a death sentence by the Ku Klux Klan who gladly carried out this unwritten sentence/law of segregation. SURELY, my father knew the ultimate consequences of his behavior; nevertheless, they both continued in it. Because M'Deah's family had some favor among Chatom's whites, the KKK gave M'Deah warning that my father had better STOP the affair and leave Alabama—if he wanted to live. The "lovers" chose to leave Alabama—but only for a short while. When they returned, they moved to live together in Pascagoula, Alabama but then moved back to Chatom. What were they thinking? The KKK took action.

Did the KKK do it themselves? No, not this time. They used coercion instead—on Big Mama's sister Aunt Daisy's adopted son. She had initially raised M'Deah, then she and her second husband, Jack Slay, adopted a son to fill the loss when M'Deah moved away. Their son grew up and later spent time in an Alabama prison—which had NOT been a good experience. Finally, he was released. Was he guilty of some crime? I don't know the exact circumstances. Maybe yes. Maybe no. Actual crime wasn't always a requirement for young black men to be imprisoned in the South. Sometimes, they just needed to be fit for the county to farm out as forced labor. Sometimes it was for some minor infraction of the written and non-written laws of segregation. Anyway, he had served his sentence and been released. And so, the KKK threatened this Slay adopted son with return to prison—if he did NOT kill my father! What treatment he had experienced there was so dreadful that he feared being returned on whatever charge, so he did as they told him. He could have left town, but instead complied with a fatal shotgun blast to my father's back in an ambush. There were NO legal consequences; he was as free as a bird. The whole slave descendant community in that area knew what had happened and were helpless to do anything about it.

CHAPTER NINE

KKK

I didn't hear this violent group mentioned much by adults in my life. They usually pronounced it as "Klu Klux Klan" and not "Ku Klux Klan." When I finally got tired of the confusion, I looked it up for clarification.

> *The Ku Klux Klan (KKK) is an American white suprema-cist terrorist hate group founded in 1865. It became a vehicle for white southern resistance to the Republican Party's Reconstruction-era. history.com*

I don't remember all the other details, like how we were given the news of my father's death. Probably by a telegram, but I don't know. What was the chronology of what happened next? I don't know. How did I feel about this life change? All I remember was that I was OKAY—as long as I had my mother and brother. My father wasn't in my life a lot during the war; he was away at other stations. So, I didn't really have a hole in my life from missing him. Plus, remember that I was angry with him from the time of the tricycle incident! I had angrily told him, "I don't love you ANY MORE!" and I meant it to the best of my young understanding. Oh, the mind of a child! But we ended up back in Alabama later to attend my father's funeral.

My father was killed on August 18, 1947, less than two weeks after M'Deah's 28th birthday. He was to be

30 years old on October 26th. I didn't know that at the time as dates don't generally have much meaning for a child. Other than their birthdays. Or sometimes the dates of great trauma.

My First Funeral

I hadn't missed my father at all when we left Minneapolis to go South to his funeral in August 1947. I was ignorant to all the drama happening with my parents. I had NO idea that my father had changed so much after the war. PTSD? No. He had always been stationed state-side and saw NO combat action during the war. He simply displayed more of who he already was. But I didn't know any of that as a 6-year-old and had no idea what any of it meant.

The Mitchell family wasn't all bad. I learned later that Miss Janie's father had been a Baptist preacher. Maybe that's how she was able to put up with her womanizing husband who had a mistress who lived down the road from them. But Riley wasn't all bad either. He had donated land to the community for use as the first Negro high school in the county and again donated land for use as a church. That was of great help to the generations after slavery.

This funeral event involved unexpected trauma. The funeral and burial was done on the land of my father's parents. My father's casket was in the center hall of his parents' home, common for funerals in that time and place. I saw some kind of liquid drip from the coffin. I assumed it was water, but I heard some adult say that it was embalming fluid, whatever that was. I have no memory of viewing his body, although I probably did, and it made no impact. There were LOTS of people there—grandparents, aunts, uncles, cousins—the house was full. But it was all a kind of fog to me, and it seemed to me that the people behaved strangely; I avoided them. My focus and point of reference was M'Deah.

My big memory of that event was that my mother was CRYING at the grave site. I had never seen her cry before! I was trying to be okay in these strange circumstances but when I saw my mother crying and heard her threaten to jump into the grave, I broke. I burst into sobbing tears because of my mother's tears. Surely, everything in the world was very scary if my MOTHER was crying! She was asking how she could possibly raise his two fatherless children alone and without him and otherwise expressing her grief. I thought she was doing just fine taking care of us! It was all very confusing to me. I was glad when we left my father's family home later that day. We stayed with Papa and Big Mama in Chatom but I never saw the home and farm I had grown up on. And I never again saw my little watermelon patch. The graveside drama left me a little tired of this whole trip! Years later, I learned M'Deah's tears were all a performance for their sympathy—which worked. Of course, I had known NONE of this at the time. I was just feeling frightened and insecure at the sight of M'Deah's tears and her grief-stricken behavior. As I joined her with my own tears, I'm sure it helped her cause too! We left the funeral and we left Alabama safely.

It was later, when I was a teenager, that I learned from M'Deah some of these above details. She had always been emotionally close to my father's family and siblings who loved each other as true family did. I don't know why, but now they actually blamed HER for his murder! They had threatened to beat her up physically and her defensive ploy was to do a performance at the gravesite. It worked. His family swore to give her whatever help she needed in raising us. They re-expressed their love for my mother and for her children. All was well; their expressions were real. My father's sister Aunt Mary Jane, in whose house I had been born, was my Godmother. She and her husband, Frank Washington, continued to be good and loving Godparents to me. Mostly, from a distance though.

But we NEVER went South to visit my father's family again. I grew up not knowing my father's side of my family, or how much help they may have been, if any, to M'Deah in upcoming years. M'Deah sent a "Care" package South EVERY year right after Christmas for the rest of Miss Janie's life as well as to some other of my father's family—particularly to Mary Jane and Georgia. The love between them all was genuine. (Decades later, I learned that Aunt Mary Jane referred to the Jim Crow era as "the second slavery.")

CHAPTER NINE

Years later as an adult, I learned more about the strange funeral day and about the family relationships. I'm sure my father's lack of faithfulness to their marriage was all very heart-breaking for M'Deah. She had moved to Minneapolis with her children because she had filed for divorce and wanted a new start in life. No matter how hard it might be, she was not afraid of hard work. Now, after his death, there would be no need for divorce. She was a 28-year-old widow with two children to raise on her own.

I sometimes wondered what had happened to the white woman my father had an affair with. It was a relationship forbidden by ruling white society—for both of them. I didn't find out until November 2022. I happened to read a newspaper clipping my granddaughter had posted on Ancestry.com. The article was about a white woman who identified the dead body of a murdered black man as the person who had kidnapped and raped her. It was the body of my father! M'Deah never told me. Neither did any others of the family; I don't even know if they knew. It doesn't matter, except to see how such incidents of "scandalous shame" were handled in 1940s Alabama in the segregated deep South.

I only have four memories of my father before his funeral—vaguely that he came home from the Army; he drove our family to visit his mother in the Jeep in the rain and mud; he helped me plant my watermelon patch; and the tricycle incident. That's not much and it's a mixed bag.

CHAPTER TEN

Harrison Elementary School (1947–1951)

Childcare

With no more Miss Luvenia, we had a neighborhood teenager who baby-sat us. Her name was Shirley, and I really liked her. She was not a long-term solution though. Soon we would not need a baby-sitter. I would be considered old enough to take care of Billy and myself when needed. But I really missed Shirley. I have the one and only professional photo of her with Billy and me. Shirley was the only babysitter Billy, and I ever had. Years later, I learned she was the daughter of someone at the church we attended. Hers was a large, active, and well-respected family, the Langhams.

A New School

In the Fall of 1947, I was enrolled in nearby Harrison Elementary School. The walk was not nearly as long as the one to school in Chatom, maybe only 3 blocks, and I was happy about that. I remember M'Deah and me meeting with my new teacher at the beginning of the school year. The teacher told M'Deah that I would be a student in the first grade.

CHAPTER TEN

I strongly protested! In Chatom, I had advanced by ability/merit to the THIRD grade, and I already knew how to read! Being placed in the first grade was now a demotion that I took very personally! The teacher patiently explained to me and to my mother that the Minneapolis school system graded students by age and at six years old, I belonged in the first grade. I had no choice but to submit to my assigned grade. Sigh.

Actually, this was the best solution for me; I had so much to learn in this new cultural environment. There were actual books to learn from, among other things. I was introduced to school water fountains and bathrooms. I learned what a cloakroom was and how it's used. And more. I learned the Pledge of Allegiance and the national anthem; both were new to me. So too were other common patriotic songs. I had white classmates and a white teacher for the first time and was comfortable with that. What's the big deal? I remember that at my mother's first parent-teacher conference, my reading ability was demonstrated to her. The teacher did so from the now-famous Dick and Jane books we commonly used then. I also read to my mother from a book that combined words and associated pictures—you would read the words and then say what the picture was when you came to it. There were a couple of pictures I couldn't identify correctly. I had no idea what they were. Some culture shock remained. I also remember my mother dressed formally that day—you always wore your best when going to a meeting with your child's teacher. That's what she knew to be proper etiquette. At this meeting, she even wore her fur coat, bought during WWII. I was embarrassed because the other kids' mothers dressed far more casually. It was the only school meeting M'Deah attended—she was always working. I didn't know or understand the great sacrifice she had made to attend this one meeting. She probably had ignored an opportunity to sleep and rest up for her next work shift. I was just another unknowing and unappreciative child. Sorry.

Health Care

Once in the Minneapolis school system, both Billy and I were vaccinated. Not fun, but they counted it as necessary. At this time, polio still raged, with the Elizabeth Kinney Hospital being very busy. This was the dreaded disease of the times, but I personally knew no one who had polio. Then along came Jonas Salk and his medical solution and the polio hospital closed. Polio was no longer something to be greatly feared.

But cancer—"the Big C"—was still the big bad beastly health giant of the times, and I knew some family members it had attacked.

Holidays

One new thing about school in Minneapolis was the holidays. I don't remember any in Chatom,

CHAPTER TEN

although I'm sure we honored them too. Now however, school was closed for every holiday, and we were taught about them in school and made keenly aware of them. My favorite month became February, not just because of my birthday though. It was the month where we had TWO holidays, honoring the birthdays of George Washington and Abraham Lincoln! (This was changed in 1968 to a single holiday, Presidents Day, honoring all U.S. presidents.)

A New Home

My mother did indeed take good care of Billy and me. I didn't know it then, but she worked very hard and often at multiple jobs both full-time and part-time. M'Deah benefited from the time we lived with George and Janie and was able to work and save money from whatever was left after probably paying them for our room and board. Soon she moved us out into our own home. Always industrious and a saver, she was able to buy a Minneapolis duplex house on Humboldt Avenue North. A duplex was like a house set on top of a house, but each had their own separate entrances. Usually, a rear staircase might connect them if wanted, or it could be kept locked and separate. It was two houses for the price of one. This one was located not too far from where George and Janie lived.

M'Deah shared this home with two of her sisters. They were Eloise Mitchell, who later changed her first name legally to Eloyce, and her husband, "Buster" Sears Mitchell, my father's brother; and Carrie Bogan, another sister, and her husband, Tommy Bogan. Eloise and Buster lived in the first-floor unit. I don't think Buster worked regularly and I later learned Eloise was pregnant when we moved in, and I don't think she worked regularly then either. On the 2nd floor was a 3-bedroom unit where Carrie and Tommy along with M'Deah and her kids lived. It worked out just fine. A typical Minneapolis duplex was a smart choice to buy. Each floor had three bedrooms, one bathroom (typical then), living room, dining room, pantry, kitchen, dumb-waiter, a 1920s/1930s era stove and a fridge. On the outside front of each floor was a porch that went the length of the house. The common back staircase was for interaction if desired. I was enamored with the green enamel stove and its warming bin and utensil storage. I thought it the most beautiful appliance I'd ever seen—and still do. It certainly wasn't the pot-bellied stove I knew in Chatom. In fact, I'd love to get one of these antiques one day! And the dumb waiter was simply fascinating and fun to use.

In our new home I was responsible for Billy. No more baby-sitter, Shirley. All the adults on our floor worked and were usually gone early in the morning. I was given an electric alarm clock to which I awoke immediately. It made me feel very responsible. (I still have it, but I don't use it.) It was then that I

CHAPTER TEN

developed the life-long habit of always first knowing what day it was on waking—in case it was a school day, and I needed to get moving. Years later, I needed to know if it was a workday or not and if I needed to get moving!

Our morning routine involved me waking up to my alarm clock and then waking Billy. Next was our trip to the bathroom, followed by our daily routine of "washing up." This mini bath included washing your face, ears, and neck. And you ALWAYS washed your underarms and private parts—your genitals—your "butt." I learned later that whites called these "sponge baths." (We always had our tub bath the night before.) That was followed by putting on school clothes and having a cold cereal breakfast. There was always enough time allowed to do this and be ready to leave for school, without stress. It was my responsibility to make sure the door was locked. The key was on a chain around my neck, so it couldn't get lost.

Growing up and later, our house clothes were not a separate new wardrobe. They were our old school and work clothes now demoted to in-house clothes.

After school, we were to take off our school clothes and put on our clean play clothes. This was a time when many mothers joined the workforce—there were MANY "latchkey kids" in America and it was common for the times. With our parents working, we had the responsibility of letting ourselves out and in our homes as well as being responsible for ourselves there too. It was necessary. We had the safeguard of definite rules to follow—and we did follow them. And it was usually quite safe. It was extremely rare for anyone to ever bother these kids who had keys to their homes as well as the adults. It was necessary for their daily lives and was generally safe, thankfully. We kids were unafraid. Even the neighborhood drunks had morals—moral teachings in their backgrounds which they still observed in their behavior. They didn't use profanity in the presence of children or women. In addition, these kids were generally covered by prayers—those of their loving parents, grandparents, and others. For all their lifelong? From even before they were born. Children too have an enemy: the devil, who is the enemy of us all. And he doesn't play fair, has no mercy, even for helpless innocent children. I learned that as I later learned his hatred for myself and for my own children. But it was not stronger than the loving care and provision of our God for them. Thank God! Thanks, forebearers and M'Deah, for your prayers for us all. Thank You, Lord, for M'Deah.

A New Church

When we moved to Minneapolis, my mother joined Holsey Memorial C.M.E. (Colored Methodist Episcopal) Church and Billy and I attended regularly. I'm sure my mother took us sometimes, but I

CHAPTER TEN

don't remember that much. She usually worked on Sundays too and sent us to church. Or maybe Carrie took us. In Alabama, M'Deah had been raised traditionally and religiously but now she had to do what she had to do to survive. I learned years later that she sang in the choir whenever she didn't have to work on Sunday, but I don't remember it. Her upbringing had been with a very Victorian ethos—you did only what is "proper"—always. After all, their family were educators and teachers. That meant something then. You followed and set a "proper" standard of belief and behavior. Hymns meant a lot to me, slowly. They were my Gospel before I knew the Gospel. They drew me to the reality of God. I began to recognize hymns in cowboy Western movies and in WWII movies. Some of my favorites that I remember were, Amazing Grace, Blessed Assurance, I Come To The Garden Alone, What A Friend We Have In Jesus, and Yes, Jesus Loves Me.

Visit To Mississippi

I think I was in the second grade when Billy and I lived in the South again briefly. We lived in Meridian, Mississippi, with Auntie and Uncle Robert Grant. They had no children. I have no memory now of how we got there, but I do remember why. We were told that M'Deah's appendix had burst, for which she required emergency surgery, and that she was okay. While she recovered, we lived with Auntie and

HARRISON ELEMENTARY SCHOOL (1947-1951)

Uncle Robert. I don't remember the train ride there or back home, but our lives were being disrupted again. Would we be going to a segregated school? Not on their watch! They had agreed that they did NOT want us to attend the segregated Jim Crow schools of the South. The only schools not segregated in the South were the Catholic schools and there was one near their home, so we were enrolled there. It was a whole new experience for us. All of our teachers were nuns and we learned some Catholic rituals. I liked the school at first and got accustomed to it. My teacher was a young nun who, like all the others, meted out punishment with her wooden ruler. We didn't have that in Minneapolis schools and I don't remember that Big Mama ever did that either—although she probably did use corporal punishment on the older students. But I was glad that I could be a good girl and never worried about being punished. That changed one day. Our assignment was to recite the alphabet to the nun teacher singly. No problem because I knew the alphabet well and was familiar with it since I was about three or four years old. But I was nervous this day, maybe because my teacher was so intimidating. I began my recitation and finished it, only to hear from her that I had missed the letter "G." I had realized I had missed it, but it was too late. No mercy. This nun told me to put out my hand and proceeded to give me a single whack to my open hand—as hard as she could. No one had ever treated me like that before!

CHAPTER TEN

I recoiled in shocked painful surprise. It's not like I was a bad or misbehaving student, and I thought my treatment was most unfair and downright cruel. If this was their norm, I didn't like Catholic school anymore. As tears fell silently from my eyes, I purposed to NEVER have that happen again. I also concluded that she was a mean nun who enjoyed punishing kids. The school wasn't segregated, true, but I was glad when it came time to go home to M'Deah. I don't remember how we got there though.

Billy and I stayed in Meridian a few months. Meridian was also big-city life. They had modern amenities like indoor plumbing and electricity and telephones. Now, Billy and I were familiar with these technologies because of our Minneapolis experience. It was a very pleasant time, and we were loved and cared for and really enjoyed our new backyard to play in. I greatly admired a glass-topped patio table they had, thinking what a beautiful glamorous thing it was. Although it was city living, there were chickens in the backyard henhouse, and I had the pleasure of gathering eggs again! Billy really liked to chase the chickens around the yard and one day the rooster began to do the same to him! They ran around and around the house with Billy getting more and more tired, afraid that the rooster would catch him and harm him. What to do? I opened the back door and held it open and told Billy to run inside on his next trip around the house. He did so and was safe. He never chased the chickens again—so they were safe too!

It's funny what children will believe. Somewhere around this time, I regularly ate apples—a new pleasure for me. Auntie or Uncle Robert told me that it was dangerous to swallow an apple seed because the seed would then grow inside me to become an apple tree. Imagine my terror when I swallowed an apple seed one day as I ate an apple. What would happen to me as the seed grew and became an apple tree inside me? Would I be able to breathe? How long could I live? I struggled with these questions all day. Later, I told Auntie what had happened. She assured me that I would be okay, to my great relief. But I still tried my hardest to avoid ALL apple seeds from then on. I was taking no chances! It was about a decade before I finally believed I was safe and relaxed from this terror! I was relieved but a little angry too. Why was I told that frightening lie? I was used to adults telling me the truth! But these adults had no children and maybe they didn't know how important that was. They didn't know any better. This was the first time I ever thought maybe an adult could say something that wasn't correct or truthful! Later, the apple became my favorite fruit. Who knew?

Aunt Mary

Aunt Mary deserves a chapter all by herself. She was the only member of Papa's family I ever knew.

CHAPTER TEN

She was Papa's sister, my great-aunt. She also lived in Meridian. While living with Auntie and Uncle Robert, Billy and I stayed with Aunt Mary for a while, maybe it was just a weekend. She was manager or custodian of the black hotel in Meridian, Mississippi. Billy and I had great fun when she allowed us to have pop from the red flat Coke vending machine WITHOUT having to put coins in it! Good times. We even had an occasional Coke! Aunt Mary also had something to do with the Madam C. J. Walker Beauty School in Meridian. It was never clear to me what her connection was. I think she may have overseen the custodial staff there. More about her later.

Coca-Cola

Why was having Cokes such a big deal when staying with Aunt Mary? One of the joys in life then was a nice cold bottle of soda! You know—pop. Of course, at the time Coca-Cola was the biggie. But so were grape soda, orange soda, and strawberry soda, the flavors usually given to children. Coca-Cola, R.C. Cola, and Dr. Pepper were mostly for adults. They were considered too strong for children. And kids only had ginger ale when they were sick. The bottles were a lot smaller then than now. But it was a definite treat! M'Deah's beauty shop in Chatom always had sodas waiting for her clients when they came for their usual every-two-weeks appointments. Billy and I were treated to them on our rare short visits to the shop and grape was our favorite flavor. Years later, I learned that it was high praise for a woman to be told she had a shape like a Coca-Cola bottle—high praise indeed! I once heard M'Deah say she had gotten such praise.

My First Epiphany

The Cambridge English Dictionary says that an epiphany is "a moment when you suddenly feel that you understand, or suddenly become conscious of, something that is very important to you." I describe it as a sudden knowing of something as true that I didn't know before. When I was eight years old, I was walking home alone from Harrison School. Maybe Billy was sick that day.—It was safe for kids to be alone then and I was in the alley.—I looked around me and strange thoughts began coming to me. I realized that man had made many of the things I was seeing—houses and cars and alleys and trash cans. But I knew that GOD had made other things though—grass and trees and flowers and squirrels and sky. This was the day that I KNEW of a certainty that God existed! I saw things that ONLY HE could make. When we studied the "theory" of evolution in school later, the Truth of God never left me as THE reality of life. That remained, even when evolution was arrogantly dropped as being a mere "theory" and was upgraded as man's "scientific" truth. Bah, humbug!

Decades later, I had another epiphany. Only when you KNOW God is Creator can you possibly conceive of Him as Savior. That's how important Creation knowledge is. Evolution has no Savior for you because it has no Creator. A very serious Truth.

Our Neighborhood

My best friend's then were the twin boys Raymond and Robert, who lived next door to us. They were Billy's age, and I remember them fondly. We played together with them a lot, usually after school and on weekends. They were also descendants of slaves. In fact, so was our whole neighborhood—with one exception. Across the street from us, a family moved in who were Russian refugees. We got along just fine with their children, despite a slight language barrier. I was the leader always and chose what games we would play with Raymond and Robert. Our house had a wide front porch that was our own little playground for the four of us. Our favorite games were "Red Light, Green Light" and "Captain, May I?" We played them nearly every day the weather allowed us to be outside. Often, I read books to them and played teacher. We also played with the normative games and toys of the day—jacks, marbles, hopscotch, jump-rope, and yo-yos. Because I was the oldest, I ruled! And I thoroughly enjoyed being the boss!

The normal week-day routine for Billy and me was that after coming home from school, we changed into our play clothes—to keep our school clothes clean to wear another day—before going onto the porch to play. We weren't allowed to leave the porch per M'Deah's rules and that was fine with us. We didn't have bicycles to ride then anyway.

Our neighborhood was an older one. We weren't poor though. It was not what I came to know later as a "ghetto." We were a working-class neighborhood. People were friendly and respectable. There was no crime there at all. Still new to this big city up North, we were taught to be cautious. But we always felt very safe.

Household Cuisine

M'Deah was a great cook. All our meals were home cooked. I don't know how she found the time to do all that she did! I just assumed it was a mother thing. No. I learned from classmates over the years that many mothers did NOT see all this as a motherly responsibility. Years later, she would advise me to do as many chores as you could the night before to make the next day easier. And, especially, start the cooking or finish it all; it makes such sense now! But I didn't make it my routine, as she did. Looking back, I wish I had! And how did she do it financially? Our dinners were of two types—beans (butter beans, Great Northern beans, black-eyed peas) and cornbread, or greens (cabbage, collards, mustards, turnips) and cornbread. (Kale were greens I knew nothing about until we moved to D.C. years later!) These were very time-consuming foods to prepare. The beans had to

CHAPTER TEN

be soaked in water for a few hours or overnight and the greens had to be cleaned and de-stemmed and cut. Both dishes were seasoned with meats alternating between chicken feet, pig ears, and pig tails. My favorite occasional seasoning meat was ham hocks. Yum. Meat as a meal entree was usually reserved for Sundays. During the week meat was only a seasoning accompaniment for greens or beans. Sunday dinners were more of the traditional: macaroni and cheese or potatoes or rice, with a featured meat of fried chicken, pork chops, or ham, Fried fish was an usual Saturday dinner. A special treat was occasional "chittlins." They required a LOT of work by the cook, but it was worth it! (More about them later.) Another Southern "good eats" was home-made hog-head cheese. Yum! I would see it years later in Denver stores as "souse" M'Deah cooked the foods she was familiar with from her slave descendant Southern heritage. Later, as a Minneapolis hospital cook, she expanded her knowledge.

Of course, we were not exempt from enjoying the occasional pop culture meal of canned chicken noodle or tomato soup—with saltine crackers! We considered it a real treat!

Once, around third grade, I objected to eating cabbage and cornbread. Mothers in this era did NOT do cafeteria-style cooking for their kids; it was definitely "one-size-fits-all" and that was it. NO individualized meals here! So, she told me that I could be excused from eating the cabbage leaves—but I would eat the cabbage "pot likker" and cornbread. That's it. You ate what food they provided. My options were very limited; I could eat as she suggested or eat nothing at all. Okay, I'll take the pot likker and cornbread. I enjoyed it too; her pot likker was very flavorful, I liked cornbread, and it all filled me up! One day, I noticed a cabbage leaf in my bowl, and I objected. M'Deah calmly told me to eat this one little ole leaf and I reluctantly did. After a few more cabbage meals that included more and more cabbage leaves I had to eat, I was happily eating all her cabbage and refusing no leaves. It was years before I realized that unbeknownst to me, M'Deah had slowly been adding more and more cabbage leaves to my servings and I was accepting them all. Wow! Not only was she a great cook, but she was a master child psychologist too! And she had never read Dr. Spock! There are definitely great advantages to not being limited by knowledge of what's popular but not wise. Cabbage is now one of my favorite vegetables to eat.

(Later, I applied this tactic of limited options in my own child-rearing! "You can go to bed at 8:00 or 8:30. You choose." They always chose 8:30, which is what I wanted them to choose all along!)

Our Health

M'Deah once caught a very bad cold during her early period up North when going to a doctor was not

CHAPTER TEN

financially practical. So, what to do? Home remedies, of course. She had heard that liquor was good for a bad cold, so she purposed to go to a liquor store. She would make a "hot toddy" which included lemon juice and sugar or rock candy. However, her upbringing had said that a "proper LADY" would NEVER go into a liquor store. So, she waited outside a downtown liquor store, waiting until no one would see her go inside. As she made several attempts to enter, someone would come walking along the street and she'd back off. She was there for a LONG time not realizing that in the city someone would always be walking by. This was NOT Chatom! Finally, she decided to go inside anyway to buy what she needed for a cold remedy. You were to also take Black Draught with it, a nasty-tasting liquid supplement. But it was a common folk remedy then and it always worked!

Occasionally I had very bad side aches. Trips to the hospital for probable appendix problems always ended up negative. Life was kinda stressful then and that's probably all these episodes were about. Later, in my teens, our family doctor would say they were psychosomatic pains, but I NEVER agreed with this—the pains that I felt were all too real.

Billy was fine although at one point he was prescribed eyeglasses, which he didn't always wear. If necessary, we had a family private doctor.

I Am a Fighter!

In all my years at school I had only one fight. It involved a classmate named Arnold, who had a reputation for violence, bad behavior, and just for being a bully. It was a reputation that he had justly earned! Arnold was half-and-half, mixed Negro and white, and life was probably not too good for him. Such children were looked down upon by BOTH ethnicities. Arnold was somewhat unkempt, probably a neglected child and rightfully angry with life. But I knew none of that.

Billy was sometimes bullied by Arnold, even though Billy was two years younger than we were. Arnold would take Billy's eyeglasses then would return the eyeglasses whenever he decided to do so. Once he returned them broken. M'Deah had to pay for that repair cost. We were in the third grade then. In that same school year, Arnold had defied our male teacher (a rare thing for elementary school!) and run from him. The teacher chased after Arnold, and they ended up on the playground where Arnold jumped off an elevated embankment as he tried to escape. The teacher jumped too, and this WWII veteran's cries revealed that he had broken his leg! Arnold was fine. Arnold reigned. Certainly, if a teacher couldn't handle Arnold, I was never gonna challenge Arnold in any way! But one day I gathered up all my little courage and decided to confront Arnold. I was angry at the extra money M'Deah had to spend on Billy's broken

CHAPTER TEN

glasses and at his treatment of Billy. I was just tired of it all. As the students descended the staircase, I was walking one stair ahead of him. I turned around, yelled at him to "Stop bothering my brother!" Then I punched him in the stomach as hard as I could—and ran for my life! The next day, I was fearful to go to school. Staying home was NOT an option and would only buy me one more day of life anyhow! I loved school. But not today. What would Arnold do to me? Nothing. I never had a problem with Arnold. No words were exchanged between us, but he seemed to respect me after that. I guess it's truly said that the safest thing to do to stop a bully is to confront them. It sure worked for me! Whew!

The Mysterious Playground Puzzle

Somewhere during this time, our school got some surface re-pavement done to the playground. It included a painted puzzle of some kind on the paved playground. No one knew what it was, but I finally concluded that it was some type of shape that appeared to be a snail or ring-shaped hopscotch game. But how to play it? No one knew—not even the teachers. I wouldn't give up—if it was put here, it was meant to be played! After a few weeks, I happily DID finally solve the puzzle and all the kids, and I got to enjoy playing on this new hopscotch activity. And we did it LOTS of times! It was fun.

School Cruelty

One lesson I learned in elementary school was that kids can sometimes be cruel. It was a surprise to me that I was sometimes on the receiving end of this cruelty and sometimes I was on the giving end of cruelty.

On the receiving end, I was often teased with chanting taunts of "You got a boy's name! You got a boy's name!" This caused me to really hate my name! Bobby. Why couldn't I have been named something else? Why couldn't Bobby at least have been spelled differently? Sigh. There was nothing I could do about it. It was even worse when M'Deah told me some time later that she had wanted her first child to be a boy, had made this her only name choice, and stuck with it when I was born a girl. Who knows—maybe I could have been drafted into the Army! Years later I certainly got lots of mail and email about my prostate and other male issues!

On the giving end, a classmate named Maxwell Bird was our usual target of choice. We teased him about his first name and called him "Maxwell House Coffee!" We teased him about his last name and told him his thin frame looked like a bird and that he was most certainly a birdbrain! It was all very cruel, and I don't remember Maxwell having any friends or any who were even a little friendly toward him. Our taunting was usually a playground group activity against poor Maxwell. I finally felt sorry for him one

CHAPTER TEN

day when I saw the sad helpless expression on his face. Also, I had been taught better than that at home and in church, particularly The Golden Rule. It was universally taught in U.S. schools too. We were to "Do unto others as you would have them do unto you." I knew what it felt like to be teased about your name. After seeing the sadness and hurt on Maxwell's face, I just couldn't participate in this behavior any longer and stopped teasing/harassing /bullying Maxwell in the 4th or 5th grade. We moved away from the neighborhood before I could befriend him though.

Teachers had used me from the second grade onwards to be an aid for students who stumbled upon encountering new words. I was an advanced reader and was allowed to read the word for them as a prompt. This can be good; it was for my esteem. But it can be bad too; I often jumped in too fast with the word. Interrupting others got to be a lifetime bad habit and hard to control!

I remember the names of NONE of my white classmates from Harrison Elementary School. But I do remember two of my fellow slave descendants already mentioned, Arnold (the class bully) and Maxwell (the class bully victim).

Frozen Fingers

One third grade incident involves frostbitten fingers. Minneapolis can be a very cold and snowy place in the winter. Schools were only closed when the

HARRISON ELEMENTARY SCHOOL (1947-1951)

temperature was forecast to be either maybe five or 10 degrees below zero or colder. There was no wind chill factor taken into consideration then. Residents were legally required to shovel their sidewalks of snow when there was a snowstorm. One day after such a storm, schools were open. The piles of shoveled snow meant children could hear the cars on the street but not see them over the snow piles on the boulevard between sidewalk and street. This could be dangerous when you reached intersections to cross. Billy and I made our way to school, and I dropped him off at his class and proceeded to mine. But by now my fingers were so very cold in my mittens. In the cloakroom, I gingerly proceeded to take off my mittens, scarf, coat, snow leggings, and boots. My fingers felt strange, and I was crying the whole time as they began to warm and ache. I decided I couldn't go into the classroom and let others see me crying. So, I stayed in the cloakroom. I don't know when I stopped crying, but it was after I heard all the class procedures: attendance, saying the pledge of allegiance, singing a patriotic song, class lessons, etc. Finally, I heard the call for recess about 10:30. Crying or not, I knew it was time for me to join my class. But how? I would leave the cloakroom and get to the end of the line as the class filed past me. It was a good plan. However, it had one flaw: my teacher saw me when I did so. I was caught. She took the class to the gymnasium where we did indoor recess. She took

CHAPTER TEN

me back to her desk in our classroom and asked me where I'd been. Crying again, I explained it all to her; my painful cold fingers had caused me to remain in the cloakroom, although I was at school on time. She explained that she understood but she would have to send me home with a note for my mother anyhow. She wrote the note, folded it neatly, and gave it to me. Then she sent me to the bathroom to wipe my face of my tears and I went to do so. A note for my mother? I had never had to take her a note from school before. That was usually reserved for students who had misbehaved and gotten in trouble. That wasn't me! I had joined class late because my fingers were so cold, and I was crying! I hadn't done anything wrong as far as I was concerned. We were learning cursive writing in the third grade, so I decided to read the note teacher was sending to my mother about me. I understood it; it was about me being late for class. I made an immediate decision not typical of me. I tore the note into pieces and flushed it down the toilet. I knew it was wrong, but I didn't feel guilty to deserve any punishment. I was a victim of cold weather. I went home after class and didn't mention the incident to M'Deah. Until decades later. By then we both had a good laugh about it though.

A Great Vacation

For my ninth birthday, Aunt Mary Jane and Uncle Frank sent me a beautiful present. It was a "silver" music box filled with chocolate candies, and I thoroughly enjoyed it. Gifts sometimes have the power to build and/or restore broken relationships. That's what happened for M'Deah and Aunt Mary Jane. They were friends again, as they had first been when they met in high school.

One day in the summer of 1950, after finishing the fourth grade, I overheard my mother on the phone with Aunt Mary Jane who was both my aunt and my Godmother. M'Deah was telling her that she didn't know about sending us there for the visit Aunt Mary Jane wanted because she really loved her children and couldn't think of parting with us for the whole summer. I was happily surprised. I had NEVER heard my mother say that she loved us—it certainly was never said TO us. A reserved "proper" family didn't do that! You were supposed to just know it! I don't remember ever being hugged or kissed either. I didn't know this was caused by M'Deah's childhood experience with the snake. I assumed it was normal. But if I had any doubts, I now KNEW that we were loved. I had just heard M'Deah say so to my Godmother! The result of that conversation was that Billy and I spent most of the summer with Aunt Mary Jane and Uncle Frank in Joliet, Illinois where I had been born. It was a most relaxed and joyful time! The next-door young lady who unknown to me then had assisted M'Deah when I was born, did baby-sitting for us and would make home-made peanut brittle for us to have as a treat sometimes. Delicious! There were fruit bushes and fruit trees on the property, and we could pick gooseberries and cherries that we were free to have and enjoy to the full. They were certainly not a part of our normal diet in Minneapolis, and we thoroughly enjoyed these new treats. I even enjoyed climbing the cherry trees! One evening I wasn't feeling so well. The diagnosis from family was that I'd eaten a LOT of cherries in the hot sunny day that had caused the effect. I was just slightly tipsy! I also discovered that Uncle Frank had a crockery jug of cherry wine in a closet. One day I pulled out the cork and secretly sampled it but the resulting headache convinced me this was not a good idea to try again. After this happy time, Billy and I were reluctant to go home but also glad when M'Deah picked us up by train. M'Deah promised to let us come again. But we never did; this was our first and only visit with them. But the good memory of this time lasted for a lifetime.

The Telephone

In my early elementary school years, there was a big advertising campaign for every home to have a telephone. There were big ads on the side of public buses, we heard it on radio commercials, and I think it was even mentioned in schools. The importance of every home having a phone was promoted everywhere. The public was inundated, and it worked. We got our own home phone, but it wasn't the black pole phone I was familiar with at George and Janie's house. It was the new style black desk phone design. The rotary dial was still there, and I memorized phone numbers that were important to us. Besides our number and George's, there was only one other number to know. You dialed "O" for operator and that gave you a live person to talk to and it was how you requested long distance, the police, the fire department, an ambulance, information, and so much more. It was a good modern convenience to have but there was no 411 or 911; just the all-important Operator who was a real live human woman.

M'Deah's Social Life

M'Deah didn't have much of a social life. Mostly, she worked and took care of family and home. She rarely dated, but there was one man I remember named Lucius. He was very likeable and kind to M'Deah, spending time with Billy and me, and giving us occasional popsicle money. Another man in the picture was K.C. Jackson. I don't know how she met either of them, however. K.C. only interacted with Billy and me occasionally.

CHAPTER ELEVEN

Buster: Who Is He?

The 1950s were a VERY busy decade for M'Deah and for me; lots of "life" happened. The Korean War was taking place—what turned out to be an unresolved war. Everything in our lives was going just fine though. As far as I knew. I had no idea it would truly be the best of times and the worst of times.

    Buster, the brother of my father who married my mother's sister, Eloise, was my favorite uncle. He was a substitute father for us, a father figure. His real name was Sears, but his nickname was Buster and that's what everyone called him. He often gave a nickel to Billy and me for popsicles on hot summer days. We would go to the nearby Swatez grocery store. The Swatez family was Jewish, and I learned they provided trustworthy customers with something called "credit." You could get grocery tabs put on their books inbetween paydays. This was helpful to MANY people including M'Deah. Their family also owned the nearby Swatez Linoleum store and Swatez furniture store too. They served this neighborhood of slave descendants well for many years.

Sometimes, I saved my 5-cent popsicle money until I could buy a 10-cent comic book. They were a new treat for me in Minneapolis and I enjoyed them thoroughly. One day, I did something deceitful. I bought a comic book, read it, and then took it back to the store for a refund saying I hadn't liked it or some such nonsense. Mr. Swatez didn't give me a refund but kindly allowed me to exchange the comic book for another one as I had requested. I suspect he knew that I was lying. I certainly knew that I was! I was so conscience-stricken that I never did that deception again!

I don't know how he afforded it, but Buster did more than give us money for popsicles. I remember he treated us to some live events. He took us to watch wrestling matches though not often because I didn't like them much because of the violence and noisy grunting not to mention the excitement from the yelling fans. He also took us to watch roller derby matches. That was violent sometimes too, but much more fun as I watched the skilled skaters go by. He was a good uncle.

The Fateful Day

On one day of normal routine on Friday, December 8, 1950, everything about our peaceful lives changed. I began my day as I normally did. I had my own electric clock with an alarm to waken me; I had a routine to follow and supervised Billy as

CHAPTER ELEVEN

I did so. Suddenly, my mother came home from work! For the first time in her life, she hadn't felt well and asked to go home on sick leave. She was still wearing her white uniform dress from her job as a cook at the Minneapolis General Hospital. I was happily surprised to see her on this unexpected occasion. Then Buster came up the backstairs to say the plumbing pipes had frozen in the cold weather and he was repairing them. He wanted Billy and me to help him carry some pipes into the basement for the repair and he'd pay us for it. This offer of money really delighted Billy, and he went downstairs with Buster immediately. I was a little slower, unusually reluctant for some reason. How heavy were the pipes? How cold was the basement? We had never been asked to do this before, so why now? Do I really want the money that badly? How long would it take? These were questions I silently pondered to myself.

Then M'Deah and I heard Billy screaming. M'Deah went to the back door and called downstairs to see what was wrong. When she got no answer, she quickly went down to see about her child. I hung back. I heard funny noises downstairs and screams and, after a while, complete silence. It was a frightening silence. I called out, "M'Deah!" several times but got no reply. Then I heard a strange voice telling me, "Come on down. Everything's fine." I asked who it was, and they identified themselves as my mother. I knew better and protested, "You're NOT my mother!" They kept trying to persuade me to come down. "No!" It was highly unusual to disobey an adult. But I did so now. Then, for no reason that I understood, I locked the back door and ran to get the telephone. I had seen telephone company ads that said how useful a phone is in emergencies, and this had made an impression on my mind. When Buster came up the stairs and began bumping against the door to break it down, I was calling my Uncle George. He answered on the first ring, which seemed like an eternity! He himself answered and not someone else in the household. I said, "George! Come quick! Bring your gun! Buster's trying to kill us!" God only knows how I knew this. I don't even know how I knew George had a gun, but I knew he did. I quickly hung up the phone and ran to get out of the house via the front door before Buster succeeded in breaking the back door down.

Our security-conscious family had THREE locks on the door—two slide-locks and one door-key lock. Wrestling with the door locks, I heard the back door come crashing down. Uh-oh, I've gotta escape some other way from Buster! I headed for the door to the front porch. I paused, knowing my only option was to jump off the second-floor porch. That was gonna be dangerous. I might break my leg. Then what?? I couldn't run from him then. I paused too long to figure out how to safely do so. Buster came onto the porch, and I was caught. Despite my protests,

CHAPTER ELEVEN

he hung onto me tightly and walked me back into the house.

He was taking me somewhere. Where and why, I didn't know. I asked him about M'Deah and Billy. What happened to them? I don't know what he said but I remember thinking, "Who is this man and why doesn't he sound like Buster?" I didn't realize he was taking me to the kitchen. I don't know how or when he got the butcher knife. It had been lying in the pantry beside the lemon meringue pie Carrie had made the night before. As he raised the knife high, he calmly said, "This won't hurt you at all." I realized that he was going to stab me! I contradicted him and said, "Yes, it will!"

As he raised the knife and brought it down to stab me, I instinctively grabbed the blade with both hands and held on tight with all my might. There was no time to think. It was simply about life or death. My survival. I felt no pain, as we wrestled over the knife, I don't know for how long. Buster was trying to retrieve it from my hands, but I held onto the knife blade as tightly as I could. Now we were no longer in the kitchen but in the small pantry, and we finally dropped the knife. Now he had to retrieve the knife or deal with me. He chose the latter. I was lying flat on my back and his hands were around my throat, choking me tightly. With my now-damaged hands I was trying to pry his hands off my throat so I could breathe. The back of his hands surely was greatly bloodied in the process, but I thought about none of that as I struggled to breathe. As in a dream I began to see African tribesmen dancing around a big iron pot on a fire. It looked like a Tarzan movie. I had no knowledge that the pounding was all in my air-starved brain and produced this scene. Then, I lost consciousness.

When I slowly came to, I was lying on the floor on my back and something big was lying on top of me, but it wasn't heavy. I don't know how much time had passed. It took a while for me to figure out what I was underneath. It was the ironing board that was kept in the pantry. How had that gotten on top of me? There was no time to think further because I heard voices and thought Buster was returning to finish me off. So, I decided to play dead. But there was more than one voice that I heard and one of them belonged to my uncle, George. He HAD taken my phone call seriously. We were rescued! Another weaker voice was M'Deah. I didn't recognize the other voices but that didn't matter to me. Somehow, I pushed the ironing board aside, got up off the floor, called to them, and ran to the back door as they were coming up the stairs. I don't know how I did all that with my injured hands. It was no time for thinking. Up the backstairs came George with Buster and three or four policemen! George was holding M'Deah's arm as she weakly and slowly climbed the stairs. My brother was also with them. A policeman was carrying him, but I

CHAPTER ELEVEN

saw no blood on him, so I wasn't overly concerned about him. Billy was strangely silent the whole time he was brought upstairs. No one was saying anything to silence Billy either; I don't know what he was thinking or feeling. I have no idea what fears were going through his mind, but I'm sure they were there.

I turned my attention to M'Deah. Although I didn't see her actual wound, it was a very bad and bloody sight. I was too short to see the damaged top of her head. It would have frightened me even more if I had. I still wonder how she had been able to walk up the staircase in such a weakened condition.

The policemen ordered Buster to sit down at the kitchen table. He did and then stood back up asking anxiously, now in his normal voice, "Who did this to my brother's children?" It was decades before I remembered and realized he had asked nothing about who had hurt his sister-in-law! Suddenly my concern turned to great anger at him. I yelled out, "YOU did! You KNOW you did it!" It was like the feeling I had when I told my father that I didn't like him anymore—it just came out. Suddenly I wasn't a child anymore but an equal. I didn't wait for any response from him. One of the policemen pulled his gun on Buster and ordered him to sit back down and not move. I really was finished with Buster and my attention quickly turned back to my mother.

I was riveted at the sight of bright red blood pooling down the right side of M'Deah's uniform that had only recently been the usual crispy white. It seemed to be coming from her head. That was my total focus as I asked if she were okay. I got no answer and listened as she seemed to only be talking to George. M'Deah was telling George that her life insurance policy was in her trunk at the foot of the bed and said some other things about raising her kids. George was telling M'Deah, "Don't talk like that!" He tried to assure her she'd be fine, but I'm sure he was fearful too. Again, George tried to comfort her by saying all that wasn't necessary. But I could see why she thought it was. None of these words sounded good to my 9-year-old ears; they were frighteningly serious. I became VERY concerned for her life. And rightly so. I felt no pain from my own injuries but just the pain of knowing M'Deah had obviously been hurt. The adults seemed to know that and really didn't give me a lot of attention. M'Deah was focused on telling George what she thought were her last wishes and instructions. George was busy trying to persuade M'Deah that she was going to survive, and he wouldn't need her life insurance policy. But M'Deah was insistent that he listen to her. As they continued towards her bedroom, she was telling him she wanted the life insurance proceeds to be used to help raise her kids. George tried to assure her she would be able to raise her own kids, but she wasn't convinced of that at all. Crying profusely, my only concern was for her welfare.

CHAPTER ELEVEN

The police were silent observers, calling for ambulances and keeping custody of Buster. All was a scene of bedlam in taking care of a very messy situation.

Pretty much, no one talked to me or paid any attention to me and that was okay. I know M'Deah was hurt far worse than I was, and all my focus was on her. Her well-being was my great concern. I assume that my hands were very bloody too and unusable, but I felt NO pain. ALL my focus was on M'Deah. I do remember that my hands felt somehow heavy as I hung my arms down by my sides. It was decades before I realized they were heavy because my mangled palms and fingers were hanging open from their usual position. I know that sounds grisly, but it's true. My focused concern on M'Deah blocked out all pain for me.

I learned years later that one of the policemen remarked in jest that, "It looks like somebody didn't cook the biscuits right!" Maybe that was his way of understanding the situation he faced in the near-deadly attack on my family. Maybe he was nervous. I don't know. But I was told later that George cussed him and said that was NOT the situation at all: Buster was the brother-in-law and not her husband. I never heard any of these words as I watched M'Deah closely; I was crying all the while. But not from pain. Again, she was my sole focus. Soon, ambulances came to take us to Minneapolis General Hospital. A paramedic asked me what had happened to my hands. I explained I had grabbed the blade of a butcher knife and held on tightly with both hands to avoid being stabbed. I don't remember ever looking at my hands as they bandaged them for transport to the hospital. M'Deah was placed into an ambulance which made its departure with sirens blaring. I was placed into another ambulance with blaring sirens, and we departed too. I was still crying profusely but it wasn't from pain in my hands—it was from the pain of my concern for M'Deah.

Before we left, the neighbors silently observed us as we exited the house on this cold winter morning. They were seeing a spectacle where everything had always been unspectacular. I was strangely slightly embarrassed at all this curious attention. It would be months before I would see M'Deah again.

A few years later in my teens I wondered HOW a 9-year-old girl was able to survive an assault by a former WWII combat soldier; one who was trained to kill and had served in actual war. It confounded me and I knew it was ONLY by God's help. No other way possible, certainly not physically! Thanks be to God; Buster had NOT been able to succeed in murdering me! It would have been easy to do so, after choking me into unconsciousness.

There were many other unanswered questions, some I didn't think about until I was in my 80s! What convinced George to believe me? Did he hear Buster trying to break the door down? When did he call the police—before or after arriving at our house?

CHAPTER ELEVEN

Who got there first? How did he even get into the house? What happened afterwards? How did he confront Buster? How did he discover M'Deah? What did he think of this murderous attack on his family, in terms of what we meant to him afterwards? What distracted Buster from completely strangling me to death? Did he assume I was dead? How was I able to use my mangled hands at all? Etc.

I don't remember having any bad feelings about Buster. I just knew I never wanted to see him again. My main feeling was simply one of great gratitude to God for being alive. That feeling or belief served me well all my life. I was always glad to be alive—having come so close to death.

I have since become convinced that God sent M'Deah home that morning from work. Buster had no way of knowing that and had already laid his plan against Billy and me. She would have otherwise come home to discover her two children murdered. BUT GOD! How had he not been successful at killing me by complete strangulation? By stabbing me with the knife I had somehow succeeded in wrestling from him? Was he somehow interrupted by hearing George banging on the door downstairs? I don't know. Only God does.

CHAPTER TWELVE

Recovery

Minneapolis General Hospital

All was confusion at the hospital. I never saw M'Deah there in ER but continued to ask about her and got no answers to my questions. The ER staff began examining my hands for the extent of the damage. Only in ER did I see my hands—a bloody sight of two red raw masses of bloody blobs of mangled skin. The medical examination of them was the source of the great pain I began to suddenly feel now that the bandages were off.

I was no ordinary case. The exam was exceedingly painful and intense. All I could do was to cry loudly in anguish. I heard continuous screaming ring out through the ER. It was coming from me! How anyone could think it was okay to examine my injuries with no pain remediation is beyond me even now.

I learned both my palms were sliced open and seven of my fingers were cut. The middle fingers on both hands were especially badly damaged. Until now, I had experienced NO physical pain. Now I saw the sight of tweezers being used and the great excruciating pain I felt at the examination of my damaged

CHAPTER TWELVE

hands and fingers. Even then I don't really remember seeing my hands clearly. Probably because of my eyes being veiled by my tears.

Finally, I heard someone say, "Maybe we should put her to sleep." Someone else agreed and mentioned ether, so they could better examine my hands and repair the damage done to me. I was glad to hear that. I had cried continuously from the time I saw M'Deah's bloodied condition until the time I was put to sleep in ER. That's a long time. At no point was I able to wipe my nose or face. Neither did anyone else. It was the least of my worries, which were all on M'Deah and her well-being. I haven't cried for so long in all my life, well over an hour.

I learned sometime later that my case was beyond the ability of the hospital staff to handle successfully. So, they had a surgeon flown in that day from the Mayo Clinic in Rochester, Minnesota to try to save my fingers and hands. I never met him. But I do know that he did a brilliant job! God had him on hand just for me no matter what the rest of his career entailed. I thank God for him. Later, I even prayed for him and his family—for their salvation and well-being. I don't know how many stitches I required—probably nearly as many as M'Deah had. The number for each of us was close to 100. M'Deah mentioned 93 stitches for her when I asked her months later. My exact number remains unknown to me. I don't intend for this to sound gory; it's just the way that it was.

I woke from surgery with both of my hands in casts that reached from the end of my fingers to my elbows, and both were attached to a traction pole raised in the air. Only some of my fingertips were visible. I was a little tired too, because I had been crying for so long. Now I was helpless and could do absolutely nothing for myself without the use of my hands. But I learned to adapt quickly. I had to be fed with a spoon by an aide or nurse. I had to have those cold metal bedpans for bodily waste removal. I had to be bathed in bed by an aide or nurse and then dressed by them. And so much more. As time went on, the worst part was the itching in my fingers that came as they healed. There was absolutely no way to ease the itch with both hands encased in casts up to my elbows! Nothing to do but grin and bear it. Later, I was able to be loosed from the traction pole long enough to get out of bed for a brief time, usually for a whirlpool treatment of my healing hands.

By observation, I learned the hierarchy of medical staff. Nurses all wore white uniforms with white stockings and white shoes. Some wore white caps while others wore white caps bearing a black stripe and were more senior in rank. The latter were RNs— registered nurses. Interns also wore white uniforms. Doctors wore white lab coats. And orderlies, who did the grunt work, had a different outfit. Metal bedpans were cold to the body and uninviting. I was happy when I no longer needed them after several weeks.

CHAPTER TWELVE

Though necessary, they may have been the least likeable hospital experience!

I later had regular visits to the whirlpool where my casts would be removed, my hands were put into the warm whirling water to remove loose dead skin, and then new casts were applied. This was done at least twice weekly. In the whirlpool events I learned that only three of my fingers had not been cut—my two thumbs and my right index finger. I was in the hospital from early December 1950 to sometime in April 1951. During that time, I came to appreciate the value of doctors and nurses and considered joining their ranks when I grew up. I wanted to do so out of gratitude rather than interest and talent—not the same thing! So, I didn't.

I don't remember what my hands looked like when the casts were removed, but I would never again be able to fully make a fist with either hand.

I thought of some movies I'd seen where someone clung hanging onto a cliff awaiting rescue. That couldn't ever be me; I would fall off the cliff long before help came. That bothered me for a long time! Yes, it's strange what kids think. Hollywood once did stories that reflected positive popular culture. Then it mixed in propaganda to mold popular culture into what it wanted to exist, to affect attitudes and beliefs regarding war, patriotism, sexual mores, gender identity, and so much more. And it was encouraged to do so by bad government and foreign investment.

Now, all of that prevails over Hollywood values of old—those of the Greatest Generation. They weren't perfect, but they were better! Who will resist this molding and why? I see only one sector of society being able to do so: Christians who look to God for Truth.

    I was in a children's ward in the hospital and other children would come and go, depending on their condition. Slowly, I became friends with other long-term patients. One little blonde girl about five or six had to be loudly aroused from sleep each morning for a long time; she never woke on her own. How strange. I don't remember seeing any other Negro children or medical staff. After my hands were no longer required to be elevated, I would ride the tricycle ever so carefully, still in casts.

    My greatest joy there in all this time was reading comic books. The supply was inexhaustible! I would request them from the hospital children's librarian and staff would read them to me. Then I would ask for another one. And another one. And another one. But that didn't last long. Staff had too much to do besides reading comic books to me! So, I developed my own system. I would have them continue to place them on my upright bed tray. Then I would read them by myself! How? I used my tongue to turn the pages. Yes, that's not what I would normally do as I would not consider the pages of used comic books to be clean enough for my tongue! But this was different;

CHAPTER TWELVE

it was an emergency need. I enjoyed seeing comic books about many characters that were new to me, as well as those that were old friends—like Superman, Wonder Woman, Batman, Archie, Dick Tracy, Gene Autry, Roy Rogers, Tarzan, Mighty Mouse, Lone Ranger, Donald Duck, Mickey Mouse, Porky Pig, Classics Illustrated, Henry, Super Boy, Gangbusters, Nancy, Sad Sack, Jughead, Tom & Jerry, Little Lulu, and Blackhawk. Blackhawk was one of my favorites though, along with Wonder Woman. Good times! Comic books of that time were often very entertaining and educational—they kept me reading. This was my most frequent and consistent activity for all the time that I was hospitalized. I saw no newspapers on the children's ward, as I had customarily read before at home. But I was never bored. I had heard that M'Deah and Billy were okay—so I was okay too.

Radio was very big for entertainment then. I was happy having my very own little radio at home—but it wasn't allowed in the hospital. I enjoyed listening to the popular shows of the time: The Lone Ranger, The FBI In Peace and War, The Shadow, The Lone Ranger, Hopalong Cassidy, Fibber McGee and Molly, Jack Benny, Amos and Andy, Gene Autry, Roy Rogers, Dick Tracy, The FBI In War and Peace, George Burns and Gracie Allen, Our Miss Brooks, Baby Snooks, Edgar Bergen and Charlie McCarthy, The Life Of Riley, Gangbusters, Superman, Boston Blackie, The Adventures Of Sam Spade, The Inner

Sanctum, Suspense, Tales Of the Texas Rangers, and so much more! There was a lot to enjoy, and it all had been available to me—at least, up until my 8 o'clock bedtime.

I don't remember anything about my hair care in the hospital either. I'm sure it was done but I have no memories of shampoos and hair-braiding by any of the aides. Maybe Carrie braided my hair on her visits, I just don't know. Maybe the nurses braided my hair, but I doubt it. I must have had some hair care, but I remember none—which may be a good thing. There was no trauma involved!

Another very special thing during my time in the hospital was bacon! We were allowed to have as much nice crispy bacon as we wanted—even after breakfast was over! I was in bacon heaven.

There was a TV in the children's lounge that I was able to watch sometimes, a treat only a few homes had at the time. A few kids at school were this lucky and spoke of the programs they watched. They would invite their friends over to watch TV with them after school or on Saturdays. It was a special treat that made the hosts VERY popular at school. I remember them as being only the white kids and I was never invited to their homes. I learned only indirectly about this wonderful thing called TV. Now, in the hospital, I was able to see who Hopalong Cassidy was but I didn't watch it much. Reading and riding the tricycle was much more fun to me.

CHAPTER TWELVE

Supposedly, we had school in the hospital. But I don't remember it being of much consequence. For most child patients, they were likely too ill to do class work. For me, except for my hands, I was fit and healthy though—one of the few.

Big Mama

The very worst thing that happened in my hospital stay concerned my beloved Big Mama. I'm sure the news was from Tommy and Carrie—the only family that ever came to visit me in the hospital. One day several weeks later, I was told that Big Mama had a stroke upon hearing the news of Buster's attack on us. She died as a result, and I would never see her again. Nor would we be able to attend her funeral. M'Deah and I were still in the hospital. M'Deah was fighting for her life and recovery and the fight was on for my fingers and recovery. It was a very sad time for us. How important is a funeral? A lost opportunity to say "good-bye" to a loved one? A non-essential? Maybe. Memories of a loved one last for a lifetime. It has often been said that funerals are for the living and not for the dead. For us, it was more about our extended hospital stay. For me, the months went by quickly. I think the time lingered for M'Deah though, sadly.

Mercifully and to my great surprise, I didn't dwell on Big Mama's death. Maybe because there was no one to talk to about her. Those in my hospital world didn't know her. No one else ever mentioned her death to me. When I went home and was reunited with my family, neither did they. It was almost as though she had never existed. I had a lot going on in my life then and maybe it would have been all just too much for me to handle.

My Hospital Visitors

I had very few visitors during this time; only Carrie and Tommy. They came weekly to see me. Of course, I would ask them about M'Deah and Billy and I was given assurances that they were just fine. I would send greetings to M'Deah through Carrie. While I had seen that Billy wasn't very badly hurt and was not bloodied, I wanted to see M'Deah. Where was she? As a child, I wasn't allowed to see her in the hospital. I was told that Billy's leg had been only slightly hurt and that was all. I learned that M'Deah's wrist had also been broken during the attack, as she had raised her arm to protect herself from the many blows of the iron pipe Buster used to bash her head. M'Deah required 93 stitches in her head and was still in the hospital as I was and was healing nicely, I was told. That was such a comforting thing they gave to me. I could now relax and enjoy myself. I had no stress or sadness the whole time I was there. I was too busy coping with my new life in the hospital. I was just very thankful to be alive and thankful that my family was alive and well too!

CHAPTER TWELVE

I was somewhat surprised that neither George nor any of his adult family ever visited me in the hospital. I don't know why they didn't. I had wanted to thank him for saving my life. I was eternally grateful that he had answered the phone so quickly and didn't fail to take me seriously. I'm sure he probably heard Buster trying to break down the door. I also thought his family would be glad that I was alive too. No visits. Oh well. Somehow, I was able to make myself be okay with that. Maybe they were visiting M'Deah; she was injured far worse than I was. Did anyone else from family maybe make a one-time visit to see me? I don't remember any.

One day during my time in the hospital, Eloyce sent me some of my favorite fried chicken on one of the visits by Carrie and Tommy. While I looked forward to it, I was also timid about it. Would it be okay with hospital staff for me to eat it? Carrie assured me that it was okay, but I wasn't so sure. Was I allowed to have it? This was my first time as a hospital patient, so I didn't know the rules. I thought the chicken might be taken from me if I were caught eating it; after all, it wasn't from the hospital menu. So, I was afraid and thus unable to eat and enjoy it. I put it away in the drawer of my bedside table. Probably it began to rot. Because one day a nurse discovered it in my drawer, and she threw it away. Sigh. I was sad to see it go—Eloyce was a good cook and fried chicken was one of my favorite foods. But I was happy to know that I hadn't broken any unknown hospital rules! That was the ever-compliant side of me.

Only once I briefly thought about the bloody mess at home—my blood and M'Deah's blood. Who would clean it up? Probably Carrie and Tommy because they still lived there.

Billy's Condition

As I said, I learned thankfully that Billy's only harm was a slight injury to his leg. When Buster attacked him, Billy had rolled under the bed there. It was a move that surely saved his life. While we were in the hospital, Billy stayed with his Godparents. They were an older childless couple that lived across the street and a few doors down from us. Mr. Martin was a Pullman car porter—a very highly respected position for slave descendants—who was frequently "on the road." Mrs. Martin was a housewife. They were both mentors for my mother too and loved Billy dearly. Mrs. Martin had great respect for Billy's fastidious ways. That was innate for him but maybe some ways were also taught to him by Mr. Martin. I remember a time when Billy cried and refused to wear a pair of socks because they had a tiny hole at the toe. M'Deah assured him it would be seen by no one, but he insisted that HE knew it was there. No, it couldn't be worn. M'Deah had to relent and give him another pair or darn the offending sock. Mr. and Mrs. Martin would buy clothes for Billy and otherwise help M'Deah out sometimes. I only speculated that then, but it was true. My mother's "village" was very small, but very helpful.

Sloppy Journalism

The newspaper accounts of this incident was something I saw decades later. It gave me a new view of journalism that I had always thought of as being painstakingly factual before. It is not! That's the impression I got from old movies about the integrity of journalists, I guess. There were so many inaccuracies printed that I hardly would have known who and what the case was about if I hadn't been there myself! Important and easily confirmable details were all wrong. One wrong detail was that M'Deah had come home from work because she was told her children were being molested! Another wrong detail was that we were all stabbed. And yet another downplayed the extent of our attack and the resultant injuries Sigh. When Buster attacked us in 1950, I was nine, Billy was seven, and M'Deah was 31 years old.

Eloyce and McCary

I had a personality mixture of being bold and of being timid. Let me explain. I later learned that Aunt Eloyce, (my mother's sister had legally changed her name from Eloise by then) had left Buster and her marriage behind with their baby son, McCary, in early

December. She returned home down South to her parents, Papa and Big Mama, and was now back in Minneapolis. Buster had not been able to provide for them. He didn't work and was on something called "reefers." I don't know all the whys and wherefores of all this—that was "grown-folks' business" that children were NOT privy to! The marriage just wasn't working out. Supposedly, Carrie had been instrumental in persuading Eloyce to leave Buster. M'Deah wasn't involved at all. But when Buster came home to find his family gone, he asked Carrie about it. And she wrongly implicated M'Deah. Her lie almost cost us our lives. I didn't know Eloyce had left him and taken McCary. Again, that was grown folks' business.

A few weeks before the incident, baby McCary had been very ill. I overheard that it was due to not having enough milk to drink and that it was Buster's fault for not providing for his family. M'Deah was instrumental in saving baby McCary's life when he went into convulsions from not getting enough milk for nourishment. I was happy that the baby was okay, greatly assisted by M'Deah, but I wasn't angry with Buster for it; he was my favorite uncle, after all.

My Deposition

On another day in the hospital, I was told I had visitors I didn't know or expect. All the other patients in the ward were taken elsewhere so we could have privacy. After the ward was cleared, I was told my

CHAPTER TWELVE

visitors were from the court and I was to give them something called a deposition. I was to simply tell them what happened in the attack on me and maybe answer some questions. I did my best. It seemed to take a long time. In this new experience, I answered all their questions and understood my words were to be used in Buster's trial. I later learned from Carrie and Tommy that he was found guilty and given a sentence in the Stillwater, Minnesota prison, and that he said he had no memory of the incident at all. I didn't know how long the sentence was for, but I felt safe that he had been put away in prison for years. I breathed a big sigh of relief. Now it would be safe for me to go to school, to play outside, to be at home alone, to go places—without fear. When I got out of the hospital, I could resume my normal life in safety. Whew!

The only time I ever spoke of what happened to me with Buster was when I gave the deposition. No adult asked me, and I never opened that conversation with anyone. Not with M'Deah, Billy, or George. It was an event not spoken of. I think I only asked my mother how Billy had been spared greater harm and she explained. No one spoke in agreement to say it would be a forbidden subject. It just was.

At some point in my hospital healing process, one finger was very slow in healing. I learned many months later that doctors went to M'Deah, and advised her to allow them to have it amputated. For that, she needed to sign papers giving her consent. She asked for a delay of just one day so she could think it over. Why did she do that? She later told me she wanted to take time to pray as well. The finger to be amputated was the third finger on my left hand. Many years later, M'Deah told me that she couldn't bear the thought of my getting married one day without being able to wear my wedding ring there. The NEXT day, my finger DID begin to heal, and NO amputation was necessary! Hallelujah!

    I had no idea all this was going on. I was given a new medicine—an orange liquid. Why do I remember it? Because it caused me to slowly gain excess weight. It was noticeable to me upon discharge. When I asked M'Deah about it, she explained that the doctors had to give me this medicine to help in the healing process. Oh. How bad could it be if it helped heal my hands? I had never had excess weight before. But it was bad—worse than I'd thought. When class pictures were taken in the 5th grade, it was obvious I wasn't that cute little girl I once saw in earlier photos. My face was chunky, to say the least! And I would be overweight for a long time—before slimming down after high school and then getting "fat." I stayed there for most of my adult life, and it was not ALL due to this medicine, for sure. It was me.

    As my healing progressed, I was given physical therapy. The one thing I remember was having to exercise by doing a drum-roll movement with each

CHAPTER TWELVE

finger tapping to the tune of the theme song from The Lone Ranger TV show! It was fun—not grievous at all. My improvement was slow but steady, but I would never be able to make a fist again with either hand. Thankfully, that is NOT a life-altering habit to be left without! I'm a very peace-loving person, so why would I NEED to make a fist?

CHAPTER THIRTEEN
Home at Last

I was finally discharged from the hospital sometime in April 1951. I had been in the hospital five months. The only bad part had been in ER! But I was glad to be home with M'Deah and Billy again. I was happy to be reunited with my family. I hadn't seen M'Deah or Billy since that fateful day of December 8, 1950. M'Deah was discharged from the hospital at some point before I was discharged. We were no longer living on the 2nd floor of the duplex though. There was a swap and now Carrie and Tommy lived there alone. Eloyce and McCary lived elsewhere. My family now lived on the first floor. M'Deah had the rear bedroom. The bedroom where M'Deah and Billy had been attacked was used for storage. I don't remember it ever really being used. Billy and I now gladly had our bedroom in what had been the former dining room. It was right off the kitchen and had no door separating the two rooms. As for me, I was afraid of the dark and was given a flashlight. I ALWAYS kept it under my pillow. At some point, it was determined that I absolutely needed it to feel safe. I had thought I wouldn't be afraid. But I was.

CHAPTER THIRTEEN

The craziest fear I had was one I never shared with ANYONE else. It was this. If someone I loved and who I believed loved me—like Buster—could one day try to kill me, could others I loved also do the same? I even wondered about M'Deah. Could she go berserk too? I allowed NO ONE to ever touch my neck. I had been choked into unconsciousness once and I would NEVER allow anyone to get even close to my neck again! I didn't even like to touch my own neck to wash it! That took some time, but not too much because of M'Deah's good-motherly hygiene requirements and because I didn't want to have a dirty neck that others would see! Vanity can have a good purpose.

I was pleasantly surprised to find my hands didn't stop me from doing the things necessary for everyday life. I had learned to squeeze out a washcloth for bathing. I could hold a toothbrush when needed. I made other slow adjustments with ease. I think now that M'Deah was greatly relieved too. I have no idea what the doctors had told her to expect. M'Deah was very patient with me as I recovered physically and otherwise.

Billy had his own fears too. Many nights he would be crying in anguish and tell of seeing someone at the transom window atop the front door. He would ask if we saw him and give a description of someone in a red suit. No one ever saw what he saw. I knew it was torment for Billy, but I couldn't help him. I saw no one.

M'Deah's healing process from brain injury is unknown to me, physically or emotionally. It was not something we ever talked about. Again, sadly.

Sibling Rivalry Gone

My prized possession before this time was a child's rolltop desk and matching chair and I was very fond of it. While Billy and I recovered from our physical and soulish wounds, I realized I had nearly lost my mother and my ONLY brother. I had a new appreciation for them both. But I also still had a heart of sibling rivalry.

One day Billy and I were arguing about something—probably something foolish. I angrily picked up my desk chair, raised it high over my head, and fully intended to hit Billy in his head! Instead, I somehow hit my own self in the head as I swung the chair backwards. I saw stars and had nearly knocked myself out! And I never tried that again! It was years before I realized I could have hurt Billy badly or even killed him with that chair blow! That was unthinkable—totally unimaginable to me. I'm forever grateful to God for this meaningful change in my thinking and behavior! Meanwhile, Billy and I NEVER had any conversation about the murderous attack on us. None. But we never had any more conflicts or quarrels either. I somehow KNEW now he was my ONLY sibling and, as such, he was precious family to me, just like M'Deah was.

CHAPTER THIRTEEN

When we moved to a new home later, my beloved desk and chair were left behind as refuse or sold or given away. I don't remember but I never forgot it and wanted another one. I finally bought an adult version from Facebook Marketplace in 2020—nearly 70 years later!

Eloyce and McCary had returned to Minneapolis, maybe after Buster was in jail. I don't know when it was, but I do remember she took Billy and me to a Billy Graham crusade in downtown Minneapolis. I didn't understand much but I liked it. Maybe a seed was planted in my heart for later development.

That Phone Call

I was quite conscious of the fact that my life was saved because George had answered the phone so quickly. From that moment on it became my life's work to ALWAYS answer any phone call quickly. My thinking was, "This may be a matter of life-or-death!" For that reason, I always attempted to answer any phone call after the FIRST ring. I made it my personal assignment and responsibility. Even years later at work. Even for a while after caller-id technology became routine.

So, when the phone rang one day, I answered quickly and heard a familiar voice. It was Buster! If he was making a phone call, I somehow knew that meant he was out of jail! In shocked fear, I dropped the phone and screamed. When M'Deah asked me what was wrong, I told her it was Buster on the phone. I'm sure we both wondered HOW he was free to be able to call us! M'Deah talked to him briefly. I was too much in shock and fear to remember what she said. I do remember that she called the police right afterwards and was told Buster had been freed from prison and told to have no contact with us. But that's NOT what happened. M'Deah told the police that if she ever saw Buster that she would kill him—shoot him dead—to protect herself and her children. They were convinced that she was serious, and I believed her myself. They contacted Buster immediately and told him that his release had a stipulation; he was to leave the state of Minnesota and never return or he must serve the rest of his sentence time. Buster immediately left Minnesota and returned to his native Alabama. Even so, I lived in fear for a long time. What if he caught me as I walked to and from school? What would I do? Would he succeed in what he failed to do before in trying to kill me? Would I be able to protect Billy on these school walks together? It was NOT easy to need to consider all this. It was a heavy load. And I thought it unfair too. I had never been told of Buster's sentence but assumed it would be many years for his nearly-successful murderous attack. Apparently, he only served about six months. Wow. Buster believed M'Deah's words the police told him. Because we never heard from or saw him again.

CHAPTER THIRTEEN

(I only learned recently that Buster was charged with simple assault. That's why his sentence was so light, apparently. He should have been charged with attempted murder!)

In those days, there was no such thing as counseling for trauma victims as there is now; no one helped regarding possible PTSD. The thinking and practice then was to just go on with life and try to be as normal as before. It's what ex-slaves did. It's what the Greatest Generation did. It was what everyone did! It was just a part of life. And the strong survived. In later years, I pondered whether counseling would have been something I/we should have had. And I think not! It may have made us more dependent on natural reasoning and resources. Instead, we had to depend on God, and I believe that this was a good thing! It had brought us safely forward thus far and prevails. I always had the comfort and joy of knowing that I was alive because of Him! I was very grateful for that. I healed physically; the healing needed in my soul would come later. Meanwhile, we just moved on! I was always glad M'Deah had come home early from work that day; very much out of the norm for her. But it wasn't until maybe 2023, that I really understood what would likely have happened to Billy and me on that day, had she not been with us. It would have been no problem at all for Buster to take out two little kids. I'm glad all over again, blessed by God to live.

After Buster it took a lot to annoy me. I now put petty grievances into perspective. Compared to nearly being murdered, it ain't no big thing. I was far less selfish than before. That new attitude has lasted a lifetime.

School Catch-up

When I returned to school, I learned that my class had learned the multiplication table in my absence! My hospital lessons had not kept me on track with my classmates. It wasn't real school but I didn't much care at the time. We were there for recovery from various health issues, so fun and relaxation were emphasized far more than academic schooling. I felt stymied. Now Mrs. Martin, Billy's Godmother, baby-sat us after school. Every day, she diligently worked with me in drilling me to memorize the multiplication table. Thanks to her hard work and mine I caught up with the other students! Still, I never felt comfortable with math for a few years. I was always unsure whether I knew enough and was totally insecure on that subject. (I had also missed lessons on Minnesota geography and history too.) It's very unsettling not knowing what you may have missed—being unsure of the exact loss. Sigh.

The Poison Pill

I didn't realize until in my 80s that a night-time conversation I overheard now was a poison pill

CHAPTER THIRTEEN

conversation. Such a pill is small but can be deadly and it is not always known by the person who dispenses such a pill. Nor is it always recognized by others for its danger. As a child, I certainly didn't know. One night, after Billy and I had gone to sleep, I was awakened by hearing voices of people talking. Carrie and Tommy were in the kitchen, talking to K.C. They were talking about M'Deah. Were they saying what sterling character she had and what an exceptional mother she had been to raise two small children all on her own and what a hard worker she was? NO! They were saying only bad things about her! The character and beliefs of my family was that one did NOT take what was called then "public relief"—welfare. That was considered to be NOT "proper" for anyone with class! It was not a resource available in the South to black folks, anyway. M'Deah had worked VERY hard to survive without resorting to this scarcely available resource in the North. So, she not only survived but THRIVED in difficult economic circumstances. (In fact, she was at work now.) Everyone knew that about her. Or so I thought.

But now Carrie and Tommy were saying what a horrible person M'Deah was! They accused her of promiscuity with the white elite men in Chatom and that she had used her body to curry favor with them. K.C. seemed to be trying to defend her, doubting what they said. But they were persistent. I remember Carrie saying she wouldn't lie about her own sister! I kept silent and gave no hint of being awake, as I couldn't help but hear this "grown folks' business." Because there was no door separating our dining room/bedroom I heard most of what they said. I didn't understand it at all. It was sometime later that I learned that they knew K.C. wanted to marry my mother. Carrie wanted to stop it, and she convinced Tommy to help her, so they slandered M'Deah. What was their motive? I don't begin to know; I have never known. Maybe they just didn't want her to be happy. I didn't know then that's how the enemy works—using whoever he can to do evil.

A Man in the House

Unknown to all the family, M'Deah and K.C. were already married. Billy and I didn't know that. They had eloped to Iowa and gotten married. Now, K.C. lived with us as a "roomer" and I thought it was just for our safety. We were told at some point that they were married but I don't remember it. Certainly, M'Deah would NOT do anything that was not "proper." We knew it by the way WE were being raised. It was OKAY that he was in M'Deah's bedroom. M'Deah said that she had thought it best for us all to have a man in the house; we would be safer. I was glad to have a man in the house too. It seemed logical and reasonable to me, and we called K.C. "Daddy." But it was to become of great danger to M'Deah's personal safety.

CHAPTER THIRTEEN

Far from preventing the marriage, Carrie and Tommy had planted a poison pill into a new marriage instead, spoiling any chance for its success. I knew none of this then. I don't remember how the evening ended but thought Carrie and Tommy were satisfied that they had persuaded K.C. to believe what they were saying. Sadly, that bitter pill would bear very bitter fruit. I didn't understand the connection for many years—decades. I never mentioned that conversation to M'Deah. I didn't want her to know how very nasty her beloved older sister had been. And I didn't want her to know that her daughter had eaves-dropped on a forbidden conversation. I didn't tattle. Perhaps I knew the pain it would bear was possibly more than the pain of any physical abuse she suffered later. Do those who plant bitter pills know the poison it produces? Do they even care? That's even less likely. Did Carrie and Tommy ever consider the damage they had done, after K.C. was gone later? Probably not.

I had another reason for being glad that we had a man in the house though. The hospital had suggested piano lessons as a further physical therapy for me. I was excited when K.C. promised me that's what I would have. I knew exactly where I would get them because the nearby Phyllis Wheatley Center offered piano lessons. I went there often to get library books to read. Billy didn't usually go with me. Books were not his passion as they were mine. But I NEVER got the piano lessons! And I never knew why. It wasn't something mentioned. I asked about them once and was given no definite answer. I just knew I would not be getting them. K.C. had not kept his promise and I swallowed my disappointment. Hard. And I hoped it would maybe happen later. I purposed in my heart that somehow, somewhere, at some time in my life I WOULD have piano lessons! It's still a dream coming.

K.C.'s Background

I came to learn more about K.C. over time. He grew up in Hattiesburg, Mississippi. His background was different from M'Deah's in some significant ways. His father was a poor sharecropper, as had been his father before him. Before K.C. mentioned it, I had never heard the word sharecropper but gathered that it was some kind of farming and farmer. It was decades before I knew it was actually just one step above slavery. The website, American Experience, provides a lot more information:

What is Sharecropping?

Sharecropping is a system by which a tenant farmer agrees to work an owner's land in exchange for living accommodations and a share of the profits from the sale of the crop at the end of the harvest.

The system emerged after the Civil War, when the southern economy lay in ruins. With the Confederate monetary system wiped out, farmland decimated, and slavery abolished under the 13th Amendment, access to labor and capital was extremely limited among Southern landowners. For former slaves, federal proposals to redistribute land fell apart in the 1860s, leaving millions without the promises of full citizenship guaranteed to them by the 13th, 14th, and 15th Amendments.

Pitched as a solution for both groups, sharecropping was presented to the formerly enslaved as land ownership by proxy. It put an end to work in "gangs" under an overseer, while keeping Black workers within the agricultural sector, preferably on the same land where they had been held captive, and incentivizing high crop yields, benefitting landowners. But even though the old plantation system had changed and some day-to-day activities were delegated to sharecroppers, sharecropping proved a fundamentally unequal arrangement, organized to keep Black farmers from ever achieving economic or social mobility.

As writer Doug Blackmon notes, many white southerners after Emancipation were determined not to pay for something they had once had for free—Black labor.

Many landowners at the end of the Civil War were furious at the idea of paying Black workers whom they'd owned only months before. As a result, landowners developed systems adjacent to slavery. On the plantations, this took the form of sharecropping, though the transformation did not happen overnight.

Black Americans in the South were eager to exercise their newfound freedoms after the war. As historian Wesley Allen Riddle writes, "the most basic and symbolic" *of these freedoms was "mobility" itself. The formerly enslaved left their plantations in droves, some looking for work in the South's devastated cities, while others looked for—and were given by the Union Army—vacant land on which to raise a farm. But work in cities was hard to come by. Only about 4 percent of Freedmen were able to find work in southern cities after the war, and many who came there were relegated to shantytowns of the formerly enslaved. As for those that were given vacant lands by the army, they were forced out when President Andrew Johnson canceled Field Order No. 15 in the fall of 1865, returning these properties to their white owners.*

While many formerly enslaved did leave the plantations after the war, many others could not. Those trying to leave faced horrific violence and intimidation from their former owners. As Union General Carl Schurz reported in his testimony to Congress in 1865, "In many instances, negroes who walked away from plantations, or were found upon the road, were shot or otherwise severely punished."

With land ownership all but closed to them, and urban service work extremely limited, many Freedmen had little choice but to return to the plantations by the end of the 1860s. Their motives for this were mixed. Though economic pressures were strong, many wanted to reunite with loved ones who had been sold during slavery and saw some appeal in working in an agricultural sector that they were familiar with.

Twenty-to-50-acre plots, a cabin to live in and farming supplies were promised to them, all in exchange for about

CHAPTER THIRTEEN

50 percent of their harvest. Freedmen envisioned a self-sustained life working a plot of land, raising a garden, and providing for their families as they wanted. But these hopes were dashed as the pitfalls of sharecropping quickly became clear.

Life as a Sharecropper

By design, sharecropping deprived Black farmers of economic agency or mobility. Although they were no longer legally enslaved, sharecroppers were kept in place by debt. As their income was dependent on both the profits from the sale of the crop and the whims of the landowners, sharecroppers had to find means to sustain themselves during the rest of the year. They were forced to purchase food, seed, clothing and other goods on credit, typically from a plantation "commissary" owned by the landlord. At the end of the harvest, when revenue from the crop was "settled up," the sharecroppers' portion of the profits was calculated against their debts. As a result, sharecroppers often ended the year owing their landlords money. What could not be paid off was carried into the next year, creating a cycle of indebtedness that was often impossible to break.

Sharecroppers in debt to their landlord were subject to laws that tied them to the land. If they attempted to move, any new tenancy contracts they signed with other landlords could be voided by their existing ones. If they ran away, they could be brought back to their landlord in chains and made to work as a prisoner for no pay at all.

Even if sharecroppers did not try to leave, they still faced massive obstacles in achieving any kind of solvency. For instance, many Southern states limited how and to whom sharecroppers could sell their part of the crop. In Alabama, cotton had to be sold and transported during the day and could only be purchased by a state-defined "legitimate" merchant. As sharecroppers couldn't afford to lose a day's work to take their crop to market, these laws curtailed their ability to sell their product at the best possible price.

In addition, individual freedoms were crushed by tenancy contracts, many of which included arbitrary clauses forbidding alcohol consumption, speaking to other sharecroppers in the fields or allowing visitors on rented land. Black sharecroppers could not seek redress through the political system either. Despite the ratification of the 14th and 15th Amendments, the southern "Redemption" that followed the withdrawal of Union troops from the South in 1876-7 ensured that the federal government would not enforce Black voting rights. Black elected officials disappeared from Congress and state legislatures, and attempts at organizing Black voters were brutally suppressed, as in New Orleans in July of 1866, where a convention of Black voters was attacked by a white mob under police protection that killed an estimated 200 people.

Educational opportunities were also sparse. In 1872, white Southerners pressured Congress to abolish the Freedmen's Bureau, a federal agency designed to provide food, shelter, clothing, medical services and land to newly freed

CHAPTER THIRTEEN

African Americans. With the dissolution of the Bureau, few resources remained for the approximately 80 percent of Black people who were illiterate.

Sharecropping, with its prohibitive restrictions on physical and economic mobility, its use of violence and intimidation and its emphasis on maximum production, denied Black Southerners the ability to gain wealth, to exercise the freedom granted them by Emancipation and to gain the education they were deprived of during enslavement. The system existed, in conjunction with other institutions, to exploit Black labor at a minimum "relative loss" to white landowners while keeping the Black population underfoot. As Black sharecropper Ed Brown said of his experience, "hard work didn't get me nowhere."

Even later, I learned that two-thirds of sharecroppers were white, and one-third were black. Both groups suffered under this system! This is reminiscent of the life of poor white coalminers as depicted in the song, "16 Tons," made popular by country and gospel singer Tennessee Ernie Ford in the 1950s. In either system—sharecropping or coalmining, there was no way to get ahead or to escape grinding poverty and bondage. Today, heavy consumer debt can do the same thing.

I assume K.C. was drafted into the Army during WWII. I honestly believe that's the only thing that gave him the courage and desire to leave the South. Otherwise, I think he would have ended up being just a bitter sharecropper. Living up North opened up a whole new world to him. But I don't ever remember him trying to get his parents to leave their sharecropper lifestyle in Mississippi. Maybe he did and they refused to leave. I don't know.

Freed slaves could choose their own names. It was common to choose as last names that of their former masters or those of past presidents. First names ran the gamut of common names in the culture or merely initials. I don't know how the name Jackson was chosen for them, but the family's three sons were named W.A., F.B., and K.C. Some freed slaves did not take on full names but used initials only. This was the practice of K.C.'s family. Other former slaves often looked down on those who had no first name.

When he was drafted, the Army required that K.C. have a full first and middle name for better specific identification. So K.C. became Kenneth Charles—"Casey". The Army didn't use initials for a soldier's name—too common and confusing. But K.C. never used that name in civilian life.

K.C.'s brothers also had moved to Minneapolis. W.A. lived nearby with his common-law wife who had several children by him, and she also had an older daughter from a previous relationship. F.B. lived in the sister-city of Minneapolis—St. Paul—with his common-law wife. Their lifestyles were looked down on by nearly all Negroes. Marriage was the norm, not shacking up nor having illegitimate children. They

CHAPTER THIRTEEN

had a beautiful and beloved only sister, Justine. She was married to a physically abusive and womanizing husband, Claude, who believed in keeping Justine "barefoot and pregnant." They had several children and were poor; Claude lacked ambition, to say the least. They still lived in Hattiesburg.

K.C. only went through the 6th grade in school although typical education for slave descendants in the South was to the 4th or 8th grade. He had a deep thirst for education, but the family had no money for "schoolin'" and he always felt shame and bitterness for it.

In talking of his own "ole days," he told of an incident involving his father. His father had a dream where K.C.'s grandfather told him of a Mason jar that was buried in the backyard filled with money for K.C.'s education. Wow! Sounds like an answer to prayer. But it didn't work out. Was the money not there? We'll never know. Why? K.C. said they were all sufficiently frightened at what might have been a message from a ghost that no one ever bothered to dig for it. Not even K.C. His dreams of an education ended, and it remained something he was very bitter and insecure about for the rest of his life. He always felt that he had been cheated out of an education. He blamed everyone except for his family and himself; it was always someone else's fault. It seemed clear to me that no one had acted on a clear answer to a clear need. They had not trusted God, to their loss. Of course, I never spoke that out loud. It would be putting my spin on "grown folks' business"—a definite no-no.

K.C. did speak slightly about his WWII experience. He was a soldier stationed in Burma, a British colony which became Myanmar later. K.C. bitterly described how white G.I.'s told the women of Burma that the black soldiers had tails to discourage their socializing with the fellow black soldiers. Most of these women were simply made curious to see such a thing and still dated the black soldiers anyhow.

K.C. Resented M'Deah

I learned K.C. held resentment toward M'Deah. Why? She had an education, and he did not. Her family were landowners and his were sharecroppers. But why be resentful of the lifestyle and blessings she inherited, and he did not? It wasn't her fault! The Bible says this about comparisons: "There but for the grace of God, go I" (I Corinthians 15:9-10). It's true. Chance and circumstance happen to us all. Unsolicited. So, no blame or resentment to any. Why would you marry someone you resent? The reasons for your resentment don't suddenly go away. So, your misery of resentment will never stop. And it will damage your relationship. Indeed, it's just another "poison pill" of your own making.

Family Medical Visit Up North

Of course, family sometimes came to visit us from "down South." The most common cause was for medical treatment that wasn't available to them there. Common thinking in the South was that if you went to the hospital, you never came out alive. I suppose it was a justified conclusion. Regular medical care wasn't available to them—just the occasional country doctor. Once, when we lived in the Humboldt Avenue house, K.C.'s mother came to Minneapolis for a medical visit about her health issues. She was taken to a doctor and had tests done. I think her diagnosis was terminal uterine/vaginal cancer. As a child, I only learned this via snatches of conversation I overheard occasionally. We had only one bathroom and one day I needed to go when she and M'Deah were in there. I discovered that she was bleeding in that area of her body, and I equated that bleeding with death. She returned home to Mississippi and died shortly afterwards. Sad.

CHAPTER FOURTEEN
The Good at Home

Our lives changed again—spectacularly. I didn't know my parents were searching to buy a new house, but one day I heard M'Deah tell someone they had finally found the house they wanted to buy. However, they could get NO bank to give them a mortgage! Was their credit bad? NO! They both had good jobs and good credit. M'Deah still worked at the city and county hospital. K.C. was a brick and block mason who had learned the trade on the G.I. bill for WWII veterans—an economic boon for the soldiers and for the country. So, what was the problem? Redlining. This was a common practice then which only became illegal years later. It was something done by white lending institutions—banks, savings and loans, credit unions—to deny mortgages to slave descendants who wanted to live in certain neighborhoods and thus confine them to what were later called ghettoes. This was what my parents were up against. M'Deah prayed in desperation.

The Outcome

One night, M'Deah had a dream. In it, Big Mama was telling her to go to a particular institution to

CHAPTER FOURTEEN

get a mortgage. It was the Farmer's and Mechanics Savings and Loan. Voila! They did so and the loan was secured—without hesitation! They bought a NEW house in the Camden area of Minneapolis. The style would be called a "GI tract home"—a small starter home for GIs to begin their lives after serving in WWII. It was just two blocks inside the city limits, just outside was the Brooklyn Heights suburb! We were the ONLY family of slave descendants on the block and only one of a very few in the whole neighborhood! It was a small cute two-bedroom, one bathroom house, just the right size for us, with room for expansion in the basement and attic if needed.

After we moved, I never saw any of my former classmates again nor any of my old neighbors—not even the Martins. It was a total cut from our former life. I didn't know why that was so.

New Family Members

Uh-oh. It turned out there was a reason our parents bought a home with room for expansion! We got another surprise after our move when we learned that K.C.'s children from his first marriage would now be joining us. This was news to me—both his having a first marriage and his having kids. It was the first Billy or I had heard of either. We got over the shock because M'Deah seemed to take it all in stride, of course. I overheard that the situation with their mother in California was not good and that maybe she'd had a mental breakdown. K.C. didn't want them to live like that and he was trying to get custody of his son and daughter. He won full custody, and we were told they were coming a day or so before they arrived. Curious to meet them, we had no problem bonding at all. These were our new siblings.

Emeal (pronounced E-mell) was oldest at nine, and I was glad Billy had another boy in the family. They were the same age, but quite different. Emeal had been the oldest sibling, the boss. Now he wasn't, I was, and it was made clear that I was in charge when our parents weren't home. I don't know how Billy and Emeal got along but I was glad I had the edge over Emeal as the eldest child. I thought it was good.

Later it would be revealed that Emeal was being a bully at school. He wasn't that way at home, at least not to Billy and me. We got along fine with him. But he was a little bossier with Linda and Floyd.

Linda was seven and was a beautiful and sweet little girl. She seemed happy to have a sister, and we got along well, despite our 5-year age difference. I enjoyed being a big sister to someone who was so easy to get along with. We worked together well, and I kept some limited contact with her over the years. So did M'Deah.

But there's more! Shortly afterwards we were told there was another son for which K.C. was fighting to gain full custody, still living with the same mother. We had heard nothing of him either!

CHAPTER FOURTEEN

Floyd was four and came a few weeks later but we also had no difficulty bonding with him.

We were now a family of five kids and not just two! I had already gotten rid of my attitude of sibling rivalry, thankfully. So, I had no problem embracing these new siblings. It wasn't something they made hard either.

Linda and Floyd were very amiable. It was easy to welcome these cute little ones. I'm sure Linda and I tangled sometimes as two girls sharing the same small bedroom must. But I remember no such incidents with Floyd. He was always genuinely amiable with everyone. And he was so cute with his smiling dimpled face and curly hair.

Billy and I were surprised to get new siblings and welcomed them gladly. We were taught and behaved as though we were all family. We even looked the part, having the same skin tones. I'm not aware that any of us showed any distinction between "real" sibling or "step" sibling. We weren't given instructions on how to treat one another. We just fell into it naturally. It's amazing how well we got along.

A New School and My New Name

We were enrolled into Hamilton Elementary School in the Camden neighborhood. On my first day there in my 5th grade class, my teacher asked if my name Bobby was a short nickname for Barbara or Roberta. I quickly saw my chance to CHANGE my name finally and I GRABBED it! I slowly but eagerly replied, "Barbara." I had a new name that I liked! That lasted for the next seven years of my life. What a relief! I would never be teased about my name again. I overlooked my deceit and was very satisfied. I told M'Deah and to my relief she was okay with it.

We used to do air raid drills in school for possible atom bomb attacks. Nowadays kids do drills for school active shooter attacks. We never had an actual bomb attack. Sadly, that is not true for active shooter attacks. They are all too frequent with great loss of life for students, teachers, and other staff.

As a 5th grader, my appearance had greatly changed. I remember the portrait with babysitter, Shirley, in which I was a cute little girl wearing a favorite, brown-checked dress. But now I looked swollen and fat. As said, I learned later that this was a side-effect of the meds I was given to ensure healing for my hands.

I continued to do well in school. There was a big school campaign for home fire prevention. Those who did well earned a fire chief's badge for their work. I got one! These students merited a spot in the parade for the annual Summer Minneapolis Aquatennial. Not just any spot, but we got to ride on the red fire engine in the parade! It was quite an honor, and I enjoyed it.

One of the things I liked about our new school was an annual P.T.A. (Parent Teachers Association) event for which mothers sent a dish to school for lunch. My favorite dish was called a "hot dish," a casserole of ground beef in tomato sauce with macaroni. Yum! It was a highlight event.

Another fundraiser at both my elementary schools was the annual "paper sale." Students brought in old newspapers from home, preferably tied in bundles. They were sold by weight to a local company and funds were given to the school. Students were encouraged to participate and did, and helped homes get rid of a lot of old newspapers. Nearly every home subscribed to a daily newspaper and accumulated more paper than could be reasonably used in home garbage and other disposal tasks. Everybody won: the school's P.T.A., the kids, their homes, the paper processing company, and the city's dumps!

Church and School Partnered

Public schools participated in a program with local churches and Hamilton Elementary School was no exception. With parental consent, elementary school students could attend a local church of their denomination for an hour of Biblical instruction every Friday. The church provided the instruction and lunch. (I loved the canned tomato soup with crackers!) Catholic kids attended the Catholic church. I suppose Jewish kids likewise attended synagogue, and so on. Being mostly of Scandinavian heritage, with some Germans, most of the students and staff were Lutheran. There was no C.M.E. church nearby so

I attended the Methodist church that was only a block from the school. Home, school, and church all taught and confirmed the same moral and cultural values. We held these in common. What was taught there flowed to all other areas of society. It worked. It was a strength we lost later. Students whose parents didn't want them to participate in religious instruction simply remained in the classroom with the teacher. There was no animosity on the part of those who did or did not attend church instruction. It was all very civil! I treasure those times.

School taught common VALUES—the values of church and home. It was a three-fold cord that united us as families and as Americans. As church and home diminished its values, so did school. Parents preferred school academic achievements without values reinforcement and all society got the fruit of that emptiness. We still suffer from it today.

Land of 10,000 Lakes

Fishing was a perfect skill/hobby to have in Minnesota, the land of 10,000 lakes! And fish we did. We would take family fishing trips to local lakes in rural areas where you could stop enroute at bait stores to buy worms and other fishing gear. The lakes were plentiful on private farms, and you simply asked for permission to fish there. Many had boats available for rent. Usually, the kids stayed on shore and the adults went out on the lake in boats. K.C. may have been the only one who knew how to swim—thanks to mandatory military training. Sometimes, he went fishing alone or with buddies. Fishing trips always resulted in good eating—fried fish for dinners. M'Deah taught me how to prepare the fish hauls—scraping off the fish scales, gutting and cleaning the fish, and frying. Yum! Sometimes there were fish to be prepped for storage in the freezer too.

Danger!

On one such fishing trip, because I was the eldest, I was the baby-sitter for all the kids. We had traveled to the lake with Eloyce and her new husband, James, and with McCary in their own car. There was another family with us as well in a third car. All the adults got into boats and went fishing on the lake. Assigned to babysit, I tried to wrangle all the kids; there were lots of them and much more than I was used to overseeing! McCary was young, surely under five years of age. He kept running to the end of the dock and turning at the end to run back again. I kept telling him to stop running, but he ignored me. On his third run, he failed to turn at the end of the dock and landed in the water. I suddenly knew that he could drown! I ran to the end of the dock and lay on my belly. McCary was under the water, and I waited for him to come bobbing up again. I thought I had read somewhere that a person drowning would come up out of the water only three times. My thought was that I would wait for him to rise up and I would grab him somehow. I missed him when he came up the first time and the second time. His hair was too short for me to grab! Then he came up the third time and I grabbed him by his shirt. Only by the mercy and grace of God! Thankfully, he cried—and the lake water in him came out. The white farm owners had seen what occurred and came to the rescue. They got McCary into their own son's clean dry clothes. Our family fishing on the lake had seen what happened from the boats and quickly rowed to shore. I was shaking with gratitude that I had saved McCary's life. I was also scared that I was in trouble as the baby-sitter! But I explained how McCary had repeatedly NOT obeyed me to stop running and all was well. They were grateful that he was alive. Whew!

Hunting

Hunting was also another vital life skill to have. A new game for K.C. to hunt was Minnesota's bountiful pheasant! Often, he went hunting with our family. These jaunts would become family picnics too. I enjoyed these times because they were less stressful events for all. I always enjoyed the lunches M'Deah prepared for these times. Most delightful to me were her BLT sandwiches: nice crispy bacon, wet lettuce, made so by juicy red tomatoes, and delicious mayo—yum! So, what if the toasted bread got a little soggy—we devoured it all! It may have been an ordinary thing for other families, but it was the only time we

CHAPTER FOURTEEN

had BLT sandwiches. It made any picnic special These hunting trips gathered all kinds of food for our family besides pheasant. Wild ducks. Raccoon. Opossum. Squirrels. Wild rabbits. Deer. Our parents modeled and passed on to us what they had been taught about eating all food set before you: "Clean your plate," and we did. Thankfully, it was always tasty! It was a lesson that endured for a lifetime. I learned some valuable pioneer skills. I can skin a squirrel or rabbit. I can pluck a chicken or duck. Etc. But I never used them again as an adult!

M'Deah taught me how to prepare all this food for cooking. Feathers were plucked. Fur was removed by skinning. Bullets and buckshot were removed. Flesh was cut up and soaked in salt water. Excess was put away in the freezer. Much was cooked by her and eaten happily by all of us! We ate pheasant for Sunday dinner as commonly as some people ate chicken. In fact, pheasant was our chicken. The freezer was full of them. It was delicious and often served with M'Deah's iconic Minnesota wild rice dish with its mushrooms, onions, butter, and seasonings. M'Deah was a great cook! She usually fried and smothered it—delicious. I had read somewhere that it was considered to be a luxury food in most places around the world. But for us it was so common that we came close to being tired of it. Pheasant again?

An interesting new product was margarine. It was widely advertised and cheaper as a substitute for butter. It was interesting to pop the dye cap in the plastic bag and squeeze it around in the fat to make margarine! But I think it became popular mostly as a forbidden and illegal item in dairy-rich Minnesota! It was a regular thing for Minnesota families to drive to Iowa on short excursions to pick up the forbidden margarine and smuggle it back into Minnesota! It was like a game. Of course, years later it was also found to be a not-so-healthy substitute after all—even if you didn't mix it up yourself but bought and ate it pre-mixed.

Joe

We also had a dog when I was growing up. Most black people did not. From our Southern culture, animals were for work or for food, not for pets. Dogs and cats kept as pets were always kept outside; NEVER indoors where people lived. You didn't usually pay money for a dog. They were free as they kept breeding! Some people had dogs they found and took in as free pets, both cats and dogs. Our dog was a pointer named, Joe. K.C. bought him from a co-worker because pointers were working dogs and very useful in hunting. Joe was good at his job; it was a treat to later watch him point pheasants and retrieve them.

It was made clear to us that Joe was bought to be a working dog and not a pet. Not that either term meant anything to us, really. We didn't have any experience with any animals as a pet. You didn't

CHAPTER FOURTEEN

spend money on animals either. Money was for human expenses. We didn't take Joe to play with us or others wherever we went. We weren't cruel or unkind to Joe ever at all. We admired Joe when he went hunting and pointed. We understood why his breed was called "pointer." It was beautiful to see, and Joe was both happy and good at it, well-trained. I think Joe's main emotion, if he could have talked, was boredom. He didn't hunt enough to really get to enjoy it much.

Hunting greatly supplemented the family meat supply. We ate rabbits, squirrels, and ducks, but my favorite was pheasant. There was always some in the freezer too. K.C. and the boys hunted and sometimes the women went too, just to have a picnic or to walk the rows of corn on the hunting grounds. They were usually in a farmer's field where K.C. would ask permission to hunt. M'Deah and the girls cleaned the catch when we got home. She taught me and Linda how to prep it. I learned to cut the meat into serving sizes. It was hard work, but we knew the reward we had coming was a delicious meal M'Deah cooked. Yum! Of course, Joe was an outside dog with his own doghouse outside or space in the garage. He was only allowed into the house in cold winter weather. I don't remember what we deemed cold weather for Joe, but Minnesota winters were sometimes even too cold to snow. Joe was always glad to head for the basement whenever we let him in.

Overall, we treated Joe like a dog. We played with him some, but not much. I'm not sure we knew how to have and treat him as a pet. It wasn't part of our culture. That was common for whites, but mostly came later for blacks. For a short while, we also had a red Irish setter to hunt with Joe. But K.C. sold him to another hunter. Later, M'Deah had to sell Joe to a hunter too. She thought it cruel to keep him and not have him be used to hunt, which he loved doing, and she needed the money.

   K.C. was raised to fish and to hunt as many Southerners were. These were NOT just sports. They were often essential skills for obtaining necessary food! And you farmed your own produce and livestock. Not only were these essential survival skills, but they could also be times of refreshing enjoyment and relaxation as well. K.C. was always calmer and in a good mood when doing both fishing and hunting. He really enjoyed these times. Maybe they took him back to times of enjoyable childhood memories. Maybe they reminded him of times with his beloved grandfather. I don't know. But I do know that NO one has a childhood of ONLY bad memories. There's always some good in there, too.

Chittlins

   You haven't lived until you've cleaned chittlins! I remember assisting in the cleaning out of fresh chittlins—ugh, what a stinky, messy job! My parents

CHAPTER FOURTEEN

bought a whole slaughtered hog from a local farmer once. It was up to the customer to deal with the fresh chittlins though. Known formally as "chitterlings," chittlins are hog intestines. They came to us ready to clean—not cleaned. So that meant the intestine contents were still present. Someone had to stand on something tall to hold them and someone else would pour water through to flush out the contents of partially digested pig food. And pigs eat anything. Yuck! Thankfully, this was my first- and only-time cleaning fresh chittlins. Usually, we buy them from the grocery store—frozen in 5-pound red plastic buckets and already empty of contents. Of course, you must clean them further and it's very time-consuming. I thought at the time that only black slaves and their descendants ate chittlins. Wrong. Yes, they ate them. For survival, because slaves were usually given scraps to eat, and then because the slaves cleverly perfected cooking techniques to make them delicious. But I learned later that all poor peoples around the world included this in their cuisine. In fact, I read in my youth that they were then a gourmet dish in France! Chittlins are something you learn to eat when you're young and don't know what they really are. For those who know, it can be hard to digest! I only have one child and one grandchild who eat chittlins with great relish. The rest avoid them. They really are delicious when cooked right though. Even today, they are on many tables of slave descendants as part of the New Year's good luck and prosperity meal tradition.

Responsibilities

I was properly prepared at home for adulthood responsibilities. I was also taught sewing and cooking at home and in school. I began cooking when I was about 10 in 1951 after we moved to our new house. I wasn't a good cooking student because I would read a book while cooking and often burned food, even when ordered to remain in the kitchen when cooking. I would be so engrossed in the book that it overrode even my sense of smell; I didn't smell burning food on the stove. M'Deah would come running in despair and try to salvage the damage done and wonder at my absence of awareness and alarm. It happened multiple times, but she never gave up on me. I didn't become a great cook then but merely an acceptable one. But I became a great baker, particularly of homemade dinner yeast rolls. It was my signature dish. I used a recipe from M'Deah's first cookbook she had as a bride to make Parker House rolls. They became a great family favorite and something I made most Sundays—delicious! I called them "pocketbook rolls" because prior to the last rising, I would cut out a circle of rolled dough, putting a dollop of butter in the middle before folding it in half. You ate a "pocketbook" full of butter! Again, I say delicious! Unfortunately, I didn't make it my lifetime signature dish! Cornbread was the first skill mastered—something we had almost daily. I enjoyed learning to cook. I also made other dishes from M'Deah's cookbook. Desserts—cakes and cookies—were occasional treats. I liked oatmeal raisin cookies with pecans or walnuts.

Alcohol

Alcohol was not used in our home with minor exceptions. K.C. drank an occasional beer. Sometimes, at rare special holiday occasions, maybe we would get a tiny bit of Kosher wine: Mogen David or Manischewitz. The portion size was that of what was used at communion. M'Deah soaked her Christmas fruitcakes in alcohol, of course, to keep it moist. Neither of these was done together. Even if they had been, it wasn't enough to get any of us kids drunk—or even high! We had no real desire for alcohol and were never in danger of becoming alcoholics.

Gardening

My parents bought the vacant lot next door and used it as a flourishing garden for okra, potatoes, corn, green beans, collard greens, peas, and butter beans. We also had raspberry bushes in the backyard and rhubarb too, which was unfamiliar but grew easily. We didn't know what to do with rhubarb—it was too bitter to eat as a snack. But I looked in an old cookbook we had, and I learned to make rhubarb pies that were tasty. I remember having to work in the garden with all my siblings—but that's it. I remembered nothing of the how-to of gardening—the hoeing, digging, watering, weeding, fertilizing, harvesting, etc. I just have the memory of the important part: eating the delicious fresh food from the harvest!

Trips Down South

Other peaceful times involved our road trips down South. These occurred most summers. And to go to the segregated South often meant traveling by car on the road/highway. It was cheaper and sometimes necessary. If you were going to rural areas, which most slave descendants did, social resources needed for travel weren't always available to you. This meant transportation hubs like airports and train stations. It meant places to eat where you could be served. It meant available places to stay like hotels. In the South, these and other facilities were NOT always readily available to slave descendants. Because of the sometimes-rural nature? Yes. But MOSTLY because of segregation! There were sometimes facilities available to the public that were 'don't even think about it' for slave descendants! They were too dangerous. So, most trips 'down South' were by your private car that involved multiple days. So, we slept in our car. We ate in our car. And we used roadside trips to the nearby woods for our bathroom necessities. So, no such trips were made without having your own toilet

CHAPTER FOURTEEN

paper packed as a necessity! And your own food too—often white bread and boloney. No showers or bathing was done along the way. And you went straight through—no stopovers. Keep going until you reach your destination. Yeah, those were good times. It's one of those things that you may enjoy, but you're glad when it's over!

Oh. When we had these trips, they were always to Hattiesburg, Mississippi, K.C.'s hometown. We never went to M'Deah's hometown of Chatom, Alabama or to Meridian, Mississippi where Auntie and Uncle Robert still lived for a while. Curious.

Prosperity

Our meals changed somewhat too. After K.C. came into our lives, we had meat entrees during the week more frequently. Billy and I were happy either way for we were always filled with delicious food. Although they looked well physically, I'm sure having regular full meals was a new and happy habit for K.C.'s kids too. Most black people of our generations were economically lower middle class. But I think we thought of ourselves as just middle class. Our family worked actively and hard for that designation—onward and upward. It was the American Dream, although they didn't think of it that way. For them, it was just the dream of the slave descendants.

K.C.'s job had benefits for our family as well. He would be given gifts by his construction company employer. One was a holiday box of food to prepare for Thanksgiving dinner—with a turkey and all else. And it was done again at Christmas. There were other things too that weren't new items: an upright piano, a Model T Ford car, and many used books were given or sold to K.C It was all a blessing we enjoyed immensely. One year, it was an old classic jukebox from the 1940s. We kids were all fascinated by it! And it was in a format/mode that did NOT require money to be inserted in order for it to play. An added benefit was that it played 78s and 45s—even some 33s later! Music heaven! While all of us kids enjoyed it, I think I got the most pleasure from using that jukebox. I would dance by myself, listening to the free music sounds, and using a pole in the basement as my partner. I looked forward to enjoying it for a long time. So, I was sad when M'Deah said that she'd had to sell it years later.

CHAPTER FIFTEEN
Changes and Puberty

One night, when I was 12 years old, I awoke thinking I had somehow wet the bed, because it felt wet. NO! A trip to the bathroom revealed that I was not wet—but bleeding! I was horrified as I remembered that K.C.'s mother had been bleeding in the bathroom too. Was I also dying of cancer? I gently knocked on my parents' bedroom door and softly called out, "M'Deah!" She answered my call and came out to see what I needed. I softly explained that I was bleeding, and my stomach hurt slightly. For some reason, I didn't want K.C. to hear me. She accompanied me to the bathroom and helped me clean myself up. She told me to lie back down, and she would come back later. I waited anxiously. Why was I anxious? Why was I waiting? I believed that I was dying of cancer, and she didn't seem concerned—she was way too calm about my upcoming death! She put some clothes on and got into the car and left! I was puzzled. Why did she go out at night and not K.C.? (Generally, in the culture then, men didn't buy menstrual items—only women did.) What is going on? When she returned shortly, she said she had gone to the drugstore. She had bought two things that she took me into the bathroom to wear: a Kotex pad and a small belt to attach it. I was still puzzled. All the while, M'Deah didn't say a word about all that had happened to my body. But I could hear her talking quietly to K.C. in their bedroom. Maybe she was letting him know that I had cancer. Sigh. After a few days the bleeding stopped, and I thought maybe I was somehow healed of my affliction.

A couple weeks later, the girls in our class were separated from the boys and we were to watch an animated Disney movie. Sounds like fun. But we weren't told why. I wondered what movie could the boys not be allowed to watch also? I soon found out. The movie was called, "The Story Of Menstruation". And it answered all my puzzled questions about why I had been bleeding! I was so relieved to find out that I was NOT dying of cancer after all. M'Deah really had no reason to show me any great concern! Whew! But why hadn't she told me about puberty changes? Sadly, she was not the only mother that skipped this in the 1950s. When I told her some five years later, how I had suffered the tormenting thoughts of my impending cancer death, she explained that she ASSUMED that I had already been taught this at school. It was the beginning of schools doing 'sex education'. Parents, your assumptions about what's taking place in school are NOT always accurate or good—even to this day! Find out! Altogether, my

CHAPTER FIFTEEN

puberty years in school were good with spikes of bad. My home life was the opposite: bad with spikes of good.

Household Chores

Chores were a part of our everyday life—a natural. During the week, they were light, and we rotated them after dinner: washing dishes, drying and putting away dishes, sweeping the dining room and kitchen floors, emptying the garbage, etc. (Once in doing dishes, I dropped a glass, and it shattered. No one was more surprised than I was. I was holding onto the glass as usual and suddenly my fingers seemed to lock in a looser position and the glass simply fell through. I explained it to M'Deah and she was very kind to me. I was relieved to not be accused of carelessness. This happened at least once more as I grew up. It was unexplainable, but probably a result of my hand injury,)

Saturday required a few more chores—cleaning our rooms, etc. It also included doing laundry. For most of the years after our washer-wringer machine died, K.C. did NOT agree to buy a replacement. I don't know why he didn't. So M'Deah and the girls went to the laundromat on Saturdays—ugh. Saturday chores also included dusting the first-floor Venetian blinds, (a chore of mine that I hated doing and I promised myself that I would never have any in my future home!), mopping floors, vacuuming floors, cleaning bathrooms, etc. We were productively busy as we learned the value and necessity of working together for the common good. To this day I don't mind washing dishes by hand. But I still don't like drying them! I never have liked dealing with the progressively wetter and wetter dish towel!

One chore that was also common for the times was the milkman's box. Yes, milk companies still delivered dairy products to your home then. You placed empty glass milk jugs there and emptied it of milk and butter that you ordered. The box was somewhat sure to keep its contents cold for a reasonable amount of time to prevent spoilage.

At some point, each child was responsible to wash and iron their own clothes. I was responsible to also do so for our parents' clothes and bed linen. Billy was always fastidious about his grooming and appearance. He was delighted to get his clothes looking suitable to his taste. I thought that he would be able to wear a gunnysack and look like he just modeled for GQ—Gentlemen's Quarterly magazine. He just had that bearing about him. I saw it later in our son, Todd, too.

I gradually learned to hate ironing. I was pleased when commercials came out to tout the new wrinkle-free clothing. Even though they really weren't so initially. After leaving home, I began to look for clothes that had labels reading 'no ironing needed' and 'no dry cleaning needed'. I didn't want to iron any longer if I could avoid it. And I didn't want to add dry cleaning cost to the initial cost of a garment. To me it didn't make sense to do so. It's funny how childhood prejudices stay with you! That became a lifelong practice.

M'Deah kept a clean house and taught us to do the same. She worked a lot outside the house, but our home didn't suffer for it. Our home had simple structure. Because M'Deah worked so much, that was the only way it could function for the good of us all. I don't remember when she didn't work two or more jobs. For us, supper was always at 5:00. When we heard later that New Yorkers had dinner at 8:00, we laughed at the absurdity of it all. Because 8:00 was bedtime for the kids, so how could we possibly eat that late? We weren't asleep by 8:00 but that's when serious bedtime prep began so we could possibly be asleep by 8:30. I was glad that my twin bed had its head at the single bedroom window. An 8:00 bedtime meant it was still daylight outside sometimes. We were required to lower the window shade, but I would raise it a few inches. Why? I delighted to read for as long as I could by the fading sunlight until the writing on the pages couldn't be clearly read any longer. Then the only choice was to go to sleep! But I enjoyed hearing the birds singing before dark as I read books by dimming sunlight and sometimes by flashlight before finally having to give up and lower the shade. Maybe finally tired, I would go to sleep peacefully—hoping not to be awakened during the night by cussing and strange sounds from my parents' bedroom. I later learned that these sounds were blows being given to my mother by K.C. Sometimes when I did, I would get up and go to the bathroom, hoping the sound of someone else being awake would stop the attacks on M'Deah. It's a horrible feeling to know you're absolutely helpless to assist someone you know needs help. Sadly.

Bath times were reserved for Saturday night. On other days we observed the morning "wash-up". We woke at 6:00 and had an unrushed morning start that always included making our beds. (Breakfast was usually cold cereal which each child could prep for themselves. A rare treat was pancakes. Even rarer was homemade waffles. K.C. always had homemade biscuits with bacon and eggs and grits—a hearty breakfast for a laborer. M'Deah always prepared him a hearty lunch for work too. Maybe those breakfast sandwiches or dinner leftovers like a pork chop sandwich, etc. It later became one of my chores to prepare his lunches.) As a student later at Patrick Henry Junior-Senior High School, that left plenty of time to leave home at 8:00 to be at school by 8:30 when homeroom started. Classes began at 9:00 and ended at 3:00. Then you'd head for home or to your extracurricular activity of choice. Or in later years, you'd head for your part-time job.

I didn't know it then but M'Deah was methodical—a very beneficial trait for her. Things needing doing got done. I only discovered years later it was

CHAPTER FIFTEEN

an admirable trait that I learned my daughter also had. It served them both well. And others whom they served profited greatly by it.

The Ice Cream Churn

Another favorite but less frequent chore was to churn the hand-crank ice cream freezer. That was maybe the most delightful chore because of the product it produced: very rewarding and delicious icy-cold ice cream. This too was a chore I assisted in doing, but it was not a regular chore—just occasional. All the kids took a turn with the crank until the ice cream was ready. Homemade ice cream is something we all enjoyed for years, wherever we went. We could always look forward to having homemade ice cream for Summer holidays—Memorial Day, 4th of July, and Labor Day—as well as for no reason at all.

School Continues For M'Deah

At some point in my teens, M'Deah decided to take a course with a correspondence school to become a Licensed Practical Nurse (LPN). She would still work in the hospital, which she enjoyed. But she would get out of the kitchen as a dietetic cook, which she did well. Today's version of the then-popular correspondence schools would be online courses. In addition to working, she now also had homework. But she did it—she successfully graduated and changed her career. Her new job worked under the supervision of Registered Nurses (RNs). It involved more of the grunt work of nursing and less of the medical side. M'Deah often did both, however. She was competent enough that nurses trusted her to responsibly do that clandestinely. One day, M'Deah hurt her back as she assisted getting a patient into bed. She suffered pain from that back injury for many years and was told it was due to a slipped disk from that event. The pain would come and go—but mostly come.

Sisterly Help

We didn't get allowances. We worked. So the boys had newspaper routes and the girls (well, me) did babysitting. It was our own money from which we were to give church offerings, to save, and to afford our own expenses of recreation, (movies, comic books, records, etc.), and snacks. It was never expected that we would buy our own clothes, except for an occasional approved item. Our parents expected nothing from monies we earned. Certainly, the boys shared with Floyd, and I shared with Linda. Sharing with those who had less was a value we were taught for living a good life.

Linda and I helped out when 'the boys' had Boy Scout camp in the summer for two weeks. Emeal and Billy had a morning paper route that we took over during these times. We delivered the Minneapolis Tribune early in the morning. The Minneapolis Star was the evening paper. We collected payments as

CHAPTER FIFTEEN

well and had to keep good records. I remember that as we delivered the newspapers, we would see people sleeping on their front porches to escape the Summer heat, as they lay secure behind their screen doors. It was a safe time to do so. We enjoyed doing this task and we enjoyed when it was over! I don't remember that we ever got any money for it though. Maybe we did but I don't think so. It was just a way of 'helping out'. Everyone did that, we were taught.

We knew nothing of tossing newspapers. Our community norm was to place it quietly on the porch and, if the porch was locked, we placed it on the front steps. Usually, porch doors were only locked in the Summer. Why? Because many residents were sleeping on their porches during hot weather. To have home air conditioning was extremely rare. I knew none who had it. And porch locks usually consisted of just a latch hook. Nothing more was needed in our safe environment.

A Crisis For Linda

When Linda was 12 years old, she did something that highlighted the state of our family life. It was on a Saturday and all of us kids were doing our regular weekend chores. I noticed that Linda was walking a little strangely—she was stumbling a lot. She was also slurring her words whenever she spoke. I had NEVER seen her behave like this before. It was strange—and frightening. Why was this happening?

I remember something I had learned earlier in the week. I don't know whether I read it or saw it on TV, but it was about aspirin overdoses. Suddenly, I knew what was wrong with Linda. Unusually, M'Deah was home this Saturday instead of working at an extra job and was also doing her own chores—maybe working on dinner prep. I mentioned to her that Linda was behaving strangely and maybe had taken too many aspirin—in a suicide attempt. In alarmed disbelief, M'Deah questioned Linda. And Linda admitted that's exactly what she had done! She had taken all the rest of the pills in the nearly full baby aspirin bottle! Why? Linda had spent the previous night in a one-time-ever privilege. A classmate had invited her to spend the night and Linda got RARE permission to go. NONE of us had ever spent the night away from home since K.C.'s kids had come to join us. Linda said that for the FIRST time in her life, she observed a family living in PEACE! This family lived in an atmosphere of LOVE. There were NO harsh words spoken, NO wife-beating abuse, and NO fearful atmosphere! She was astonished to discover that some real families actually lived like this. And she couldn't bear the contrast with her own family. She wanted to die. So, she took the whole bottle of baby aspirin that were kept in the bathroom medicine cabinet. That's why she was behaving as she did. M'Deah told K.C. and they got Linda immediate medical help to make her vomit. That was followed by a trip to the hospital to have her stomach pumped.

CHAPTER FIFTEEN

Again, it was ONLY by the Grace of God that I could even conceive of this possibility for the reason of Linda's behavior. It's as though I suddenly KNEW what was going on. And her life was spared. And it was ONLY by His Grace that I had even learned of and remembered that very week of this possible aspirin danger. God is Good.

It was very humbling for K.C. to learn why his beloved Linda had come to a point of wanting to die and not live. Of course, Dr. Schwartz, the family doctor had to become aware of this too. Things SEEMED to get better. For a short while. Convinced of M'Deah's love for her, Linda never did this again. But K.C. was still K.C.

The Slap

Around this time, I did something both common and unthinkable for a teenager. It was common at the time among teens to have this reply when given an assignment by their parent. Parents usually heard, "Just a minute!" It was usually said in irritation at being disturbed in their own private little world and in being treated like a child—which we were often in denial about that as our true ID. One day, M'Deah and I had that interaction. I don't think it was because her request was about anything difficult at all. My reply of teenage irritation not only said I didn't regard her request as something important or urgent, but also said 'How dare you interrupt me?' too. For some reason, we were in the bathroom. I looked at M'Deah's face and saw a pain in her eyes that I had never seen before. Maybe it was pain of being so badly treated by her own daughter whom she deeply loved and had done so much for. I had never treated her so badly before. M'Deah did something she had never done before too. She slapped me! I knew that I had it coming. I quickly did what she had asked of me. No words were spoken between us about the incident. But I never spoke to her in that disrespectful 'grown' way again. I was about 14.

My Sweet 16

16 was a big year for me—a year of meaningful small events. I only knew it looking backward decades later.

A major childhood friend in our new neighborhood was Marsha. She lived about two blocks from us and was about a year younger than I was. She had a sister a year older than me. Like me, this sister was also the only class Negro when she graduated from Henry a year prior to me. And she was smart too. Each generation is unique with unique experiences in school and in life. It was also Marsha who taught me the only card game I knew: War. With only us two players, it was the most boring game I had ever played! I told myself that I just wasn't a card player. It wasn't my thing!

I'm unsure of the timing, but M'Deah decided that I should have a Sweet 16 birthday party. She

CHAPTER FIFTEEN

arranged for me to have it at our home. I'm sure she tried to involve me in the planning, but I don't think I was of much help. Invited guests included my friend, Marsha, and Linda, of course. I also invited a 'family' member: Eugenia (not her real name). I understood Eugenia's disdain for my party with no boys. I made a feeble excuse that I didn't know any—which was the truth. She said I should have asked her for some to invite. No. I wasn't greatly disappointed. I knew I could never have a typical teen party, because of K.C. But I would never have said that out loud to anyone—not even to myself!

I was just grateful that M'Deah had insisted I have the party and for all her effort at providing food, etc. Maybe she compared it to her life at 16 when she was free enough to elope and I had very little freedom by comparison. I was very aware that I was behind in social skills and development and that it would remain so—I accepted it. M'Deah told her sisters about the party and they all honored me in some way. Eloyce told me she was 16 when I was born and had looked forward to us celebrating my 16th birthday together—maybe having a beer. But now her party days were over, and she felt old as a 32- year old woman with a houseful of kids! She brought me a beer anyway and tried to get me to drink it with her. I tasted the beer just to please her. But I hated the taste and that was the end of that! Auntie gave me three of her clothing items as hand-me downs:

a beautiful pink brocade dress, a pair of green silk lounging pajamas, and a pink peignoir set. I felt very fancy and grown up! It was the only birthday party I ever had, to my remembrance, and I was very grateful for it. They were the only gifts I remember receiving from Auntie. They were adult gifts I later definitely used as a newlywed. At some point, even Carrie gave me a very nice no-iron print dress.

A few months later on a visit to me, I had a very serious conversation with Eugenia about a rumor I had heard. But she vehemently denied she was pregnant, even swearing by God and assured me she would tell me if it were true. I believed her. A few weeks later, I heard that she and her mother had gone out of town for a vacation. That was strange. Why would her mother leave all the other kids and her man behind? Then I learned Eugenia was indeed pregnant. I was dumbfounded! Why did she lie to me and make me feel like such a fool for believing her?

About a month later, Eugenia and her mother came back from their vacation. We were told that her mother had given birth in that time to Eugenia's 'little sister'. That's how some teen unwed pregnancies were handled back then. As for me, our friendship was over. She never apologized for having so blatantly lied to me. There could never again be trust in our relationship. It was over. Apparently, she just wrote me off as someone who was naïve and easily deceived. I was thus deemed as unworthy of an

CHAPTER FIFTEEN

apology. I was just naïve and trusting. That sealed something else for me too. I hate lies! It's as though you aim to deceive me by stealing the truth and giving me a lie in its place—so you gain some advantage over me. I hate that!

I Almost Swim

Also at 16, I decided I needed to learn to swim. I would do so in the warm summer weather. I don't know where he had learned, but Billy knew how to swim very well. I thought it was a very important survival skill. Besides it was a recreational activity many people enjoyed in the land of 10,000 lakes. I took lessons with the Red Cross. They were done at one of the city lakes. One day while being taught to float, it was on a very windy day. The wind was so strong that it was nearly impossible to float. In fact, it was downright scary being helplessly pushed around in the water by uncontrollable wind. I made that my last lesson!

Zion Baptist Church

At 16, I asked M'Deah if I could join the Baptist church most Minneapolis blacks attended. There were more teenagers there and more teen activities/programs. Our A.M.E. church I attended offered NO outlet for teens and seemed to even resent our growing up! I had volunteered to serve with the children's teacher and helped her out with various duties. I later began to want out of this church where I felt unwanted.

So, I looked elsewhere and learned most black teens attended the Baptist church. So, I sought to do so too. M'Deah agreed and I found a wealth of things teens there could do. Of course, there was a teen Sunday school class. In addition, there was a teen choir I enjoyed being a part of, and a teen Sunday evening activity called BYU which I only attended once. I felt welcome and stayed there until I got married three years later. The only thing I lacked was an answer from my Sunday School teacher, when I asked him a question. He was a Christian bank officer so I thought he should know the answer. I asked him why God didn't talk to His people anymore as He had done in the Bible—surely, we needed to hear from Him too and like never before. I didn't know his answer was the stock weak theological answer so common then. My teacher said, 'God doesn't need to talk to us anymore because we have whatever He would say in written form—the Holy Bible.' I had to accept his answer, having no counter answer/ explanation. But I didn't really agree with it. Where were the people who knew God and could give me an answer? Did they no longer exist? Did that mean I would never have any conversation or get answers from Him either? I considered that a dismal prospect. But I went on as the compliant church member that I was.

I also joined the Junior Choir. I liked to sing and thoroughly enjoyed the choir. One of my favorite times was when we marched in on a Sunday morning

CHAPTER FIFTEEN

to take our place at our part of the choir loft, singing all the way. And I did get acquainted with some other black teens at last.

My pastor was Rev. Raymond Botts, an older man. He had as his assistant the young Rev. Stanley King. I preferred the dynamic personable sermons of his youth and kinda thought of Rev. Botts as too old to be relevant to me. I was happy when he retired and Rev. King took over. However, another man was soon elected to be senior pastor, Pastor Hollowell, because Rev. King left to start his own church. I saw our new pastor as an OKAY boring middle-aged man. Of course, he had my respect. That's what I had been taught as part of my upbringing. Gradually, I heard that Rev. Botts had regarded Rev. King as too immature and lacked the heart necessary to be a senior pastor. Rev. King and his wife actually lived in the apartment above my Aunt Eloyce and her new husband, James. She told M'Deah of frequently hearing him and his fellow young pastors gossiping about and laughing at their church members. Eloyce lost all respect for him then. It affected the spiritual growth of both her and James. Sadly.

Going to Zion meant we had to take the city bus, because it was much further away from home. By then, it was usually just Linda and me. We would take the bus to church, but we'd walk the two miles home in nice weather. We thought it was fun. We'd usually stop enroute home at the Hires root beer stand near the church and I would buy us a treat with my babysitting money. My favorite was a root beer float. Yum! More often the boys stayed home. I don't know or remember why. Sometimes they would be required to give K.C. some slight help with whatever project he was working on at the time. Bottomline, our parents left church attendance up to us as a choice. For me, I had a genuine gratitude to God for saving my life from Buster. Surely, I could go to His house in thanksgiving for that! And He was keeping us all alive in a household with K.C. Besides, church had always been a part of my life that I enjoyed. Even back in the Chatom days.

I had heard of the BYU—Baptist Youth Union, I think. It was the youth group that met in church on Sunday evenings. I thought I would be involved in that. But the evening meeting time was not convenient because I had city bus transportation only. I would never inconvenience my parents by asking them to be my transportation.

My Summer Job

Like most teens, I longed to have a job. I began babysitting jobs at age 12 (ending with about three regular clients). Initially, I asked a few other classmates about what they charged for babysitting. And I charged the customary 35 cents per hour plus 50 cents an hour after midnight. That increased later to 50 cents an hour plus 75 cents an hour after midnight. It was enough to meet my needs and desires.

CHAPTER FIFTEEN

I usually bought a few paperback books and a few treats. I also shared some with Linda for her minimal needs. I heard adults say not to worry about working because it would last the rest of my life once it began. But I wanted a job. It progressed to library volunteer, to short-lived truck farming, and to a part time paid library job. That was my journey.

At 16, I was legally eligible to work. And I was very anxious to finally get a real job! I somehow heard at school of jobs available at a local 'truck farm'. I think it was through the guidance counselor that I learned a local farm was hiring kids for the Summer. I don't know why it was called a 'truck farm' but it was the only door that opened for me. So, I applied and was hired. Our duties were digging potatoes, picking and shucking corn, picking tomatoes, watering vegetables, etc. Altogether, it was hard work under the hot summer sun and I gave it my best. I traveled to and from the farm by city bus.

One day the sun really did a number on me, but I didn't know it. I just felt strange and very tired. Because of the heat, workers were sent home early—around noon. As I waited for the public bus to go home, I began to feel cold too, although I knew it was still hot. I thought that was strange. On the ride home, while waiting on the bench for my second bus to arrive at my transfer point, I still felt super-tired and somewhat dizzy, and my eyesight was a little blurry. The sun seemed extra hot and extra bright.

The last bus reached its final destination, about two blocks from my house, and I walked home slowly. I was clearly not well when I got home.

    Thankfully, M'Deah was home. She took one look at me and knew something was wrong. She began to ask me about my symptoms. M'Deah told me I seemed to have had a heat stroke—something I was totally unfamiliar with. M'Deah knew the proper treatment from her experiences in the hot Alabama sun. She had me get undressed and get into a tub of cold water she ran for me. The water didn't even feel particularly cold to me, even though she had added ice cubes to the bath water. But it cooled my body down. I slowly got better and recovered. After some time, I was able to get out of the tub by myself and felt much better. This was followed by a long nap to recover—M'Deah put me to bed. I went to sleep quickly and slept for hours and hours that afternoon. M'Deah did not allow me to continue working at the truck farm and explained why. I wasn't mad. I didn't care about the loss of income and was glad to settle for lesser monies from my few babysitting jobs.

    But I did notice something different about myself from that day forward. My eyes were particularly sensitive to bright sunlight and even to the glare from snowdrifts. And from that point, I began to wear sunglasses as something I needed—for every glaring position, bright sunshine, bright snow on the ground, etc. I never needed them before and thought of them

CHAPTER FIFTEEN

as somewhat of an affectation or style statement people wanted to make. They were now a definite need for me—for clear sight by light sensitive eyes. I bought cheapies at first and then the better Polaroid sunglasses. At least, I looked stylish!

M'Deah's Happy Time

On rare occasions, maybe just a handful of times, M'Deah SANG—usually in the kitchen while cooking/baking. Years later, she told me she had sung in the adult choir of Holsey Memorial C.M.E. Church, when she first moved to Minneapolis. I didn't remember that at all! I came to love the song she sang most often—usually it was the only song she sang:

"Pass me not, O gentle Savior, Hear my humble cry
Whilst on others Thou art calling, Do not pass me by!"

Was it a cry for help? A prayer? Wondering what went wrong in her life? Memories of a life without violent abuse? Hope for a better future? I don't know. Probably all of the above. I just remember that she seemed happy as she sang and how much it touched my heart to see her joy and peace then. Unforgettable. I think the last time I remember was the Christmas that K.C. went South to visit his family. I don't know why he went alone. He had gone away from our home then and there was great peace and joy in his absence. I think I was about 14 or 15 years old at the time.

CHANGES AND PUBERTY

I have a couple of photos of M'Deah taken during that time. She had asked for her picture to be taken. That was done a lot back in Chatom. She looks as though she had no worries but was beautiful, young, and happy as she smiled. And she was. For a short while—until K.C. returned home. I don't remember that she ever had a recreational or social life after marrying K.C.

One of M'Deah's rare pleasures was to get her beautiful hair done every two weeks. Her beautician was either of two sisters who lived together and had a salon in their basement. My beautician was M'Deah! I remember going to the salon of the sisters only a very few times. They were friends to M'Deah and she enjoyed her time there. It was really her only social activity and time of peaceful relaxing.

CHAPTER SIXTEEN

More Teen Home Life

This visit came a few years later, when I was in my teens. It was made by Papa. His health issues were also diagnosed as terminal cancer. I don't remember for sure, but probably prostate cancer. We tried to re-connect to the closeness we enjoyed when I was younger—with mixed results.

(I had overheard many family discussions re Papa over the years. After Big Mama died, his kids—mainly Carrie, I think—discovered that he had a girlfriend. They were not happy about it and accused her of being merely a gold-digger who would benefit from all the things their mother should have had! The plan was to go 'down South' and beat her up—or rather, have my mother beat her up! To them, M'Deah's great value was that she was bold and courageous. But they always tried to manipulate these traits for THEIR selfish use. Not this time. She didn't do it. Papa was told about this plan. It became unnecessary—they broke up. M'Deah deeply admired both of her parents and may have gotten some of her courageous attitude from Papa.)

After Papa was diagnosed with incurable cancer, he returned to Chatom. Maybe it was to set his affairs in order. Because he came back to Minneapolis later—maybe staying with Carrie and Tommy—and died there shortly thereafter. He is buried in Minneapolis in our family section of the Camden Cemetery. Sadly too, I have no photos of Professor Lawrence. I have never even seen a photo of him, and no other family member has a photo either. I've asked. Sigh.

Before that, Papa gave me his portable typewriter, which I kept for many years. And he gave me a book to use for my continued learning—which we both enjoyed. It was an old book that was sort of a one-volume encyclopedia. I held onto it for quite a while too. I finally decided that it was outdated and had nothing to teach me. I don't know what became of it. I think it was disposed of along with some other childhood items I'd put in a footlocker and left at home, when I moved to Denver as a newlywed. Papa was always a big inspiration in my life during the limited time I knew him. And ever afterwards. He made great impact on all who knew him—certainly on his children and grandchildren. I remember him telling me of the importance of education and that what was put into your head could never be removed by ANYONE. It was yours to keep and to use.

Brave Papa

Papa certainly was familiar with the restrictions of Jim Crow. It had greatly negatively affected his life.

CHAPTER SIXTEEN

But he badly wanted to vote for Eisenhower when he ran for president in 1952. The campaign slogan was popular nationwide as was Eisenhower—the hero of WWII. What was the slogan? "I Like Ike"! But it was unthinkable for a Negro in the Deep South to even consider voting then. But he tried anyway. The results? 'Professor Lawrence' went to the courthouse polls to become a registered voter—and was badly beaten for it. But he was just one of the many who believed the Republican campaign slogan that swept the country: 'I like Ike'. But KKK don't play. He didn't try that again. Carrie led the charge in telling him how foolish he had been to even THINK about voting in Alabama rather than thinking about what the loss of his life would mean to the family. Only a successful civil rights movement uniting all races and religions of people could change that. Only God could change that. And He did.

Slavery Terms Hang On

There were terms used in our world/lives that were unique leftovers from slave times. For example, "whuppin'/whippin'" was the slave term for "whipping"—a throwback to when slaves were actually beaten with whips. Now, it was about parental corporal punishment for their mis-behaving children. This came not in the form of an actual whipping though! It could mean being hit with a leather belt, a tree switch (small tree twig), etc. A belt was more common—especially in cold Minneapolis weather when all tree switches were usually frozen in the winter. Really cruel parents used an electric cord, a coat hanger, etc. I thought that was abusive and was happy it didn't apply to our home! Billy and I got very few whippin's. I don't know what Billy's thinking was. But I thought a perverse K.C. would sometimes beat M'Deah for OUR bad behavior. We always tried to be 'good' so that wouldn't happen. We all did. K.C. was VERY harsh in his whippin's of his own children—particularly of Emeal. His son, Emeal, got it worst for some reason. Maybe K.C. used him as an example of making him manly/tough. I don't know. I always felt sorry when he did, because K.C. never failed to leave 'welts' behind. These were red bruise marks on the skin caused by blows. Sadly.

Or maybe it was likely that K.C. was now giving Emeal the same type of whippings he himself had received as a child. It was cruel I thought, and no other child was ever treated that way. These whippings always left welt marks behind that lasted for days on Emeal's body. I was glad these whippings were applied to no one else and wondered how Emeal felt about them. Of course, I didn't ask him.

Another leftover slave terminology was "head of chillen." It was about how many children you had—like heads of cattle. During slavery it was profitable for your slaves to produce as many children as possible. And because you weren't regarded as fully human

CHAPTER SIXTEEN

(only human enough for the white men to have sex with the slave women), a cattle term was used to refer to the children. During slavery, the number was often in the teens or higher. Even when I was growing up, it was common for slave descendants to have large families. (Famed civil rights activist, Fannie Lou Hamer, was one of 20 children of a sharecropping family.) Birth control pills were to be invented in the future. It was often considered economically detrimental to do so. But those with large families weren't generally fearful—just trusting God to provide. And for those, He always did.

Another common leftover slave term was 'M'Deah'. All my classmates referred to their mothers as 'Mom". That's the motherly name that I wanted to use too. One day in my late teens, I asked God about it and came to realize that the slave meaning of "M'Deah" was 'Mother Dear'! Amazingly, it was not so foreign to me now! I was OKAY with it forever afterwards.

"Nothing beats failure but a try" was a popular saying I heard adults say often. I didn't understand what that meant because I thought they were saying, "Nothing beats failure but a trial." But I finally got it. They meant don't give up when you haven't even tried. I'm sure many former slaves and their descendants lived by that ole saying! It's how they made it.

S & H Green Stamps

One iconic phenomenon of the 1950s was S&H Green Stamps. This is what Wikipedia says about them:

> S&H Green Stamps were a line of trading stamps popular in the United States from 1896 until the late 1980s. They were distributed as part of a rewards program operated by the Sperry & Hutchinson company (S&H), founded in 1896 by Thomas Sperry and Shelley Byron Hutchinson. During the 1960s, the company promoted its rewards catalog as being the largest publication in the United States and boasted that it issued three times as many stamps as the U.S. Postal Service. Customers received stamps at the checkout counter of supermarkets, department stores, and gasoline stations among other retailers, that could be redeemed for products in the catalog...S&H Green Stamps had several competitors.

Our family, like most others of the time, freely used these stamps. We collected them to get items for the house. One such was a set of colored aluminum water glasses. The colors were great because each family member was assigned a glass by color, and it cut down on a lot of confusion! Another was a set of green sherbet dishes. They were great for desserts. M'Deah usually served lime sherbet with creme de menthe in these glasses. And we got a big and complete set of green dinnerware dishes. These last two

CHAPTER SIXTEEN

items may have been things M'Deah later sold to get necessary funds. I never saw them again in later years. Happily, around 2015, I saw two of them (serving bowls) at my local Goodwill and grabbed them up. I still have these childhood mementoes. The pattern is called Colonial Homestead by Royal.

Christmas Times

These were magical, as they should be for children! M'Deah and K.C. busily did their secret shopping. There was lots of baking cookies. And M'Deah always made a fruit cake, generously soaked with liquor before the holiday. I may be strange, but I liked fruitcake. And I liked eggnog too. We decorated the live Christmas tree our parents bought with glass ornaments used from year to year. The tree lights were colored—varied or the color of the year. I remember the blue year well! They were beautiful indoors and outdoors. We toured by car the neighborhoods known for beautiful Christmas outdoor decorating—usually in the suburbs. Every year involved a trip downtown to visit the department store window Christmas displays, which usually included some moving items. And don't forget the visit to the department store Santa and a possible photo with him for your parents to buy! That was lots of fun. We opened our presents on Christmas morning. The rule was we could get up early for Christmas, but we had to have been asleep before then, and it had to be after midnight for sure. Often, M'Deah and K.C. would be wrapping presents and assembling some gifts at or after midnight. The first child who woke was allowed to wake all the others after getting permission, so we would open our presents together by turn. I don't know how they did it, but our parents were great gift-givers—but not extravagant. Presents were thoughtfully picked and always included some clothing items. Our Christmases were good and full of great childhood memories. And the Christmas tree was always taken down on New Year's Day. New Year's dinner always included the Southern standard good-luck meal: black-eyed peas for many coins throughout the year, greens for much folding money throughout the year, and pork for plenty of food throughout the year. Good times. Oh, yes, we each had our own bike that we got one Christmas. Most kids in our time did—it was the norm.

Our Toni Dolls

My stepsister Linda and I had always usually gotten along very well in spite of our 5-year age difference. We shared a bedroom, even though our twin beds made for a fairly tight fit! I was happy to have a little sister and another sibling. Being older, I could teach her things too. We didn't always share toys, but one Christmas we both were very pleasantly surprised to each get a Toni doll! It was every girl's dream gift. It came with a Toni hair perm kit, and you

CHAPTER SIXTEEN

could style her hair—comb it, brush it, perm it. It was ideal! We were both delighted with our new dolls! We considered re-naming them to our own liking. 'Toni' was just the trademark name. But we didn't.

On one visit from company, a couple came from St. Paul with a couple of their little daughters. Linda and I were commanded to let them play with our Toni dolls. For me, I had already purposed to save my doll in her original box and maintain her in her pristine condition. Why? I was saving her to give to the daughter I would have someday. Where this thought came from, I don't know. But I was firmly fixed on it. But now I'm commanded to SHARE her with another child? And I have NO choice. I had no more ownership—she was taken from me. Even though I protested that I was saving her for my daughter someday, M'Deah ignored my protests to her. Because you shared with company. Always. And you obeyed your parents. Always. As I handed my doll to one of the visiting girls, I was saying a good-bye in my heart. The other child mangled my Toni's fresh-as-new hair. I got my doll back as they ended their visit. But I never played with or touched her again. I no longer regarded her as MY doll. She had been violated and my daughter would never see this now-mangled mess of a toy. I meant it. I packed her back up in her box I had always kept her in and placed it on the closet shelf. Linda frequently styled her doll's hair—until it was bald. No more Toni to play with. I gave my doll to Linda after she killed her doll with kindness and too much care from a child mother. Plus, in my heart, I no longer owned her anyway.

I think M'Deah probably knew how I felt when our company left—but it was too late. Because like most 'bad' happenings with our parents, it was not a pattern—rather, it was a one-and-done. Because I never again was ever forced to share anything that was mine. It was left up to me. When the doll was finally thrown away, I don't even know. I didn't care.

Camden Library

In addition to the school library, I also regularly visited the local public library too. Camden Library was about a mile away. I usually went there twice a month and got at least a dozen books to read before my next visit. (The only time I didn't was the few times when I had chosen to read the Bible from beginning to end.) My favorite topic got narrowed down to historical fiction. But I decided to try exploring other types of books. For mysteries I read a couple of the Nancy Drew and The Hardy Boys books but I didn't particularly like them. So I tried a few Perry Mason books and they were better. Then I decided to explore some short story books. I remember that I read two science fiction short stories. One made the point of explaining why humans hate rats and snakes. It seems these animals were transplanted

CHAPTER SIXTEEN

here from another planet. So, we innately hate them as being aliens to us. We just don't know why we hate them, but it's natural. Interesting. The other short story made the point that a good teacher has an eternal effect. What she teaches is passed on to the next generation who then pass it on to their children. This is successively repeated so that the teacher's influencer never ends. Also, interesting. And true. After a few months I decided to stick with what I knew I enjoyed most: historical fiction. I delighted to see and imagine how people lived in other time periods without knowledge of certain truths or without certain technology advances. For example, these books left out simple things like how they brushed their teeth or went to the bathroom, and I would wonder about these things. One thing I didn't do though. I never imagined them living with the values and customs of our times. They were who they were in the context of their own times.

Our Play Time

Near our house was a big empty lot of land where all the neighborhood kids would gather to play. We mostly used it as a softball lot and played lots of games there. It was a destination for short bike rides. Oh, yes, we each had our own bike. Most kids in our time did—it was the norm. They were a symbol of transportation and of freedom. All we needed was good dry weather. Not that we rode far—maybe in a

4-5 block radius from home in nearly any direction. It was great fun. Every kid had the task of putting your bike away safely after use. It was easy for us after the attached garage and breezeway were built. We all knew how to fix bike flat tires too. It was a necessary child life skill.

The field was a great place to lie in the green grass, gaze into the sky, and daydream as you looked at the cloud formations. It was about the size of a city block. One day, I noticed lots of dust particles in the air. They were revealed by the sunshine. I suddenly realized that just as fish swim in water, we people swam in air! But we didn't 'drown' in it! What a thought! I had lots of thoughts too about our home situation. Maybe that's where I got an idea later to do something about it and not just be silent.

When we needed popsicles, there was a small shopping area nearby that had a grocery store, a variety store, a drugstore, as well as a gas station, etc.

House Projects

K.C./Daddy was VERY creative and industrious. I believe K.C. honestly tried to overcome what he saw as a deficit—but I don't believe he succeeded. As a WWII military veteran, he used his G.I. Bill benefits to become a brick and block mason. That gave him an excellent well-paying and respected career in the construction industry. He was very good at his job. He often had non-work time during the winter when

CHAPTER SIXTEEN

it was too cold for masonry work. At other warmer times, he would paint the house interior and/or exterior, around every 2-3 years—it always looked fresh and stylish. Our house had many colors over the years and even once was covered in stucco that K.C. added on. My favorite color was the brown and yellow wood combination—outside and in the kitchen.

He finished the attic to be a bedroom for the three boys—even added a bathroom there. He inserted the girls' dressers into the wall, so they appeared built-in. (We didn't go into the boys' room, and they didn't come into ours—it was an unspoken rule.) He finished the basement to be a family rec room with knotty pine paneling and wainscoting. He added onto the house an attached garage and breezeway. He added on a back room sun porch with a wood-burning fireplace and Jalousie windows. He added on another room to the basement beneath the sun porch for storing M'Deah's home-canning produce from the garden. One of her favorite canning projects was a combination of corn, okra, and tomatoes. It was a side dish of its own or used for homemade vegetable soup. Delicious. He built a 2-sided room divider bookcase and stained it the 'blonde' finish that was so stylish in that time.

K.C. believed in cutting the grass every two weeks. He was very diligent about it. Doing so often stirred up our whole block to also do likewise—whether it needed it or not. There was NO way the whites would have the house of blacks looking better than theirs. Our property would NOT become the best-kept on the block. We just laughed to ourselves at the ridiculousness of it all.

The sun porch fireplace was very useful for cold Minneapolis winters and the chill of the Jalousie windows covering its three sides. It was soothing and relaxing to watch the various patterns of flames. Maybe its warmth reminded me of bedtimes in Chatom when Billy and I had snuggled under the quilt warmed at the fireplace there. Those were good times!

I came to regard K.C.'s many projects as acts of remorse that gave him satisfaction too. He also did so by buying something for the house: a TV console, a sofa and chair, a new carpet, a new bedroom set, a new electric mixer, etc. M'Deah's taste and style was for the modern mid-century look so popular then. M'Deah always had lots of healthy house plants around too. As she said about gardening, she loved seeing things grow. It was later that she chose to prefer the vintage classic look of the 1930s and earlier furniture and decor. I would prefer these 'gifts' never be necessary. Rather, no abuse of my mother at all! Strangely, he never bought a new washer and dryer after the old wringer-washer machine died. I don't know why.

I don't know if this could be considered a project or not. Maybe it was a family fun project. But we had other occasions for laughter at whites too. Once, K.C.

CHAPTER SIXTEEN

had the opportunity through his job to buy a used Ford Model T car. I loved that car! The classic *ooga-ooga* sound of the horn, its design and old age—just everything about it. Sometimes, we would all crowd into it and K.C. would drive to neighborhoods as nice as our own that had houses for sale. We would stop in front of the houses and just look at them. We never got out of the car. It was so funny to see some white residents really look distressed at the thought that a large black family might make a purchase in their neighborhood. We would laugh uproariously. Other times, we would do the same thing, using K.C.'s pickup truck with all the kids piled in the back. We saw no danger to doing this, as there certainly would have been in the South. It was our idea of harmless free fun. I had hoped to own the Model T car when I grew up. But M'Deah had to sell it later to make ends meet. I would have loved to drive and own it.

Our Neighbors

Our neighbors were varied but all white. Across the street were a Jehovah's Witness family with two daughters and a son. The father was an auto mechanic. They were fairly poor compared to all the other neighbors. We played with them a lot with no problem. One of their daughters later married into a very wealthy family. Also across the street was a more prosperous family with one young son who was my first babysitting client. The mother was a nurse who had another child later. She had a singular distinction. For both pregnancies she only wore maternity clothes in her last month and that was just so we knew why they brought home a baby. She didn't show at all ever! I had never seen anyone like that before or since.

Life did NOT go on to be as pleasant and peaceful as I had hoped. Life with K.C. was often difficult. I just wanted peace in my home and life. It was more than was possible for me to control. But I did have the pleasure of still making my weekly trips to the local Camden Public Library. It was my one enduring pleasure in life—along with school, which I dearly loved. They both were my safe happy places.

CHAPTER SEVENTEEN

Cause and Effect

I had always kinda liked K.C. He was nice to me and Billy, although he didn't interact with us much. But he changed. He became abusive toward my mother—something I saw no hint of in him before that kitchen conversation took place. I was not aware of any of this until after we moved and were living as a separate family from any other relatives. For years, the cause puzzled me. Decades later, I think it was the 'poison pill' I referred to earlier—that conversation I heard as a 10-year old.

    Our lives had seen good and bad. But as K.C. took on the persona of domestic violence toward my mother, we were now to see the ugly. As a worker in heavy construction as a brick and block mason, he was still GI-fit at 6 foot 3 inches. He was very strong. We never SAW the abuse. But we heard it going on behind closed doors. It was frightening to hear what we knew were blows being dealt to M'Deah. And we heard profanity that was never a part of our everyday lives. I remember hearing, "You think you're so damned smart!" What was going on and why? It was foreign to us. And the whole thing was never spoken of by ANY of the family. I knew that Linda and I heard it, often being awakened from sleep. I wasn't sure that the boys heard it from their upstairs location though. I would later learn that they did indeed hear it all too.

Otherwise K.C. seemed normal. But in this one matter, he was crazy. Where had he learned that this behavior was acceptable? I don't know. I saw none of it in his family of origin.

I don't remember when the abuse began. I only remember being surprised later that it happened when his kids were living with us. He wasn't embarrassed to do so with them present in our household? What kind of father was he? I began to question in my mind what I'd overheard about his first wife. Did he abuse her too? No wonder he was divorced and I bet it wasn't all her fault that the marriage failed. Her kids seemed well fed and well cared for. Maybe she was the lucky one to have gotten out of marriage to K.C. Of course, I could never know all the truth about that. Her kids seemed not to miss her and happily embraced M'Deah as their new mother. Knowing M'Deah, that wouldn't be hard to do.

Over the years, K.C.'s violent treatment of M'Deah was continuous. Once, he beat her as she lay in bed recovering from hemorrhoid surgery. Sadly, the accounts are too many to mention. Sigh. We never SAW any of this. But we often heard it going on

CHAPTER SEVENTEEN

behind closed doors at night. And/or we sometimes saw the results the next day.

One such event involved the time when M'Deah had a full-time job at the munitions plant in New Brighton, Minnesota. It was during the Korean War. Many left their regular jobs for the higher salaries here. I think this is when M'Deah had to meet the requirement for her birth certificate. But she didn't have one! The courthouse in Mt. Sterling where she was born had experienced a fire in which some records were lost. So, M'Deah was required to get an affidavit from two people who would know of her birth directly. She used Aunt Daisy and Aunt Mary. One day, an important general came to do a walk-through inspection of the plant. Naturally, photos would be taken. One such photo involved him observing M'Deah at her workstation. This photo appeared in the local newspaper, the Minneapolis Star and Tribune. (It was K.C.'s routine to read the morning Tribune newspaper faithfully every day.) Somehow this enraged K.C! We heard the open fury of angry accusing words he threw at M'Deah. Why had SHE been in the photo? Who was this general to HER that he would stand over HER? Etc. M'Deah's words to K.C. meant nothing to him—they could NOT penetrate his unreasoning thoughts. In spite of her protests, M'Deah did get a beating that night. It was HARD for us—me—to live with, knowing how unreasonable it all was. And how cruel. Sigh.

Why are such matters kept secret? It's the silence of helplessness! It's not just silence of shame or fear, but that too.

I don't remember ever seeing M'Deah reading the newspaper. She would have considered it the wrong use of her time. But she always was up on the news. From watching broadcasts of TV news? I suppose. TV news was much more reliable then. It was mostly balanced, fair, and unbiased. In coverage? Maybe. In presentation? Definitely! You wouldn't know a broadcaster's personal views by the way they did their job! Who knew that would become a rare thing one day? Rather, they reflected the national majority views. They reflected natural common values. Most Americans were in agreement with the values of the civil rights movement. The reporters were too. Most Americans admired the Kennedy family. So did the reporters. People were in awe of the American space program. So were the reporters. Most Americans agreed with the Supreme Court decision to integrate the schools. So did the reporters. It was impossible to see the news media as strange entities from us. They were not foreign, but one of us and we could safely encourage our kids to be like them in terms of a career. Americans admired such as Edward R. Murrow, Walter Cronkite, etc.

K.C. NEVER apologized to my mother regarding his abysmal/poor/wrongful beatings he gave her. That was out of the question for a 'man' in his

CHAPTER SEVENTEEN

thinking. But there were times when we knew he was genuinely sorry. He would BUY something for M'Deah! Oh, it wasn't always something personal for her. Maybe it would be a new piece of furniture, new carpeting, etc. Or he would build or do something for the house: paint the exterior, add on a room, build an attached garage, add a fireplace, etc. Nothing was ever said, but we could see "cause and effect." I remember thinking that I would prefer he keep all this and just treat M'Deah right!

It turned out that M'Deah did have a side-effect from her surgery to her head. She began to have horrible migraine headaches at least once a month. Doctors said this was probably because a few strands of her hair had accidentally been included in the 93 stitches she got. And there was no remedy. When these headaches came, her only remedy was taking aspirin, binding her scalp tightly with a scarf, reducing the light which hurt her eyes, and having it to not be noisy. All these things only added to her already-miserable pain. Sadly, all we could do was to sympathize. Sometimes, K.C. would even beat M'Deah at these times too. No escape, no mercy.

Years later I wondered how it was even possible to make love with someone who seemingly hated you and deliberately inflicted pain and harmful abuse to you. It seemed inconceivable torment. And how can you defend yourself against unknown lies they believe about you—lies that came from your own beloved sister? It must have been very puzzling as well as disappointing to be so indefensible. You married someone you loved who spoke of his undying love for you. And then they changed so drastically soon afterwards. What? I couldn't have done it. Each person has their own strengths. I didn't have any for that.

And I saw that M'Deah was isolated too. Family seldom visited—some never visited. Friends were absent too, except maybe by occasional phone calls. Abusers isolate the abused, so they have no outlet to tell and to appeal to for help.

M'Deah was trapped in her bedroom. What should have been a sanctuary became a hell far too many times. And it was seemingly always unexpected. That could only add to the terror—not knowing when it would come and definitely not knowing why. What became of the man who had expressed his great love for her? Nothing she had done caused this change in him. And I never said a word about what my 10-year old self had heard that night I was awakened from sleep to hear folks talking negatively about my beloved and innocent mother.

Seeing what M'Deah went through forever hardened me to refuse to ever be treated that way by anyone. Thankfully.

New Neighbors

Next door to us was a new neighbor who was a police officer. His wife, Shirley, was a stay-at-home

CHAPTER SEVENTEEN

mother of their one child. When they moved in shortly after we did, I was very hopeful. K.C. had begun his beatings of my mother and I wanted the neighbors to hear that and somehow intervene. I don't see how they didn't hear but it made no difference. I soon discovered why that was so. Bill, this policeman, was also guilty of domestic violence. His wife was loud in trying to defend herself and ward him off of her, usually successfully. We had no problem hearing them, so I know they heard our family as well. Having a police officer next door was no comfort. He was a wife beater too. Sigh.

Mama Bear

Once, when we'd lived in our new home for a few years, the back doorknob which had been loose for a while, fell off in Billy's hand. K.C. wanted to give him a whippin' for it. M'Deah stood firm in saying that was wrong and unfair—the doorknob fell off because it hadn't been repaired when it was known to need repairing. Now, its repair was a must and merely had to be put back on the door. K.C. didn't like her stand at all. He did NOT give Billy this undeserved whippin'. But he did beat M'Deah that night. I believe he even hit her with the doorknob, and this was when her cheek was broken. It affected her vision, and doctors told her she was required to now wear eyeglasses for the rest of her life. Sigh. But Billy and I never had to worry about our being abused by K.C. We had M'Deah being there for us.

The Phantom

The phantom in our home was known to others as domestic violence. We didn't know that was its name or anything else about it. Except that we didn't like it. It was something strange to us. Seldom did it occur in the daytime and never did it occur before our eyes. It was something that happened in the middle of the night unannounced. Linda and I would be sleeping soundly and then suddenly be awakened by the sounds of K.C. cussing M'Deah out and the dull thuds as he hit her repeatedly and cruelly. She seldom made any noise. But we would occasionally see evidence the next morning of the blows he left. Or sometimes the blows left hidden marks. These all varied Seldom were the blows clearly seen. There would be bruises that clothing could cover them. Sometimes there was a rare black eye. I don't know all the pain she suffered but it was a lot. And always at unexpected and unprovoked times. This went on for eight years. Some think of domestic violence as a sickness. I don't. Having lived with it in my home, I see it as the pure evil that it is. It is satanic and cruel—the very opposite of God Who is Love. (I John 4:7-8)

Living in that environment was horrible. It was in strange contrast to the good we enjoyed in our home life and greatly diminished it. As kids I think we constantly walked on eggshells in our behavior. That happened increasingly as we became verbal targets of his wrath. We would sometimes hear K.C. speak of his intent to kill the whole family. That included us kids!

CHAPTER SEVENTEEN

No reason was ever given and we never knew when it might occur at some capricious moment of his. None ever wanted to say or do anything that might set him off. I took it upon myself to always try to keep him in a good mood. I knew good grades helped in that area. Plus, it fit with my desire and propensity to do well scholastically. But it was a hard job to keep him in a good mood. It didn't always work. I tried humor. I tried asking questions about his childhood. Etc. I didn't always succeed. Then I felt bad, a failure.

My Out

I knew K.C. had made a threat that was not idle. Obviously, he had thought of killing us all even before he said it. How can you think of killing your whole family—including your own children? He had never threatened to kill us before! I believed him. If he said it, he meant it and one day would do it. What to do?! I would make sure he didn't get away with it. I would leave a note in my locker to identify our killer, I didn't take the threat likely. I would make sure that he never got away with it. I couldn't bear the thought of him not being held responsible for the crime. It was always hanging over our heads—the final danger of K.C. snapping and carrying out his many threats to kill our whole family. When would it come, and would he get away with it? Weekends would be the most likely time. What if he killed us and claimed an intruder did it? Again, I was determined he would not get away with it. So, I began to leave a note in my locker every Friday at the end of the school day. "If we are found dead over the weekend, Daddy did it.". That's all it said. Every Monday morning, I tore up this brief note. I don't know how long I did this, but it was for more than a semester. Maybe for the rest of the school year. During Summer vacation, I knew of no safe location for such a note. I was afraid K.C. might find it. Consequences for that would not be good at all. I had to trust that his crime would be caught, and he would be punished. Not that it would do us any good. But he would not get away with our murder. When the next school year began, I abandoned the notes. Not because the danger had gone, but because I thought he would be caught by the obvious. And I recognized that this practice was making me fearful and anxious. No. So I went on, as though things were normal. But they weren't.

The Scary Incident

Gradually, over time, K.C. would spill his anger issues outside of their bedroom. On these occasions, as I said, we would hear him threaten to kill ALL of us! That included M'Deah AND us children—even his own three! A frightening possibility we totally believed him capable of doing. These episodes were NOT rare. Sometimes, he would go to the basement in rage, and we'd hear him cussing and loading a hunting rifle. At first, we stayed quietly upstairs. One day, his rage was

CHAPTER SEVENTEEN

so high, that all of us kids just ran from the house in great fear—hoping to escape before he left the basement to come up and shoot us ! M'Deah didn't run at all. How do you dodge a bullet when you're the target? Her running would only anger and provoke him. Thank God, He protected us. As I recall, we all ran in different directions. Linda may have gone in my direction but definitely wasn't with me. Each was on his own island. Before we got far, we saw that company was coming to visit us! It was Carrie and Tommy. Aunt Daisy was with them. We knew we were safe and that K.C. would never kill us now. He was much too polite for that. He had never displayed anything before company other than being a good host. And he was always super-courteous to his elders. Apparently, that was important to him. And it would cause his murderous rage to disappear. For now.

So, we all came back home—after they parked. Last to leave, I was also first to return. I heard them ask K.C., "Where are all the kids?" His reply? A sheepish, "I don't know—they're around here somewhere". And so, we were. After they visited a while and left, K.C. was no longer in a murderous rage and we were no longer in danger. We could relax. For now.

This event led me to make an important decision. I too had run in fear. But M'Deah was still in the house. What if he had shot HER? I purposed to NEVER leave her alone in such a dangerous situation again. And life went on.

Entertaining

Like most families, we occasionally had 'company' to come over for visits to our home. Mostly, they were only people K.C. knew and approved. That included his two brothers sometimes. It included their cousin Curtis (pronounced Sir-tis) and family—wife Voncile (pronounced Von-seal) and son, Junior. These were usually good times. Both my parents had been raised to honor company—to be as hospitable as possible and to regard them as important. Strangely, the only company of M'Deah's was her Aunt Daisy later who was usually accompanied by Carrie and Tommy. I don't remember anyone else of her family or any of her friends. I was puzzled sometimes but otherwise gave it no thought.

These visits usually involved a meal or dessert at the least that M'Deah obligingly provided. And K.C. was always completely civil at these times. For those reasons, we kids enjoyed having company. But K.C. wasn't always positively affected by them. So, his reactions AFTER such visits was mixed and dreaded. That made us regard as fearful what should have been pleasant experiences. And we were taught to be good hosts and to be unselfish with our things whenever children came with these visits. Whether we liked it or not. And usually, that wasn't hard for us to do. We were good obedient kids. We had what was known then as 'home-training'!

CHAPTER SEVENTEEN

Different Coping Ways

I observed that children who grow up in homes where there is domestic abuse of a parent are deeply affected in different ways. Especially when their own safety is threatened. Feeling helpless, they handle it in their own ways. I noticed at some point how all of us kids handled our family stress in different ways. I threw myself into schoolwork and hid in the safe world of books—a bookworm trying to escape to a better world. Emeal deeply admired his father and tried to be like him—he became a bully at school. Billy was quiet and withdrawn. He was short—always the 'shrimp' in class and his physical growth was stunted. Linda was the sensitive stressed one, quick to be empathetic to others—even above her own problems. She always seemed to put the well-being of others as first priority. Linda was deeply sensitive and became suicidal when she found out that other families did not all have homes where domestic violence was the norm. Floyd was always the cute congenial and loveable little boy with soft curly hair and a friendly smile, who became a bed-wetter. We did the best we could with our own unique 'therapy'. Each in our way and each in our own world. We were separated as we each dealt with a common trauma. For that reason, I realized much later that I was not a very good big sister. Sadly, I couldn't be there for them very well. Did Billy ever feel I had abandoned him? I don't know. I'm sure it seemed as though

I had. Each of us kids tried to navigate a home of domestic violence as best we could, not really knowing how to deal with something we never should have known. Like everyone, our lives were separate at times and overlapped at times. Sometimes this occurs in the same chronological timeframe, strangely. No man is an island, yet each man is an island. At the same time. We are part of a group, yet we are individuals. God values both the group and the individual. It's up to us to agree with Him—to recognize them as separate but equally valuable. To Him and to us—His copies of Himself.

At some point early during this marriage, M'Deah lost twins by K.C. I remember that they were stillborn. This was before we moved to our new home where he was violent and abusive. How do you mistreat a life partner you could and want to have children with? But they wouldn't have to worry about how to cope in this abuser environment. Later, M'Deah had to have a hysterectomy.

Strange Abuser Trait

A side question: how did K.C. feel as we kids got past his educational level? He seemed to be proud of our achievements but was he secretly resentful? And would my mother have to pay for that resentment? It was not an idle concern. But things seemed to be okay. It shouldn't have even been something to be concerned about, but I was. You just didn't know with

CHAPTER SEVENTEEN

him. He was very much pro-education for all of us kids. But there was some real small change of attitude towards us as we progressed past the 6th grade. Was it resentment? Jealousy? I don't know.

Looking Back

What did I learn from the life I grew up in? Domestic violence is much more and much worse than any single incident. It's the inescapable constancy too. I learned by experience what some possible warning signs are regarding the abuser's behavior. They isolate/separate their victim from family and friends who could possibly be a way of rescue and escape. They apologize for incidents with gifts and not with words acknowledging their guilt. They blame the victim and take no responsibility for their own behavior. They're often very likeable from the outside. There are others. All of this I would read about years later. But I lived it. Not directly but vicariously through a loved one. It's very damaging mentally. It's designed to be so by the enemy of our souls, satan. Look to God. He wants us free from all enemy oppression. Including this one. Keep hope alive. It's worth it.

My Summary of K.C

What did he and M'Deah have in common? Both were raised as slave descendants in the rural segregated Jim Crow South. They had some common values. But they also differed in some cultural values and experiences as well. As we were to find out, sadly. M'Deah was raised by a family to whom it was unthinkable to have domestic violence or to even use profanity and to whom church was seen as important. K.C.'s specific upbringing is unknown to me. I don't know if domestic violence was in their home, but I know they weren't opposed to it. Because it did exist in the home of their only daughter, Justine. And they did nothing about it. The three sons would talk to and about the daughter's husband. They accused him rightly of wanting to keep her 'barefoot and pregnant'. But they did absolutely nothing to help her escape the horrible situation that was her married life. Their thinking seemed to be that the wife would stay with such a husband, of course. It was very puzzling to me.

Their educational backgrounds were different too. Both were taught the value of education. M'Deah was given every opportunity for all the education she wanted and she took it. K.C. had a desire for education, but no resource. Thankfully, there was the G.I. bill for him to have an opportunity later. And he took it. But he never regarded it as valuable as the high school education he never got.

M'Deah and K.C. had some similar upbringing experiences. But K.C. was far more bitter regarding the Jim Crow South and the white man though. He truly hated the treatment there of blacks by whites,

CHAPTER SEVENTEEN

as well as hated the whites. I knew he could appreciate the distinctions between whites, but I never heard him say anything good about them. M'Deah was well aware of circumstances there, but she had no hate.

M'Deah was given the value of God and church. I don't think K.C. ever had that. In fact, I don't ever remember him going to church! M'Deah's kids were raised in church. K.C.'s kids went to church accompanying us. Billy said I always went to Sunday School and church. It was part of our life. We could walk to Holsey until we moved to Logan Avenue. Then we attended a church in our new neighborhood. It was a basement church—like nothing we'd been to before. But we went. For at least half a dozen years. All five of us kids.

My parents and their peers showed the pioneer spirit was still alive in the middle of the 20th century. Is it alive today? Yes and no. Yes, for those who were raised in and retain the same values as they. No, if you threw all that away to be more 'relevant/progressive'. Yes, if you were educated. No if you were indoctrinated. We keep what we were given in the modeling before us by those who gave it—IF we valued them at all.

I Still Had Questions

Why did K.C. stay married after hearing all Carrie and Tommy said about her? I don't know. Perhaps it was what he knew about her otherwise. She had been raised in the South as had he, so they had that cultural background in common. For example, they both regarded their elders highly,—with great respect and deference. She had Southern values of being a good homemaker and mother. She was a hard worker and a good cook. She was skilled, practical, disciplined, a planner, achiever of goals, and very generous. She loved her children and would be a good mother to his children and a good partner for him. Maybe he saw those things. I don't know. She was not a California girl with a more laid-back and less ambitious approach to life, as his first wife had been. Why did M'Deah stay with K.C. when his behavior towards her changed? K.C. was a good provider, liberal to meet the house/family needs, fulfilled his desires regarding equipment for hunting and fishing, etc. And she was overly mindful of the children's needs and welfare.

My Stunted Puberty

How to sum up my puberty? It was anything but typical. I was socially stunted in my development. Additionally, M'Deah and I didn't have mother/daughter talks about what womanhood was like. I was advised on how to wear deodorant, use feminine hygiene pads, and that's about it. She trusted me to remain a virgin—it wasn't even spoken of. Douching was popular for married women at the time, and I remember seeing the equipment in the bathroom. But

CHAPTER SEVENTEEN

I wasn't married so I didn't need to even know about it. When I did marry, I imagine M'Deah assumed I already knew about such things. In her defense, few women had mother/daughter talks then to prepare the daughter for her future. And, being only one generation from slavery, I doubt Big Mama had the talks with M'Deah either. Ah, ignorance!

I did have one bad incident during this time. I didn't like M'Deah's cream deodorant and thought it messy. I much preferred to use the newly advertised roll-on deodorant,. So, M'Deah bought some for me. After a while, I began having boils form on my underarms—messy smelly boils that were also painful. M'Deah applied all the home remedies she knew but nothing helped. She also took me to our family doctor, Dr. Schwartz, and he was unable to help. I told him I thought they were worse when I ate sweets and that probably caused them to grow after being formed. He pooh-poohed that I would even suggest such a thing. (Decades later, I learned that I was right!) Finally, they routinely grew to the size of a small egg. That's too much to be able to go about your normal daily routine! So, our doctor had me admitted to the hospital for them to be surgically lanced. It was an overnight procedure, and I was never bothered with underarm boils again. Our doctor also suggested roll-on deodorant was too strong and I should switch to another form and brand. I did. Later, I remember reading that the one I'd formerly used had a formula that proved to be too strong, and it was being changed. I didn't care—I'd already been 'bitten' once and didn't care to risk it again! Lesson learned: not every new thing is good for you. Let it be tested and proven first—preferably it's done before coming to market. I know that's the law, but it's not always common practice. How do I know? There are now too many drug and product recalls.

The Medicine Cabinet

The contents were simple and common. There was always aspirin, of course. It was touted and I thought of it as being good for whatever ails you! Items common in 1950s household medicine cabinets were: Aspirin, band-aids, Mercurochrome, sweet oil for earaches, Milk of Magnesium, Pepto Bismol, castor oil, Alka Seltzer, Black Draught, etc. That was about it. White people may have had the same, except for castor oil. Additionally, they would have had Tums maybe.

CHAPTER EIGHTEEN
Other Changes

Popular TV shows of my youth that we watched included:

I Love Lucy, Alfred Hitchcock Presents, The Honeymooners, Perry Mason, Gunsmoke, Dragnet, Leave It To Beaver, The Ed Sullivan Show, The Lone Ranger, The Adventures Of Superman, The Red Skelton Show, Maverick, The Rifleman, Lassie, Father Knows Best, Wagon Train, Candid Camera, Captain Kangaroo, The Mickey Mouse Club, Have Gun Will Travel, Zorro, The Jack Benny Program, The Adventures Of Ozzie and Harriet, Highway Patrol, Sea Hunt, 77 Sunset Strip, What's My Line?, Amos and Andy, The Roy Rogers Show, The Jackie Gleason Show, Make Room For Daddy, Our Miss Brooks, You Bet Your Life, I've Got A Secret, The Perry Como Show, Peter Gunn, The Millionaire, Bachelor Father, The Lawrence Welk Show, The Life and Legend Of Wyatt Earp, The $64,000 Question, General Electric Theater, The Honeymooners, The George Burns and Gracie Allen Show, Lassie, Cheyenne, Loretta Young, Dinah Shore, Andy Williams, Hee Haw, Jimmy Dean, Julia, etc. There was a lot of wholesome TV to watch then.

We watched some more than others. But we didn't watch much TV then—it was seriously restricted.

TV Alternative

As I said, occasionally K.C. was given a few books by bosses on his job and he always brought them home. They accumulated to the point that we needed a bookcase for them. So he took on the project of building a 6-foot long double-sided strong wood bookcase that he finished in the popular faux blonde. M'Deah shipped it to me decades later and I used it and kept it for a while. I always liked it and thought it very practical.

One Sunday afternoon when I was 12 years old, we were expecting company to come. I don't remember who it was but some family K.C. knew. All of us children were told to get dressed before they came, of course. We were told to sit down in the living room and not get our clothes dirty. Sitting was boring. So I decided to get a book from the bookcase to read. Strangely, I chose the Holy Bible that was always there but never read. I decided it was a book and knowing that I read books, why not this one? In the following weeks I continued to read it until I had finished it cover to cover. I had never done that before! I didn't understand it all, was shocked by some things in it, but I thought reading it all was a satisfactory accomplishment. In it I saw some things I had been taught in church and in school. They were the 10 commandments, the Lord's prayer, Psalm 23, the

Golden Rule, the Christmas story, the Easter story, and more. At that time in the common culture, teaching of values was held in common and taught by home, church, and the public schools. They were agreed upon values and on one accord. There were common problems, of course. But far less division, strife, and confusion than what sadly came later. I miss that. In my following teen years, I read the entire Bible at least twice more. I didn't know it was done by anyone except maybe clergy. I'm not sure my understanding increased significantly but my knowledge of it did. It bore fruit later.

I read all the other donated books on that bookcase too. It was a rich source that introduced me to Perry Mason before the TV series did. It also introduced me to the historical novel, "Forever Amber", which was above my maturity level. But I learned history of the bubonic plague and the London fire too! It was not wasted on me. After all, history was my favorite subject!

Pop Culture

We were not taught to be a part of most pop culture. Not the boys. Not the girls. Because it was popular didn't automatically mean it was for us. That was not the norm. Parents made that choice. Popular foods were chow mein and pizza. It was a rare treat to eat fast food. White Castle was the most favorite. I only remember buying chow mein at a shop maybe once. It was often a weekly item on our school cafeteria menu, but we didn't buy our lunch at school for a long time. Then I found an old chow mein recipe in M'Deah's cookbook she'd gotten as a bridal gift, and I made it at home. Pizza was so new that I only knew of a couple of remote places that sold it. They weren't in our neighborhood, so we didn't buy pizza. A&W or Hires root beer stands were infrequent locations. I knew about the new and few McDonalds that came later but we didn't frequent them. I didn't have my first McDonald's until I had married and left home. Dining out was not something you normally did. We ate at home. When you ate out, it was usually at someone else's home. That was our norm then. For most whites. For most blacks. Unlike others, we didn't attend many movies in our childhood. In my adult years, I loved to watch old movies on TV, usually from the 1930s and 1940s. I was surprised to learn years later that M'Deah's age was very much like the film and music stars of her/those times. They were truly her contemporaries.

The Johnson Publishing Company

Johnson Publishing Company (JPC) was founded in 1942 by John H. Johnson with a $500 loan, using his mother's furniture as collateral. He created his first publication, Negro Digest, in 1942. In 1945, he created what became his flagship monthly publication, Ebony magazine. It was followed in 1951 by his weekly

CHAPTER EIGHTEEN

Jet magazine. He and his wife, Eunice (creator of Ebony Fashion Fair and Fashion Fair Cosmetics), were blessed to do remarkably well. During its peak from the 1960s until the early 2000s, Johnson Publishing Company was the largest Black-owned public company. It was commonly found in every black household and business. It was our major source of accurate black news happenings, trends, and culture. It was a source of things about fashion, celebrity, recipes, black music, education, etc. It was for the 'upward bound' Negro. My parents and I were avid readers of Ebony. Like most Negroes, our family had a subscription. For me, I religiously read the Ebony magazine with an occasional guilty read of what some Negroes regarded as their lower-class Jet magazine.

I learned from the Ebony magazine my news about what race title Negroes preferred. (More about that later.) Ebony magazine was a great source of Negro accomplishments—it was inspirational to many. As an adult, I too later subscribed to Ebony. It was only natural to do so. But gradually it became corrupted. It became the ugly 'black' that was PC and tried to be militantly 'with it', as it became 'woke'. It denigrated the whites and Jews who had supported both it and other Negroes and their issues. Somehow, it threw out the baby with the bath water and became something really ugly to me. It lost its soul and was no longer something inspirational, but hateful and proud. Sadly. I canceled my subscription years ago.

Equally popular, but thought of as less classy, was the smaller Jet magazine. Its tone was more 'regular folks'. You read it only when there were compelling news stories you just didn't want to miss. These were stories like the murdered criminal who was buried sitting upright at the steering wheel of his Cadillac. Contrary to popular belief, he did take it with him. In Jet, I learned about stories of murders and lynchings. I think few subscribed to it—you just picked it up at your local store. I haven't read one in years. And I don't miss what it became.

Camden Cemetery

Oh. This is how we got the family section in Camden Cemetery. M'Deah saw an ad in the paper for cemetery plots for sale there. Mindful of laws/covenants that might restrict blacks from buying plots in 'white' cemeteries, she took action for what she wanted to buy. So, she donned her white work uniform, went to the cemetery, and bought the plots for her 'white boss'. It worked. Later, the plots were used for Papa, Aunt Daisy, Billy, Carrie, Uncle Robert, Dan, George—as I remember. There were two plots left that she intended to be used for herself and for me. Much later, the cemetery tried to claim she had no right to buy the plots and thus the sale was illegal. That's still pending, sadly. Sigh.

CHAPTER EIGHTEEN

Race Labels

I have referred to us previously mostly as the 'descendants of slaves'. We have been mostly called 'colored'. As a child, I used to wonder what color that was exactly. What race is that? None. Our desire as a people was to at least have the dignity of being called 'Negro'. Ebony magazine said so—it was our collective spokesman. I preferred the dignity of being called Negro too—although it was non-descriptive as to our place/country of origin, which other ethnicities had. In the South, Negro was certainly an upgrade from 'colored', even when it was changed to "nigrah". At least it wasn't their usual "nigger." And we did NOT want to ever again be called 'black'—that was very insulting! That is, until near the end of the civil rights movement. Then we embraced being called 'black'. It was embraced, being popularized by a hit song by James Brown, etc. I never thought I would see that happen—it was unimaginable to be so insulted! But that's pretty much where I've stopped and parked. When others like Jesse Jackson urged us to embrace being 'African-American' as our preferred title, I was done. Enough already of the merry-go-round. What's gonna be next? Will there be no end? I gotta call it quits. And I did. I decided that I'm a 'black Negro'—or just 'black'. Oh, wait: Negro MEANS Black in Spanish! Black works for me as my permanent race designation. If we could have a 'white' race, then we could have a 'black' race. The end.

Emmett Till

Emmett Till was murdered in August 1955. I'm not sure from what source I first learned of him. But it was Jet magazine that kept me informed most about such things, I think. What happened to Emmett was horrible, heinous, unjust, cruel, evil—and so many other adjectives. It was the news story of the day. What kept me intrigued was more than that though. I soon learned that Emmett and I were the same age! We were children! Could someone conceivably kill ME at age 14, as they had him? It was a question I had to face. And the answer was an inescapable 'yes'. I realized that there are people on the Earth who would have had no moral hesitation to kill me—if they chose to do so. There had already been killing of children in slavery and of Jewish children in the holocaust. It was a very sobering thought. I got a little older just thinking about it—and I never forgot it. I knew Buster had tried to kill me. But he was 'crazy' then—he was another person and yet the same person. Nevertheless, some people can and do kill children. Deliberately. Even babies. Even in the womb. And they never give it a second thought—it doesn't phase them at all. Sad.

The Civil Rights Movement

As for my part in the civil rights movement, I read of the lunch-counter sit-ins, the marches, the bus boycott, the students attending newly desegregated

CHAPTER EIGHTEEN

schools, etc. I truly admired the courage of these people—especially the young ones. I knew the dangers they faced. I disagreed with those who complained that past generations should have done this long ago. No. To do so then in their times meant their sure death—and that accomplishes nothing. Now, when it could all be seen on TV, was the better time. I thought for about a minute of somehow going to join them. No. That would just be a new worry for M'Deah. I wouldn't put that on her.

But what could I do right here in Minneapolis? I began by joining the youth NAACP. At a meeting, we agreed to picket the downtown Walgreens in support of those picketing Walgreens stores in the South. We got our signs together and went downtown on the appointed Saturday. As we marched, bystanders regarded us curiously. I felt bold and brave—but safe. One little ole white lady in tennis shoes angrily asked why we were doing that in Minneapolis because, "We're good to you up here!" I tried to explain to her that it was a sympathy march in support of those in the South. She was having none of it and cussed me out! I was shocked at how 'good' she was to us up here. Aside from that one march, there wasn't a lot done by our group. I remember nothing else. But even this was big at the time.

The NAACP was formally founded in 1909 by both blacks and whites, but its leadership was mostly whites. Its later field secretary was Walter F. White, a light-skinned black who could pass as white. Many times he risked his life for the organization, to obtain information on the lynching of blacks. Few know this. I learned of it decades later. Wikipedia says:

> 'Of mixed race, with African and European ancestry on both sides, White appeared to be of European descent. He emphasized in his autobiography, A Man Called White (p. 3): "I am a Negro. My skin is white, my eyes are blue, my hair is blond. The traits of my race are nowhere visible upon me." Of his 32 great-great-great-grandparents, only five were black, and the other 27 were white. All members of his immediate family had fair skin, and his mother, Madeline, was also blue-eyed and blonde. The oral history of his mother's family asserts that her maternal grandparents were Dilsia, an enslaved woman concubine, and her owner, William Henry Harrison. Harrison had six children with Dilsia and, much later, was elected president of the United States in 1840, but served for only 31 days. Madeline's mother, Marie Harrison, was one of Dilsia's daughters with Harrison. Held in enslavement in La Grange, Georgia, where she had been sold, Marie became a concubine to Augustus Ware. The wealthy white man bought her a house, had four children with her, and passed on some wealth to them. White and his family identified as Negro and lived among Atlanta's Negro community (despite White and his siblings inheriting a bit less

CHAPTER EIGHTEEN

than 16 percent African ancestry and being able to pass as white).'

White headed the organization as Executive Secretary for 37 years. The NAACP was the premier black civil rights organization for most of the 20th century and has many accomplishments.

Later, it was strange to see how the civil rights movement changed. This historic organization that I had always esteemed highly became unrecognizable. They disdained their former help from the Jews and acted as though they never had any part in forming their organization or their subsequent help over the ensuing decades. I was puzzled and disappointed. These two marginalized groups of society had much in common—especially persecution. It was only natural for them to come together and work for change. Now the blacks wanted nothing to do with them. It didn't make sense. But it was what it was. I doubt many blacks know of the origin and help this organization got from Jews and whites. During the civil rights movement I was struck by how many non-blacks joined forces for values held in common. It was to do what was right that united us. Not race.

The change reminded me of the old song, "The Old Gray Mare": 'The NAACP ain't what she used to be'. For sure—and sadly. Help was once welcomed from all. Now, it was rejected from all and only accepted from some.

Black Muslim

Carl Rowan was a Negro newspaper reporter whose columns appeared in the Minneapolis Tribune. I read them often. Once, he did a series of articles on this new group called the Black Muslims that was led by someone named Elijah Muhammad. I had never heard of him or of his group. They were extremely negative articles, and I was intrigued by that extreme. Surely, NOBODY could be that bad! I decided that I wanted to attend one of their meetings and see for myself. I got permission from M'Deah and I went. The gathering was small, and someone I assumed was the teacher was instructing us as to what they were about—what they believed and purposed to do. I heard some really 'crazy' things about their version of creation and about how the races came to be. The white race was deeply demonized. At the end, they asked visitors to stand, and I was one of less than a half dozen. We were asked, "Don't you want to join your brothers and sisters—black Muslims?" It was done with lots of pressure to join. I demurred that I wanted to think about it. They weren't satisfied with my answer but had to accept it. I had absolutely NO intention of joining them! I never attended another meeting. But, at least, I found out for myself what they were about. Carl Rowan wasn't just being negative, as I'd thought. I was surprised later when Malcolm X became newsworthy and spoke with such reason—far from the 'crazy' I'd heard at that meeting. I was sorry when he was killed.

Post Civil Rights Movement

Sadly, much good has happened since and much garbage has happened since. Some 'Jackleg preachers' and others became professional Negroes and race hustlers. Not of the fiber of truly heroic leaders who were justly and genuinely admired. No more MLK, Fannie Lou Hamer and the like. Those all died out. Did any take their place? Not yet.

Lifetime Decisions Made In My Youth

During my formative years of life, there were some things that shaped my persona in very real ways. I made some QUALITY decisions then that would last a lifetime.

In the 5th or 6th grade, I remember deciding that I would **never smoke**. Our science book had a section on smoking that told and showed what it did to the body. There were color pictures of lungs: of a blackened/sick smoker lung and of a clean/healthy non-smoker lung. The differences were clearly seen! One person had voluntarily inhaled poison and the other had not. Who would choose to have a smoker's diseased lung? Not me! (With one minor exception that I'll explain later.)

In the 9th grade, I decided I would **never get drunk**. Sharon, a seemingly demure classmate did.

She got the reputation of NOT being a 'good girl' because of her loose moral behavior when she got drunk at teen parties. Her name was very much disrespected in teen gossip. I never wanted to be out of control of myself. As a newlywed, I wanted to learn to drink and asked my husband to teach me. I only imbibed on mixed drinks—like the daiquiri—and had a total of maybe half a dozen dinks in my total adulthood. You can't get drunk if you don't drink alcohol!

Also in the 9th grade, I decided I would **never commit suicide**—no matter what. Linda and I were doing the boys' newspaper route while they were at Boy Scout camp. One day in October 1957, there was a new headline. It was about something called Sputnik—a scientific breakthrough rocket. The advent of Sputnik persuaded me of this decision. It proved that things can change overnight, so never give up hope! Even those faced with the dreaded "Big C" of cancer could learn overnight that a cure had been found! It changed something big in my thinking—thoughts I didn't even know were silently in my mind. I firmly decided that I would never commit suicide, even if I got a diagnosis of cancer. Such a diagnosis was regarded by many as being a death sentence. Many expressed they would then prefer not to live any longer. It was preferable to descending into the sure suffering that was to follow. No suicide for me, even then. Suppose the next day's headline read "Cure for cancer found"? I don't ever want to

CHAPTER EIGHTEEN

risk checking out needlessly a day too soon! Because I had no knowledge of imminent change and rescue. Because I lost hope and weakly and foolishly took what deceptively appeared to be a reasonable exit. Nope. I could go on in all circumstances. I thank God for expelling any suicide thoughts from my mind. It gave me hope for some unseen change in the circumstances of a household of domestic violence.

As a youngster, I also decided that I could/would **never be a racist**. There were white people in my life that I genuinely liked and who liked me: my classmates, the Swatez merchant family, librarians I often interacted with, the medical staff I met in private practice and in the hospital, teachers, etc. That also included those I interacted with casually: bus drivers, merchants, neighbors, etc. I remember Bible truths I was taught in Sunday School and in church sermons, and in my private Bible readings—God was Creator of ALL men, God is Love, you must forgive your enemies, etc. I remember what happened to Emmett Till because of racism. I heard what Martin Luther King, Jr. and others said about it: don't stoop to that level or you're no better than the worst white racist. Of course, I knew of some racists—white and black. No. Being a racist is ugly. Racism was not taught in my home, in my church, nor in my schools. I learned that people believe what they are taught—right or wrong. And, what they believe, they will act on accordingly. I wanted none of that racism.

And, of course, I would **never be a domestic violence victim**. That's true victimhood. But it is NOT inevitable or unavoidable. Only your choices make it so. God did give us each free will. It's about what YOU do with it.

I made another weird decision. I thought one had to **choose between being physically attractive or being smart** and that you couldn't be both. So, I focused on being smart and considered being average or lesser in attractiveness was just fine for me. I considered myself 'chubby' at wearing a size 16 and accepted that. For many wasted years.

Being an avid reader, I made another decision. Maybe in Pearl Buck's book, "The Good Earth" and elsewhere, I learned that a supposed traditional Chinese curse says, "May you live in interesting times—times of pestilence, war, famine, and such trouble". I decided then that I want the opposite of interesting times—peaceful times. **Quiet boring times**—free of danger and drama—were just fine with me!

I made another choice that lasted for decades. I chose **not wealth but just enough**, along with PEACE in my home. That was my priority. Later, God showed me that I could have much more! I didn't have to settle for crumbs. I could have His prosperity for me AND I could have His Peace. And I have enjoyed both, to my great delight.

Even later, at age 70, I decided that for the rest of my life, I would **do what God says**. Here, sadly, I've

CHAPTER EIGHTEEN

had some hits and misses! Every time that I didn't has always been a negative, either of bad consequences or of missed blessings. User-errors. Likewise, every time, I do what He says, I'm always blessed. Father really does know best!

These decisions may seem to have been made too soon—when I was immature. God has corrected me when I was wrong. He surely turned to good what the enemy meant for bad/harm in' my life. So, these decisions have still served me well all my life and turned out to have been mostly very wise decisions. I am grateful to God for giving me this foresight so early in life.

PART THREE

The Henry Years

PART THREE

The Harley Years

CHAPTER NINETEEN
My Happy Place

I was blessed to have two happy places! They differed in how much time I was able to spend in them. They were the library and school. For me, school had always been my happy place. It certainly was true at Henry. I entered Patrick Henry Junior- Senior High School in September 1953 as a seventh grader. I would leave six years later as a graduate in June 1959. It was quite an adventure.

I really loved school. It was a challenging place to enjoy learning. It was a friendly place with non-violent people. It was an active place with lots of activities to do. It was a safe place for me and my siblings. It was rare for me to miss school. I loved everything about it. As I said, it was my safe place, and it was my happy place. From elementary years to college years.

I attended Patrick Henry Junior-Senior High School for six years. As a combined junior-senior school, it included grades 7-12. Students were fed into this facility from three different nearby elementary schools. So, you got to meet lots of new classmates and to have new learning adventures. At least,

CHAPTER NINETEEN

that's the way I looked at it. Plus, I would have access to a whole new library with lots of new books to read! It meant new social changes too, as we grew up. But I dimmed my thinking on most of that though. Slave descendants had come to be called Negro now. I was the only Negro in a senior class of nearly 300 students and only one of less than half a dozen Negroes in a building of 2,000+ students. There were usually no two Negroes in the same class/age. But ever since I left Harrison Elementary School for Hamilton Elementary School in the 5th grade, that was my situation. I would befriend students who were new to Henry—introduce them to others, be their building guide and school information source, etc. Often these friendships were appreciated—but abandoned by them as they got to know the white students, I introduced them to. I got used to it.

I could have had closer relationships with some at Henry, but I didn't push it. I sensed some were open to more in a relationship but if they didn't make the first move, I certainly wasn't gonna do so. Carolyn, Judith, etc. were rare exceptions. We had no real close social relationship and I just left it that way. I knew nothing of their private lives, their home lives—just of their school lives. And they knew nothing of mine. We were really just acquaintances.

I knew NO Negro boys to date and accepted that K.C. would likely never allow that anyway. White boys were out of the question. So, I had no thought about attending the prom, etc. It was what it was. So, I only regarded puberty in terms of clothes and make-up. It was for me to live out the time enroute to adulthood without the typical experiences. And life would go on!

One of the things I did in school was my own game of picking out a classmate who I deemed to be smart and then unknown to them, I would compete to see if I could get a same or better grade than they did! Often, I succeeded. It was a distracting goal that occupied my thoughts during this time.

Among the many activities I enjoyed at school was one that I also enjoyed most at home. It was to read books. I was in the school library a lot, really daily. The library staff got to know me well and I would be allowed to date-stamp the book-due-date check-out cards. One day I volunteered to further help out in any way they wished. They happily accepted and I began to shelve books, etc. The library was my happiest place of all.

Built-in Exercise

The distance between home and Patrick Henry school was 1.5 miles each way. Walking alone, I could easily do the walks in 15 minutes. That's three miles daily. It was challenging fun as well as great exercise—for all six years. Patrick Henry was a combined junior and senior high school—the only one in the city like that. I particularly enjoyed

CHAPTER NINETEEN

the Spring walks and the smell of blossoming lilacs along the way—especially on Camden Highway. Neighbors didn't mind you picking a few blossoms to take home—and I did. It became and still is my favorite scent. Avon's lilac powder became my favorite scent choice for orders of their products. But my favorite time was the Fall walks with the beautiful changing leaves and cooler temperature—what I called 'sweater weather'. I have loved Fall ever since!

I know there's no definitive evidence for it, but I think that those six years of exercise bore fruit that impacted my health all the rest of my life. And I'm grateful for it.

Some Favorite Classes

My 7th grade math teacher was Mrs. Melrose. She was unforgettable and what some students considered to be a 'hard teacher. I came to sincerely appreciate and respect her. Why? Mrs. Melrose gave the class a test—Pop Quiz—every Friday. She took students from various elementary schools who were now all put together. She didn't know what previous grounding we had been given in math. So, she saw to it that we were well-grounded in the basics! She taught and she tested. That was her way. I, for one, deeply appreciated that because it was exactly what I needed. Ever since my hospitalization and recovery from Buster's attack, I had gotten behind my class in many subjects—math being the most meaningful one. Now, I was grounded in math and much more confident. No one who went through her class could say otherwise! It would prove very helpful in future classes—math and otherwise. I never had the belief that there was something I could not do—as I had once thought about math. It was genuinely helpful in life.

My 7th grade Geography teacher was Miss Emily Anderson, another favorite. She always smelled of lilacs and that delightful scent made me want to wear it when I grew up. She had a blank world map on the wall—no location names were displayed—and one of our tests was to come to the board and name as many sites on the blank map as we could. One day, she asked for volunteers to come, rather than choosing kids in turn. About halfway through the group of volunteers, I finally volunteered. Those before me had gotten to maybe 70 locations, at the most. I named 107. To her amazement and mine! That record stood for many years before being broken. They had the advantage of knowing what number to beat. I hadn't had that.

History was my very most FAVORITE subject in school. AND in my library reading: I read historical fiction most. This genre was a 2-edged sword:

1. It gave me a connection to understand why some things were the way they were.

CHAPTER NINETEEN

   2. It made me, unknowingly, somewhat of a fatalist: I know how it ends—everybody dies, so what's the point of it all?

Unfortunately, my favorite school subject once became my worst school experience. It later propelled me to get involved in my own personal extracurricular activity too. It began with an incident in 10th grade history class. The teacher, Mr. Larson, was conducting class on the Civil War. He began talking about the Negroes who served in Congress during Reconstruction after the war. He totally mocked them, calling them dumb, unfit, and a joke. He often laughed as he did so. He had NOTHING good to say about them. Absolutely nothing. This lasted for the entire class. I usually sat up front in all my classes—didn't want to miss anything by being distracted by those who sat in front of me. It felt like I got the full brunt of his mocking. My eyes began to fill with silent tears. When the class ended, I looked at Mr. Larson directly. I had always liked and respected him before. Now my look said, "Is that how you really think of me too—just an unfit joke?" He had to see the pain on my tear-stained face as he looked startled, seeming to suddenly realize he had a Negro student in his class. He had just taught this class as he normally did, degrading Negroes. I remained silent, saying nothing to no one.

I'd always liked Mr. Larson and enjoyed being in his classroom. Now this. I had to realize that he was merely doing what he always did with this subject in all his classes. My being there was a rare event in his career. He was simply expressing himself in his view of freed slaves serving in government. And that was ridicule that came from seeing them as figures in a minstrel show. He didn't really take them seriously but saw them as being put in place by carpetbagger's hostile to the genteel Southern whites. I doubt that his attitude ever changed. He taught what he had been taught somewhere in his background. He strongly believed what he had been taught. Even though I was an A student in his class, it meant nothing to him. I was just another ignorant and unworthy Negro. I continued to get As in his class.

    I believe other students told the teacher of my next scheduled class. Another kindly Miss Emily Anderson taught 10th grade English. After class, she asked to speak with me. She said some sympathetic words I don't now remember. But it was indirectly about the experience in my history class. I told her that I knew nothing much of Negro history—my family never spoke of Negro history. Apparently, there was much Negro history that I knew nothing about. She assured me there was much there that was glorious and suggested names of some people I should read about from the Harlem Renaissance of the 1920s as well as history of the 1930s and 1940s, along with famous contemporary Negroes. I'd never heard of any of this before. She mentioned Countee

CHAPTER NINETEEN

Cullen, Langston Hughes, and others. I was off to the library to study more on them and on Negro history. I made it my own extracurricular reading and research activity. For what I learned in the process, I have been and will forever be grateful to Miss Anderson. Truly a teacher, she saw a student needing to know more, needing to have dignity and pride about who she was, and provided me with it. I learned a lot that I never knew before.

How did my ancestors make it once freed? Only in America! They prospered by the willing sweat of their brows and hands. This time it was for themselves and not being forced to labor for the benefit of another. The American dream was realized by them. Wow. They were ambitious, hardworking, overcomers and not victims, compassionate, God-fearing, patriotic new citizens. Slaves learned from whites how the free culture worked. Where else would they learn it, cut off from all other sources? And the cultural mores of the time were Victorian. Children had their 'place' in society and it was well enforced.

Our past was NOT something mentioned in most Negro homes. So, we generally remained ignorant of our own history. We were rightfully proud of contemporary success stories, but knowledge of those in the past were generally lost to us. Sigh. However, other students all seemed to be proud of their lineage with parents coming from multiple countries—all proud of who they were. Why couldn't I be allowed to be proud of who I was? My forefathers had survived slavery and reconstruction. Who else could say that? That was before I learned that the enemy satan hates ALL people and that ALL people have been oppressed by those he uses at one time or another and by one way or another. ALL, without exception. Search their various histories and you'll see that it's true.

Maybe it was the norm for the times or maybe it was just something they thought better forgotten, but family history among blacks was not passed on to future generations. I have no idea what plantation my great- great grandparents came from or who their owners were. I certainly have no specific information of what their lives were like in slavery. Most interesting to me is how they fared once they were freed. How did people who had nothing survive? How did they come to have food, shelter, family, land and homes, and all else necessary to living as free citizens in America? How did they make the journey from being fully dependent on someone who owned them to being independent enough to take care of themselves? How? I don't know and never will. It's information that is all lost to me along with them—maybe forever. Because nobody ever talked about it. I believe it's helpful—maybe even vital—to know your family history and even your people's history. Not everyone thinks that way, I know. But that's how I'm wired!

This Miss Anderson also taught us about Shakespeare. It was required for those taking 10th

CHAPTER NINETEEN

grade academic English. Our class turn came to study his play, Hamlet. It was both fun and challenging trying to understand this Elizabethan English. Was it the same language as ours? It hardly seemed so. I did find it helpful in giving greater understanding of the KJV Bible and vice versa. Our big test was to memorize Hamlet's soliloquy which we had to recite individually before the whole class. My favorite part was "Oh, that this too too solid flesh would thaw and melt away!" It said exactly what I thought of my appearance. At size 16 and later size 18, I thought myself a huge unattractive blob of flesh who had better keep her expectations low. I know I'll focus on my academic strength. That gave me value.

I had another favorite too. I had always liked music. Would I join the school choir? I considered it seriously. But when the school announced formation of a school orchestra, I immediately signed up. I wouldn't learn to play the piano, but I would learn to play some musical instrument after all! We were given choice in selection of which instrument to play. I wanted to play the cello—but others chose it first and there were no more left. I really liked the cello sound, so I chose the viola for my second choice. But during the first week of classes, a viola string broke and it couldn't be played. The orchestra director had no idea when a replacement string could be obtained. So, I had to make another choice. For some reason, I chose the big ole string bass! I liked its sound too. It was fun to play. The only problem I had was in taking it home to practice there. It required two people—one at each end—in order to reasonably transport it. I usually walked alone the 1.5 miles each way to and from school, so I had to find someone to help me in this chore—and I usually did. It was fun! Orchestra also provided additional opportunities to be away from home. We also went to concerts of the Minneapolis Symphony Orchestra. Playing the string bass seemed an oddity for a girl but I didn't mind—I embraced being different.

I can't say I was the most diligent musical student, but it was something I saw as a pleasing distraction. Our music teacher, Mr. S... was a very pleasant and kind Jewish man who enjoyed music and enjoyed his students. Occasionally, we made field trips (to watch the Minneapolis Symphony Orchestra performances, etc.) and he always gave a few students a ride with him to our destination. I guess he wasn't a bad driver, but these were frightening moments for us. We discovered he could NOT drive and talk at the same time! When talking, he drove very slowly. When this would irritate other drivers, he would pull close to parked cars and drive even slower—giving drivers opportunity to pass him. This may have seemed to him a courtesy to other drivers, but it was a nightmare for us! We usually would practice silence—so he wouldn't talk and could better focus on driving. I have never met another driver like him—thank God!

CHAPTER NINETEEN

One thing I learned about teachers as I progressed through different grade levels was that I had no respect for 'easy' teachers. I regarded them as cheats who stole from me and the other students. How? They didn't do their best or challenge us enough to be properly prepared for the next grade. I regarded that as cheating us from important life skills. Some students liked 'easy' teachers. I didn't. They weren't doing their job. Blessedly, I had many fine teachers who did their job!

My 9th grade Civics class was taught by another Mr. Larson. He was the most popular teacher of the students and later became the Assistant Principal. In Civics class, we learned about the American government basics. We learned about the American Revolution and how our nation came to be. We learned when it happened and the root causes. We learned about its major events and who the major players were. We learned about the process that led to our founding documents: the Declaration of Independence, the Constitution and its Bill of Rights. We learned about our national anthem and the Pledge of Allegiance. We learned about other national songs and national monuments. We learned about the Civil War, the Underground Railroad, the Pilgrims and the pioneers, the Pony Express, the two railroads that united the physical nation, the suffragettes, and so much more. I'm surprised we learned so much, because I regarded him as one of those 'easy' teachers! But we did indeed learn in his classroom.

I never understood the removal later of this once-required subject from America's public-school curriculum. It was a deliberate move to induce ignorance. What kind of citizen would be the result of such ignorance? It could not be one who knew the basic facts about his nation and its values. Instead of "I know", we could only produce a people of "I think, I feel" that has anything as its fruit. Anything but order. This kind of chaos happened repeatedly in many societal fields besides education. Chaos was indeed its fruit. And great denigration of our nation. What the Greatest Generation and others before it produced slowly and inexorably became the Self-defeated Generation. Sadly. And we pushed that defeatism onto other nations. Misery loves company.

Other Classes and Experiences

Every Friday pep rallies were held in the auditorium and all students attended. It was as mandatory as any other class was. I learned all the pep songs but attended no games in any sports. It was something I didn't deem I would really be a part of. It was an extra-curricular activity I didn't even ask my parents for permission to attend. I rejoiced when we won games and celebrated them when we touted them in the pep rallies, just as any true Henry Patriot would. But I was always an absentee to the games.

CHAPTER NINETEEN

Other events occurred in the auditorium too. We saw old movies on occasion. There were pep events for homecoming and its talent show. Teens were blossoming all around me. Rick was one. He sang "Blue Moon" as a solo and we were astonished at what a good voice he had, Sharon got a complete new school wardrobe over one Summer and became a popular fashion plate. One girl got famous for another reason: she refused to wear her proper shoe size, and her shoes always split apart at the rear seams. She never seemed embarrassed as she wore the shoe size she had chosen for herself.

Henry Culture

The most operative word and societal value in mid-century Minneapolis was "nice". It was the biggest compliment possible. Likewise, it was the biggest/worst accusation. How dare you not be nice! It was a very urgent conforming tool. I only saw how damaging it was years later. It put pressure on you to be 'nice' even if it meant not being your real self and saying or doing things you didn't really want to say or do. Electing our Homecoming Queen in my senior year was interesting. We non-elites wanted her to be someone who was 'nice' and not just popular. Actually, we wanted to prove that being 'nice' made you the most popular! That was the criteria we sought and were determined to elect and honor. And we happily succeeded at getting such winners in the whole Homecoming court! Oh, happy day.

School fights weren't a big thing at Henry. Nearly every boy carried a pocketknife. It was commonly utilitarian at the time. But fighting was done with fists. Weapons—knife or gun—were unthinkable for use by boys or girls. This was in the days when bullying was not common as it became later. The most vicious fight I ever saw was between two girls. It was several blocks from Henry, of course. You didn't fight in school because that was a definite no-no. The two girls pulled hair, tossed blows, and tore blouses apart so as to lose buttons. We thought it was all very risqué. A neighbor intervened to stop the fight—by spraying them with a water hose! For which I'm sure both girls were grateful. It was a one-time event.

Driver's Ed

There were teens who drove their cars to school. I remember the beginning of Driver's Ed as a new school subject. We were eligible for student driver's permits at 15 but couldn't get a driver's license until we were 16 years old. Somehow it was deemed necessary that the boys get this class first. Girls had to wait.

My Extracurricular School Activities

I joined many extracurricular activities at school. To keep busy, to be away from home more, etc. One of my favorites was the forensics debate team. We went to various colleges in Minnesota for these speech tournaments. Our coach was Mr. Hoerschgen, one of my favorite teachers. I learned a LOT—about the lifestyles of other students as well as about debate. It was a chosen escape from my shyness and sometimes timidity. It helped me a lot. Being on the debate team included lots of trips to colleges and opportunities to be out of town and to see how other students lived. It was wonderful and turned out to be one of the best things in life that I ever did.

Another activity I was involved in was Junior Achievement—teaching teens to be entrepreneurs. More about that later.

Summer School Once

I did something new for me the summer after the 10th grade. I went to Summer School! Normally, that's thought of as something mandatory for failing students—to catch up and avoid getting a failed grade for a subject. But Minneapolis also used it as a time for students to take EXTRA classes that your schedule had no room for during the regular school year. Good. So, I saw it as an opportunity for me to take typing. My regular classes were all academic courses. I wasn't aiming for office skills or jobs. Besides, what if my hand injuries meant I couldn't type at all! I didn't want to get a bad grade during the regular school year for what was beyond my control. This Summer School grade wouldn't count against me if I failed—it wasn't a REQUIRED course. I needed to find out if I could type with injured fingers. Whew—I felt it was safe for me to try in summer school. How'd I do? Better than I would have ever thought! Typing doesn't require much bending of the fingers, so I wasn't handicapped at all. Homework wasn't required. I didn't have to really apply myself that strenuously. I wanted to learn typing as an essential skill—it seemed to be needed more and more in society. Even before the days of computers—personal or otherwise. And I just wanted to be able to use Papa's portable typewriter he'd given me. When he did, he told me it was something I should know how to do. He was right. My final grade was a "D"—I hadn't applied myself much at all in the class and I knew it—no surprise. But what would my parents say about a "D"—from ME? Out of five subjects, my usual grade was 4 "As" and a "B". Usually, the lower grade was for math—up from my usual "C". Remember, I got behind in that subject while I was hospitalized with my hand injuries. Even though I caught up, I never felt confident in that subject. And the few times I got a "B" in math, I was more pleased than for any "A" grade! Now would I be in trouble for getting this low grade in typing? To my great surprise, my parents hardly batted an eye. Either they thought it was due to my hand injuries—or they really loved me! I was glad either way.

 Life is strange. I ended up using typing for much of my career! My final job was as an executive secretary at a major corporation. By then my typing speed was in excess of 100 words per minute. I had acquired a genuine sought-after skill! And it all started with getting a "D" in typing for a non-required Summer School class. Who knew? It reminds me of this Bible verse:

> *Zechariah 4:10a For who hath despised the day of small things? KJV*

Term Papers

When they were assigned, I would read all needed material and somehow remember salient points. Then the night before the paper was due, I would write it all out at once. This meant a late night for me. It was the only time I was allowed to ignore my bedtime. If I was up until 3 o'clock or 4 o'clock in the morning, it was allowed. I would be the only one awake in our household. It wasn't easy, but I had a trick to aid me. I would buy a box of my favorite Cheez-It crackers. Every time I felt sleepy, I would eat a few crackers. I had discovered that you can't eat and sleep at the same time! So, I would finish writing out my term paper and grab a very few hours of sleep, wake up at my scheduled time, and head off to school to turn it into the class that had assigned it—English, Civics, History, or Social Studies. Thankfully, I generally got an "A" on my term paper. I enjoyed doing these papers. Maybe it was the whole experience—the research, the writing, and being allowed to break a rule. It wasn't the best way though.

My Grades

As I said, they were generally 4 A's and a 'B'. That was true after the 7th grade. That was when Mrs. Melrose made sure w e were solid in basic math fundamentals. Though none were fond of her technique that included a test every Friday, I deeply appreciated it. It was invaluable. Now the 'B' was usually in math.

I didn't take intellect as something I achieved. I believed rather that it was a gift from God which I gratefully appreciated and tried to use—mostly. My grades were evidence of HIM as a reality. But it wasn't always the way I saw the truth.

At this time, I foolishly and ignorantly thought grades were a measure of intelligence. I was to learn later that nothing could be more wrong! I guess I got this attitude by the importance placed on grades by teacher, parents, and others. I came to know that "common sense" was often the mark of the highly intelligent. Their intelligence shows in practical ways and not just in esoteric/academic knowledge. I think the best intelligence values and displays both. But if you gotta choose, academic knowledge alone can be of lesser value in this adventure called life! Good grades are the result of a combination of many things. Brain power, interests, effort to please, competitive nature, curiosity, effort made. Common sense, etc. are mostly God-gifts.

For example, M'Deah could outlast any educated city-slicker in a survival situation. She could sufficiently garden, fish, hunt, cook, and otherwise feed herself. She could clothe herself. She knew enough folk medicine to stay healthy. Etc. She had the skills and temperament of a survivor. None of that is academic knowledge! How's that for true intelligence?

CHAPTER TWENTY

Other Family Now

At some point, Aunt Daisy had moved from Alabama and was living with Carrie and Tommy. Then, when she had a problem with breathing issues and because Aunt Carrie thought it was TB (tuberculosis), they didn't want her to live there anymore.

While she still lived there, I interviewed her once. I made a special trip by public bus to see her. I wanted to know more about our family history. She gave me lots of names and relationships I didn't know. This was a real treasure trove, and I was delighted to have it! I went home and carefully placed it in my dresser drawer. But, to my surprise and dismay, it was gone when I went to retrieve it the next day. I was devastated! Maybe it went behind the drawer. So, I removed every drawer in my dresser to see if my notes had fallen into the bowels of this built-in piece of furniture. Nope. I asked my roommate, Linda, if she'd seen it. Nope. I asked M'Deah if she'd seen it. Nope. I had to admit that it had mysteriously disappeared and was gone forever. What to do? I would have to interview Aunt Daisy all over again. And I was too embarrassed to do so! This information surely

CHAPTER TWENTY

would be known by some other family member. I would just get it from them later. But I never did. Sigh.

So, Aunt Daisy came to live with us. We kids loved having her with us! She was very creative, and I liked talking to her. One day, we found ourselves without lunch. M'Deah hadn't mentioned what we were to have. We might just get some things out of the garden. What to do? We told Aunt Daisy of our dilemma. She resourcefully and creatively used leftover cornbread, onions from the garden, spices, etc. to make a lunch for us of cornbread dressing, I don't know what-all she used but it was absolutely delicious, and we happily devoured it all—wishing for more the next day!

I remember one of the vital things she taught us was to never throw anything away—paper bags, string, buttons, safety pins, etc.—because "you never know when you might need it again". We thought her ridiculous and old-fashioned, but it was a very valuable life lesson! It's just a cautious way to live! And a way I adopted as my own. I'm so glad they saved things like photos. I regret they didn't save family history in any written form. At least, the part that they knew.

My kids say that I am a hoarder. They're at least partially right, I admit. I save items I think MAY be important, memorable, or useful in the future. With that outlook, some things may be saved needlessly.

The results? It all just looks like a hoard! But often, one man's trash is another man's treasure—it's true! In addition, I was raised by people who lived in scarcity—raised by descendants of slaves and former slaves and of those who had survived the Great Depression of the 1930s and the rationing of WWII. They knew the necessity and practicality of holding onto things and they passed that attitude on to their children, of which I'm one! It can be very useful.

Carrie

One thing I learned about Carrie later was regarding her health. She had what the family referred to as "spells". She would sorta space out sometimes and was on some kind of medication for it. Supposedly, it began when she was a young attractive woman in love with a young man whom another woman also loved. The rivalry led this other woman to "work roots" against Carrie. Carrie became sick and her appearance as an attractive young woman changed very badly. She lost her health and her looks. Her mouth twisted like that of a stroke patient and these "spells" began. Who would marry her now? Certainly not the young man she had loved. But Carrie DID marry later. His name was Tommy Bogan. Tommy had grown up as an orphan and had little education—maybe just through the 4th grade. This wasn't that unusual for his time and place as a slave descendant in the rural segregated South. More typical for such was an 8th

CHAPTER TWENTY

grade education. High school for such was rare, in the absence of existing high schools for blacks. He also had a sister too, but I know nothing else about their lives. As an uneducated man, Tommy was considered by Carrie to be "beneath" her socially. It was something she never seemed to let him forget. Even as a child, it was humiliating to watch her constantly correcting him about one thing or another. But Tommy was kind to Carrie and provided for her—she occasionally worked but never had to do so. I believed she often took him for granted. In her condition, she could have no children. I never knew her medical diagnosis, but it seemed to be a type of epilepsy combined with some type of stroke. Later, as a teen, I often talked to her on the phone—I sorta befriended her, thinking she led a somewhat lonely life. I soon noticed that there were times when she seemed to "freeze" on the phone. (It's like what happened to Senator McConnell in 2023.) She would make kinda "grunting" noises but say nothing, even when I would call out her name repeatedly. Then, she would snap out of it, as though nothing happened. Sometimes these episodes lasted so long that I would just hang up the phone. When I mentioned it to M'Deah, that was when I was told Carrie was ill because someone had worked "roots" on her, causing her to have these "spells". Oh. I didn't believe in such things. But I don't know everything. Maybe it's because Carrie believed in "roots" and that belief had her manifest what they were supposed to do. Maybe it was a coincidental medical problem. I don't know. I just tried to befriend her because I felt sorry for her. Sadly, she had a very peculiar personality that delighted in creating family chaos and then observing it as for amusement, as though she weren't at fault. I don't know what that's called, but I've never seen anything like it. Close maybe, but not as bad. Somehow, I never had any animosity towards Carrie—just sympathy. In her earlier years, as the oldest, she had more influence with her siblings. Naturally, that ceased after her illness came upon her, but she still saw herself in that role. She thought they should seek out her advice. She was more than willing to give it for their child-rearing—even though she had no children of her own. She regarded herself as an expert in all things. No. Their lives had gone on without her.

I do remember that Carrie used to work outside of the home sometimes. But now she was a housewife and had been for some time. Maybe this was why, especially if her "spells" actually occurred on the job. Tommy had a good janitorial job at the University of Minnesota, and they fared well financially. She continued to berate him though, openly correcting his grammar and etiquette, etc. She behaved more as his domineering teacher than as a loving wife. I don't remember much about Tommy's family but knew he had a sister. I think their parents died when they were young children.

CHAPTER TWENTY

M'Deah was protective of her big sister, Carrie. She regarded all her bad behavior as being caused by her bad health—her "spells". For a long time, I knew nothing about them. The only time M'Deah ever made a negative remark about Carrie was years later. She remarked that Carrie's lie to Buster nearly cost all our lives. But there was no bitterness or hatred in the remark.

CHAPTER TWENTY-ONE

The Big Questions

There was an unexplainable code of silence in our home. We never spoke about what bothered us most. Maybe that's what fear does. It didn't occur to us to ask what someone thought about a troubling issue, like domestic violence. We were each in our own little bubble of hidden emotions—hidden even from us, from each other, and certainly hidden from all the world. Yet subsequent times and culture has given students much focus on how they felt about something—little or big, good or bad. How they thought about something didn't matter. How do you feel? That's all that mattered. How times have changed!

When I was 16, I somehow couldn't take the "silence about the violence" in our home anymore. I needed some answers. It suddenly seemed to me that it took TWO crazy people to live in that crazy situation. One person is obviously crazy for thinking that it's OKAY to cruelly beat another person who was also an adult as well as weaker in strength than you were—it was abuse. The other person may also be equally crazy in ALLOWING themselves to be treated that way! Was I wrong?

CHAPTER TWENTY-ONE

M'Deah worked a LOT—full-time and part-time. Sometimes, she had two part-time jobs in addition to a full-time job! Over the years, I figured out that it meant she had LESS time at home then—LESS time in a very dangerous environment. One of her part-time jobs included cleaning house for people. As we grew older, she would take Linda and me along with her to the home of a seamstress for an airline company who sewed stewardess uniforms. Her home was one of those that we cleaned on Saturdays.

I had wondered how M'Deah felt during and after beatings. The man she loved who supposedly loved her and to whom she had given the future lives of herself and her kids was in no way being loving protector but a hateful abuser! Did she know all the kids were aware of her treatment and really cared about it all and about her? I'm glad 16-year old me got enough courage to ask her why she let him beat her!

I also wondered how K.C. felt about beating her. Was he getting revenge on a deceiving woman whom he loved? The whole thing was weird.

Again, as time went by, I saw each of my parents as being "crazy". K.C. was crazy for beating my mother—a woman who posed no threat to him and who did him no harm, but only brought benefit to him and his children. And I thought M'Deah was crazy for allowing herself to be beaten. There was nothing like that in her birth family! She hadn't grown up with that at all!

It seemed cruel to think of M'Deah as being crazy. She was the victim of abuse, so why did I think that was crazy?! Because you agree with your abuser to be a victim and do nothing to change that position/status. Suddenly that's how I saw it. And I knew I wasn't just being cruel or misjudging. What to do?! I seriously asked myself that question for several days. The solution? Ask! I didn't know the WHY of it all and I wouldn't until I asked those involved. That would likely be risky. But I had to ask—it was inescapable.

I thought M'Deah was too passive in staying with K.C. and remaining to be married to him. Why stay with him? (I learned later that there were other circumstances of which I was totally ignorant.) I needed to know. So, I gathered up my courage.

Question For M'Deah

Enroute to the seamstress' house on one such Saturday, I asked M'Deah very hesitantly if I could ask her a question. (I was hesitant because I knew it was about "grown-folks business". I also knew Linda would be discreet and never tell her father about this conversation.) Sure, she said. "WHY do you allow K.C. to beat you and WHY do you stay with him?" I could tell it was NOT a question she had ever expected to hear from any of the children. Slowly she said that staying with him made a better life for her kids—she could never give us the lifestyle we had without two incomes. I told her that we would prefer to have LESS

CHAPTER TWENTY-ONE

if it meant we could have peace and her safety—hot dogs and beans would be just fine with us! That seemed to surprise her. Then she told us of once before talking to him about divorce. He threatened to somehow find and kill her if she ever dared leave him. She didn't want to leave any of us motherless nor see us hurt or killed too. So, she stayed and endured painful mistreatment. Sigh. And she worked the many jobs in order to have a legitimate reason to be away from home. It was safer for her. Oh.

I asked why she'd married him, seeing he was so abusive. She said he hadn't been like that when they dated. When they went for a ride in the country one Sunday, he asked her to marry him, and she declined. She had no plans to remarry then. Her focus was on raising her children. Then he accelerated the car and declared he would run into a highway bridge abutment and kill them both if she refused to marry him. Supposedly, he loved her so much that he couldn't live without her and didn't want anyone else to have her. So, she quickly accepted. What?

It was mind-blowing to hear M'Deah say why she endured the suffering of domestic violence to her body and soul. To make for a good life for the kids—all of them. She believed it could only happen with a 2-income family. Maybe remembering the struggle of single parenting was something she really didn't want to repeat. And he had made it clear that leaving him would be a death sentence for her—and maybe for the kids too. She truly couldn't foresee just taking me and Billy with her and leaving his children behind. She loved them as her own. He would surely take that as further justification for killing her. She felt stuck in her situation. And so, she just endured it.

The Lord told me later, when I asked Him, *"She chose to trust man for safety instead of trusting Me"*, after the attack by Buster. Wrong choice, as she was to find out rather quickly. I'm sure she prayed for safety and for an end to her torment. But trusting God wasn't something she was easily accustomed to doing. It was difficult. She had always trusted in her own strength and hard work. It had gotten her this far. But she slowly learned to trust God fully with everything. The Lord answered her prayers. And it's the Goodness of God that leads to repentance - to change of thinking and believing in Him.

After I got M'Deah's answer, I was relieved for two reasons. One was that I hadn't gotten a blow for being so "grown" as to question an adult about "grown folks' business". Two, there was more at stake than I ever realized. Sigh.

(Years later, I wondered if M'Deah had thought the violent behavior of K.C. was from his WWII experience—"shell shock?" Maybe she made allowances for him in thinking that. But that wasn't the reason for his behavior.)

I decided that if M'Deah could go on, so could I. And I always had school as my safe place and books in

CHAPTER TWENTY-ONE

which to escape. Yes, I could go on too in an unhappy life. Linda's only response was to ask M'Deah that if she ever left, "Please take us with you!" She was speaking on behalf of all us children.

I still had questions that I asked to myself. I thought to myself, how could someone proclaim love for you and profess they don't want to live without you and then want you harmed by them? I'll kill us both? Do you regard that as the expressed depth of their love? Or do you run for the hills as fast as you can to get away from this crazy person? For me, the latter—a definite deal-breaker. For M'Deah, maybe she believed it was a genuine profession of his love for her. Nope, it wasn't, as she was to learn later. What was it then? Did K.C. love her so much that he didn't want her to ever leave him? Or did he think of her as his personal property, having no right to leave him? Selfish dogged determination to have his way? Maybe.

At least, M'Deah now knew that we were aware of her situation and deeply cared for and about her. She was LOVED! I had told her we'd rather eat hot dogs and beans in a home of peace than have anything else. She was shocked to hear that. I also had told her that her situation required TWO crazy people: him for beating a woman as a bully who knew that he could and her for taking the beatings without opposition. After what M'Deah shared that day I had another question—for K.C. I had NO idea how our situation could ever be changed. I saw no way out. Yet I wasn't hopeless. God, help! I still looked to Him to somehow rescue us. And He did later. In a most unusual way.

Decades later, I wondered if K.C. had attended Buster's trial. I never thought about that before. But how do you not—to learn what happened to your loved one and what they went through? The trial would have been pretty cut and dry. I didn't know then what Buster's plea was nor how long the trial took. But K.C. had married M'Deah quickly. I believe he then truly wanted to be the man in the house to protect her and her kids.

Question For K.C.

After my question to M'Deah was answered, I was somewhat both emboldened and relieved, I made another decision. It took longer to work up my courage though! A few weeks later, I asked K.C. if I could ask him a question. As I prepared to ask K.C. the question, I stood in the kitchen doorway—far from him—and was prepared to run from him and out of the house if necessary. I asked, "WHY do you beat my mother?" He was shocked and silent. He slowly said, "There's more going on than you know." And he too didn't give me a blow for being so nervy and "grown". Whew! I was GREATLY relieved, to say the least, and didn't push it any further! I think K.C. was somewhat embarrassed too. I don't think he ever considered that the kids were actually aware of his behavior—or that they cared. I don't know if he ever shared my question with M'Deah. But I do know that he did NOT take the incident out on her and beat her for it—this time. I had considered that he might do that. But I needed answers—real answers. And I never got them. Nothing more would be forthcoming from him about this. When he replied, I asked NO more questions. I was too happy to have escaped great peril. Okay.

Another One

Years later, one of my relatives married a young man who grew up in a home with domestic violence. His father would beat his mother. That's the only home lifestyle he knew. When he tried to replicate that behavior with his new wife, he got quite a surprise: a cast iron skillet to his head. She quickly dissuaded him of any notion that she would submit to being a domestic violence victim. He got the message and that was the end of that. It confirmed for me that women did NOT have to be victims. Stand up for yourself courageously THE FIRST TIME because you value yourself and you deny any man the right to punish you as though you were his wayward child. What kind of sick relationship is that? Who would want such a relationship with someone who was also to be their lifetime lover and the father of their own children? There could be no true intimacy. It makes no sense. I once heard old folks say that "If you take the first blow, you'll take the rest of them too". They meant you MUST seriously protest when you're hit the FIRST time with a domestic violence blow. You MUST take it seriously before it becomes a lifestyle. Accept NO excuses. Make NO allowances. Be NO victim. At the FIRST.

I learned later that it's not always that simple though. M'Deah was put in a position of remaining in a bad marriage, so she thought, to protect the lives of all of us children. Unhappily, she settled. For far too long. It didn't ever get better for her.

My Memory Of The Two Traumas

What two traumas? Buster and K.C. Again, I have heard that the traditional Chinese curse is this: "May you live in interesting times." That would be times of pestilence, war, famine, etc. NO! I would rather live in boring times of peace! And I have. There may not be many memories there, but I enjoyed the trip! And those are times when great lessons are learned too. That's the memories I have of those quiet and mostly uneventful times.

I greatly admire the generations that went before me. They NEVER saw themselves as victims though they lived in times when societal customs and experiences did everything to indicate otherwise. It was a time when racism truly was endemic—written into the laws. Amazing. The power of agreement for non-victimhood is powerful!

CHAPTER TWENTY-ONE

Also, I always remembered that God had kept me and my family alive in the attack by Buster in which we should have been sure and easy victims. So I prayed simply as best I knew how, holding on weakly to that slender thread of hope. And it was not in vain. God is Good. God is Faithful. And I am thankful.

The threat of Buster was sudden. The threat of K.C. was a constant background possibility. But it was a threat of gunshots and not of an iron pipe or knives. Who could defend themselves against that? So it was actually more frightening. And it was a constant—a daily reality and possibility. In a sense, it was death by a thousand knives. Not an easy thing to endure and not show any signs of distress. It was a life of pretense. The show must go on. Unseen damage to your thinking of life continues silently. I don't wish that for even my worst enemy—for no one. There seemed to be no possible way out. No exit seen.

CHAPTER TWENTY-TWO
What Happened?

One evening in January 1959, I heard "funny" noises coming from our parents' bedroom. I considered that Linda didn't get anywhere near the opportunities I did to be away from home, and I suddenly felt sorry for her. She looked particularly sad and lonely as I prepared to leave home for an extracurricular activity. I thought it would cheer her up to get away from home for a little while. Unsure, it prompted me to ask if I could take Linda with me to my Junior Achievement meeting that night, I had never done that before and was unsure what the response would be. But I was given the okay! How did Linda react? She seemed relieved. Our parents were in their room preparing for a visit to attend the annual Auto Show downtown with K.C.'s cousin, Curtis, and his wife, Voncile, who were enroute to our house. Linda and I left to catch the city bus to another high school way across town where the meeting was to be held. When we arrived, Linda was with me and yet not with me. She was not actually in the room where the meeting was held. Rather, she was assigned to sit outside and was able to see and to be seen through a large glass window. Our Junior

CHAPTER TWENTY-TWO

Achievement group took a scheduled group photo that night. I still have a copy of that photo. In it, I have the biggest happiest and most joyful smile ever. Or so it appeared. I was looking through the window, trying to cheer up a very sad-looking Linda on the other side. I was trying to give her some sense of hope because she seemed to be in such deep despair. I suppose we were both wondering and worried about what might be going on at home. M'Deah had seemed to urge Linda and me to leave. Why? I only knew that when Linda and I got home, the house had a strange feel to it—although all seemed quiet and peaceful.

The Event

The next morning, M'Deah was preparing breakfast. I was in the kitchen with her. At some point, she stopped cooking and went downstairs to the basement. Not unusual. Then I heard the front door open, and I heard her voice. She had left the basement, exited out the back door, and gone around to the front of the house. That's unusual. K.C. was sitting at the dining table reading his usual morning newspaper while waiting for breakfast to be prepared. His back was towards her as he sat at his place at the head of the table. I assume she called his name. What was M'Deah saying? I heard her ask for a divorce and to say that K.C. was gonna listen to her. What? I knew that wasn't gonna work—NO peaceful end to this request was possible!

WHAT HAPPENED?

All the kids were coming for breakfast—Linda from our bedroom and the boys from their upstairs bedroom. M'Deah was unexpectedly holding one of K.C.'s rifles. I guess they all saw the gun scene because they all began running towards the back door. I was the last. But as I went to join them in running too, I remembered my promise to myself from the last time: I will never abandon M'Deah again when she was endangered. Suddenly, I stopped in front of the stove, frozen in my tracks. I had only taken two steps from the dining room into the kitchen. From the kitchen, I had heard him as he suddenly rose from his chair, called her a profane name, and ran towards her in rage. I had no doubt about what would happen if K.C. got ahold of the gun. I don't know what I can do but I've gotta go back to help M'Deah. Then I heard it before I could even move. BANG! A single shot. But who had shot who? Had K.C. overpowered M'Deah and gotten the gun? That's very likely. I went back into the dining room. M'Deah was still standing. I was so relieved to see her there. But K.C. was lying face down nearly at her feet.

He had maybe only taken three steps before she pulled the trigger, and he dropped face down very near her. What was he thinking? What did he expect? Certainly, it would have been no good outcome for M'Deah. He really did intend to kill her. I heard no sound from him, so I assumed his death was instant. I only knew he posed no threat to anyone. Knowing

CHAPTER TWENTY-TWO

him, it was truly self-defense. I am forever grateful that he didn't succeed in doing what he wanted to do—to kill M'Deah for sure.

I was glad to see that M'Deah was standing, holding the rifle. Immediately, I asked her if she were okay. I knew she hadn't been injured so it was mostly about her state of mind. She replied that she was alright and instructed me twice to call the police. I did so, amazingly calm because she was OKAY. I saw that K.C. was lying face down on the floor, almost at her feet. Was he bleeding? I was too stunned to know what to do. The next instruction I got from M'Deah was to get towels from the linen closet. I did but I don't remember ever using them to staunch his blood flow. I never saw the wound, but I think I knew he was dead At some point, M'Deah leaned the rifle to rest it upon the wall. Otherwise, she never moved. I also worried about Aunt Daisy, who was living with us at the time. I think she slept on the sunporch—there was room nowhere else in our small house. How would this trauma affect her? But she was absolutely calm. Maybe it was an outcome she had expected. I called the police to report a shooting in our home.

Gradually, the other kids came back inside the house. We were all dazed. I have no memory of anything the other kids said or did. I think the boys went upstairs to their room. I vaguely remember Emeal being angry and confused. Everyone else was silent. Surely, Aunt Daisy knew even more than we kids did

WHAT HAPPENED?

about what was going on in our house. The wisdom of the aged being observant? Probably.

There was a lot going on. I wouldn't look at K.C. lying on the floor. What happened afterwards was mostly a blur to me—I remember very few details. How quickly did the police arrive? I don't know. But they came quickly. They arrested M'Deah, as she and I knew they would—as we all knew they would. What would happen to our family? I wondered. Surely, K.C.'s brothers would want M'Deah to have nothing to do with K.C.'s kids. Would they take them in and raise them? It seemed logical, but sad. M'Deah loved his kids, for sure, and they knew it. But how would they react now? I think M'Deah told me to call Auntie to get me, Billy, and Aunt Daisy. She expected K.C.'s brothers would get his kids. Linda was clear on wanting to go with me and Billy. But that decision was not in her hands. It's all very blurry, even now. My thoughts were on the welfare of M'Deah. Surely, she would be deemed innocent by reason of self-defense. Surely?

The police came and M'Deah was arrested, as we knew she would be. The newspaper photographer showed her wearing a fur coat enroute to jail. It was an "apology gift" K.C. bought M'Deah buy for Christmas a few days earlier. I never saw it again. I assume she later returned it to the store of purchase so she would not be saddled with paying for it.

CHAPTER TWENTY-TWO

Astonished at what had happened, I also knew there was no other way out from under the situation of domestic abuse. None would have been allowed by this crazy man. I only knew that we were free from its horror. Forever. It certainly wasn't the ideal solution. But it was a solution. Instantly, I was glad that K.C. was gone from our lives. I didn't celebrate the way that he was gone—only that he was gone. In 1959 I got something I thought would never be possible. I had a home in which there was peace—blessed peace. It was a wonderful new experience. I looked forward to having more of that in my life. I didn't hate the person, K.C. I hated what he did to M'Deah. But when he was gone, I didn't grieve for him at all. I don't ever remember shedding one tear for him. I was sorry only that Linda's father was gone. But I wasn't grieved because of it. I didn't know what the future would look like but eight years of hell were over. And I was glad to know that he was gone from our lives forever. I know of no other way that would have been possible.

Of course, we didn't attend K.C.'s funeral. We weren't even notified of anything about it. We didn't get an obituary later either. It was as though we didn't exist. His family would be there, and they had made it clear that they had no love for us at all. I guess they assumed we hated him and them. I thought surely, they cared for his children though and would take them in as family and raise them. Nothing could be further from the truth. I somehow heard that their only interest was in his life insurance. Of course, M'Deah couldn't inherit it legally, and she didn't want it anyway. She wanted that money to go to his children. How it all worked out, I don't know. I only know his family refused to step up and turned his kids over to the government to enter the system for dependent children. All three became wards in the foster care system, sadly.

Again, I shed no tears for K.C. but I had no hate for him. Later, I tried to remember him for the good things he had done. I tried to remember the childhood hurts he had sustained because of Jim Crow and poverty, denying him the education he had so desperately wanted. And the discrimination he encountered in the Army while at war. But I never saw him as a total victim. His choices were his choices. Slaves and former slaves endured such and more. And usually made better choices. So could he. No excuses. I was just glad that he was gone out of all our lives and that he could never hurt M'Deah again. Or kill us all. I felt safe again. But I wondered what would happen to his kids, my stepfamily. Would they really not be allowed any more contact with us in the future by the bitterness of their father's family? M'Deah dearly loved them all and I think they know that. I believed Linda would still love us. And maybe Floyd too. But what about Emeal? Not likely. I knew our family would never be the same again. I knew there were big changes ahead for us all.

CHAPTER TWENTY-TWO

The Relocations

This happened for all of us, of course. I had unanswered questions though. Who called and arranged for Billy and me to go to Auntie's house and how did we get there? I don't know. Who arranged for K.C,'s family to have his kids and when did they leave? I don't know. Who arranged for family to get Aunt Daisy and when did she leave? I don't know. What role did the police play, other than arresting M'Deah? I don't know. It's as if it all happened to another person—not to me. At 17, a flood of emotions and thoughts overwhelmed me. It all boiled down to one big question. What would our family look like in the future? Nothing had prepared any of us for this. We had no discussion about what had just happened or what was to come. What could we say? I have little to no memory of much that happened afterwards.

As I said, when the police arrived, M'Deah was arrested and taken to jail. But somewhere/somehow, she had arranged for Billy and me to live with Auntie and Uncle Robert. I think K.C.'s family came to take his kids away. To repeat, I learned later that they were only interested in any life insurance money his kids may inherit. At the time, I thought it was because they loved him and his family and were gonna use it to take care of his kids. To my knowledge, his kids received zero benefit from his life insurance. I don't know who did. It was many years before I learned

WHAT HAPPENED?

that not all families had the same value for each other that M'Deah had modeled and taught us. Sad.

Shocking to me—and to the kids—K.C.'s family did NOT want to raise his kids. They also wanted my mother to have NOTHING to do with the kids. Floyd was placed with a good and loving family. Emeal went to another family for foster care. Linda was placed in foster care and moved from family to family and occasionally to some group homes—she was placed in several locations. ALL were unsatisfactory for her. It was so sad. She was treated like a throw-away child. That she lost none of her human pathos in the process was absolutely miraculous. She was nearly overly capable of feeling the pain of others. Maybe because she went through so much pain herself. Loving and being loved meant a lot to her.

How did we learn of what happened to K.C.'s kids? Maybe it was from M'Deah's lawyer who would have found out at her request. M'Deah and us really hated that there was nothing we could do for them. I don't know the details but M'Deah had a good relationship with Linda's welfare case worker. Actually, Auntie worked for the department and could have gotten this information for M'Deah. That was more likely. Either way, she was able to be informed of their welfare.

Again, Floyd was a really good-looking child—a real delight. He had beautiful soft curly hair and a sweet demeanor. He was almost always smiling (I

CHAPTER TWENTY-TWO

think he had dimples) and he was very easy to get along with. He was a cute little brother. To repeat, I only have rumors of what became of Floyd. He was young, controlled by adults, and I have had absolutely no contact with him since his father's death. Neither did M'Deah. One rumor I had was that he was adopted shortly afterwards by his foster family—into a lovely farm family in the nearby suburbs. I pray he had a good life.

Emeal was shifted from foster home to foster home, I think. So was Linda when foster parents were available and willing to take in a teenage girl. Otherwise, she was being placed in institutional settings. Somehow, as I said, M'Deah was always able to keep up with what was going on in her life. It was later that I learned from Linda of the trauma of being transferred from place to place, whether private home or group home. Never again to have a sense of being a beloved family member who belonged with anyone. I learned of how your belongings were not treasured and you carried them from place to place in trash bags. That was your luggage. I felt so sorry for Linda. And for her brothers. But there was nothing I could do. Indeed, there was nothing M'Deah could do either although she loved them as her own and would gladly have raised them if she could. Linda and Floyd would have been receptive. Emeal was bitter. His father had been his hero. Sadly, life growing up would never again be pleasant for them. We would hear about K.C.'s kids. But we never saw his sons again.

Depression?

I didn't know what depression was, but I think I got depressed during the brief time we were at the home of Auntie and Uncle Robert. By this time, their oldest brother, Dan, and his family had moved to Minneapolis from Coffeeville, Alabama. They were also living with Auntie and Uncle Robert during this transition time. We were a big family now. (Dan's wife was also named Janie. I had asked once how we could tell Janie's apart in conversation. I think it was M'Deah who suggested tying their names to their husbands: Janie-Dan and Janie-George. It worked! There was never any more confusion or doubt as to which Janie you were referring to when you mentioned them that way.) Billy and I adjusted to life elsewhere. I remember that I lost all interest in taking a bath—which had never been a problem before in all my life. I wasn't going to stink, of course. So I did the bare minimum of a daily sponge bath upon waking. I hit the hot spots, the highlights. My cousin, Ruby, noticed and mentioned it to me. I was unaware of and puzzled at my strange behavior too. I didn't know the reason at all and it just continued for a few months.

I mentioned that Ruby and I became close friends. We spent more time together than we had before Billy

CHAPTER TWENTY-TWO

and I went to live with Uncle Robert and Auntie after K.C.'s death. We didn't attend many movies in my childhood. I remember one that K.C. may have taken us to see before the Buster attack. It was called "The Thing". And I thought it was very scary. I decided then that I didn't like scary movies. I remember a time when Ruby and I decided to attend the latest movie craze one evening after work. All the talk was about this Alfred Hitchcock movie called "Psycho". So, after work, we had dinner at the popular Chinese restaurant downtown and then went to the movie. It was indeed scary—I had forgotten that I didn't like scary movies! And unlike "The Thing" movie that I had seen in my early childhood, this involved real people—a real human psycho. At the movie's end, we were both frightened. And we continued on in the silly decision we had made earlier. Ruby would go to her home in South Minneapolis. And I would go to my home in North Minneapolis. Alone. We both came to regret that decision. It was about 10 o'clock, pitch-black night, and a time when most decent people were in bed. The bus route that delivered me nearest to my house—about a block—had stopped running for the night. So I had to take another bus route that dropped me off about three blocks from home. That night it was a very long three blocks. Not only that, but it included a walk over the Shingle Creek Bridge. I was sure a psycho could be hiding under the bridge as I ran across it. The walk also involved a lot of looking over my shoulder too—to be sure I wasn't being followed. I was incredibly relieved to arrive home safely and swore I'd never do that again! And I went to no more scary movies—certainly nothing that included a solitary trip home. Once was enough!

Cousin Juanita (Ruby's younger sister) and I became close at this time too. Our most frequent activity was to take long walks in the neighborhood. They were fun. We would walk and talk. Good times. Juanita was years younger than we were.

Family Migration

From the time of Negro migration to the North from the South during slavery and during the civil rights movement, it was common that families helped each other in the movements. George and Janie did so for M'Deah and her family. And maybe briefly for some others. Auntie and Uncle Robert did so for Dan and Janie and their family. Juanita was two years younger—Billy's age. They were a great help to M'Deah and her kids in a time of trouble. Carrie and Tommy helped Aunt Daisy briefly and I think Aunt Mary too. M'Deah took in Aunt Daisy and Aunt Mary at different times. I remember that Aunt Mary had her own apartment above M'Deah later and worked as a cook at the major downtown Chinese restaurant. The restaurant where she worked would throw away chicken livers—they had no use for them. So, she would bring them home and use them herself. We had

CHAPTER TWENTY-TWO

many delightful helpings of her fried chicken livers and her smothered chicken livers. It was in the tradition of slaves and their descendants, wasting nothing.

The migration practice slowly died out as older family members died out. Finally, no one needed this kind of help. I remember the overall family getting seemingly less and less close. Ruby and Juanita noticed it too. We promised each other that we would not follow in those footsteps but would keep the cousins together. That was our sincere intention. Which is what the road to hell is paved with: good intentions. Sadly, we did not follow through on our good intentions. We made some weak talk about it from time to time. It's something we never forgot but never did. Sadly.

At age 80, the Lord gave me the idea that we could have a family reunion via Zoom—better than nothing. Zoom was not something I was into much— I think I had used it only once! Scott had arranged for me to celebrate my 80th birthday via Zoom with family and friends. It was delightful! But Zoom also seemed useful for this event too. This reunion would involve no costly need for transportation, hotel room, meals, etc. Particularly, we wouldn't have to use any physical energy for air travel—an advantage because we were all getting older! And no Covid-19 issues will be a concern for us. I made mention of it minimally. But, seemingly, there was no corresponding interest. I love my cousins and generally address them as "Cuz". We cousins all still know each other, of course. But our children—the next generation—don't know each other at all. Except for those whose parents are siblings. Sigh. Family is important.

To understand the significance of this migration, I offer this excerpt from the website of the U.S. National Archives:

> *The Great Migration (1910-1970):* The Great Migration was one of the largest movements of people in United States history. Approximately six million Black people moved from the American South to Northern, Midwestern, and Western states roughly from the 1910s until the 1970s. The driving force behind the mass movement was to escape racial violence, pursue economic and educational opportunities, and obtain freedom from the oppression of Jim Crow.
> The Great Migration is often broken into two phases, coinciding with the participation and effects of the United States in both World Wars. The First Great Migration (1910-1940) had Black southerners relocate to northern and midwestern cities including: New York, Chicago, Detroit, and Pittsburgh. When the war effort ramped up in 1917, more able bodied men were sent off to Europe to fight leaving their industrial jobs vacant. The labor supply was further strained with a decline in immigration from Europe and standing bans on peoples of color from other parts of the world. All of this afforded the opportunity for the Black population to be the labor supply in non-agricultural industries.

CHAPTER TWENTY-TWO

Although the migrants found better jobs and fled the South entrenched in Jim Crow, many African Americans faced injustices and difficulties after migrating. The Red Summer of 1919 was rooted in tensions and prejudice that arose from white people having to adjust to the demographic changes in their local communities. From World War I until World War II, it is estimated that about 2 million Black people left the South for other parts of the country.

World War II brought an expansion to the nation's defense industry and many more jobs for African Americans in other locales, again encouraging a massive migration that was active until the 1970s. During this period, more people moved North, and further west to California's major cities including Oakland, Los Angeles, and San Francisco, as well as Portland, Oregon and Seattle, Washington. Within twenty years of World War II, a further 3 million Black people migrated throughout the United States.

Black people who migrated during the second phase of the Great Migration were met with housing discrimination, as localities had started to implement restrictive covenants and redlining, which created segregated neighborhoods, but also served as a foundation for the existing racial disparities in wealth in the United States.

Records in this topic cover migratory information and trends captured by various branches and agencies of the government, including employment and housing. There are also records reflecting cultural and social aspects of the lives of those who participated and were impacted by the Great Migration.

It was indeed a GREAT Migration! And our family was a part of that—as were so many other families.

My Childhood Seasons In Minneapolis

How did I see the Minneapolis seasons of weather? Statistically, living in a part of the world that had the beauty of four distinct seasons is a good thing. I've read that people living in such weather enjoy a longer life than those who don't. Longer can be a good thing. Or not.

Fall was my favorite season. It was relief from the Summer heat, the beauty of leaves changing color and the rustle of them underfoot as you walked outside, etc. And being away from home and back to school was a highlight. I loved what I called "sweater weather". But Fall was also hunting season. I enjoyed trips we took as a family to the hunting grounds and watching Joe point in the fields of Fall foliage and dried cornstalks. But hunting also meant more guns. And more work cleaning game the hunters in our household shot. More danger from K.C. too. It hung over Fall like a bad shadow.

Winter was worst of all. When cold winter weather made it impossible for K.C. to work his housing construction job because the concrete mortar would freeze rather than set, his days at home would be generally spent in two ways. Either he would become more violent to his family OR he would become more productive! This is when he would take on big projects and small projects. They kept him busy and otherwise mentally occupied and thus we were all safer at home. If he took on a big project at home, it was usually okay. He did good work on them and exhibited his skill and creativity. If he didn't have a project, tension was awful in our home. We never knew when his mercurial temperament would set him off to abuse M'Deah in the night. Anything or nothing could set him off. I tried my hardest to distract him. I used humor. I tried to get him to talk about his childhood days in the South, his Army experiences, anything. It didn't always work. I loved to hear adults talk about the old days of their childhood and young adulthood. I found it fascinating. M'Deah had no problem telling us of her old days. Her family wasn't wealthy but they never seemed to be without. They produced their own food on their own small farm. They may not have always had what they wanted but they were never without either. Usually the community provided the teachers with donated food stuffs. They didn't lack. K. C.'s childhood was different. He never spoke of largess growing up. I didn't understand sharecropping at the time. I would be puzzled as he often withdrew from our midst to go into their bedroom. I didn't understand that it probably depressed him to remember his childhood. Also, after my hands were frostbitten in the third grade, I wasn't a fan of the cold blizzard Minnesota Winters either—unless I was inside looking out! That's when

WHAT HAPPENED?

I most enjoyed one of K.C.'s finished projects: watching wood burn in the sunporch fireplace.

Spring was a joyous time. It was warm enough for K.C. to work consistently and be less volatile. It was truly a delight for me to smell and to gather lilac flowers from trees along the way to school and to watch the Earth come alive again. They were a beautiful sight and beautiful scent always.

Summer was a mixed bag. K.C. would be working steadily. But I missed school safety and activities. We spent more time at home. Fishing trips and picnics were welcome breaks. I was usually glad when Summer was over because I didn't like the hot weather either.

CHAPTER TWENTY-THREE
The Big Life Change

After K.C. was gone and our family structure changed, we all came out of our shells. I was ready to become a real teenager and also free to be so. It was many more years before I no longer felt the need to excel and throw myself into activities outside the home trying to earn the normal life. I don't know what happened to Emeal but heard he had gotten on drugs. Linda remained vulnerable and frequently sacrificed her own welfare for what she thought was the good of others she deeply sympathized with in their plight. It was obviously enough to break a person. I heard that she later turned to drugs for relief too. She moved to California after aging out of the foster care system. She got pregnant at some point and gave birth to twin girls—one of whom she named Barbara, after me. Linda was strong in adversity, however—especially now that she had her beloved daughters. She went on to overcome all that and was able to live drug free. Floyd was always a delightful child and had a short stay in foster care. A loving couple adopted him. I never knew any of the adoption specifics or anything of his later life. Rumors heard said that he didn't live long into adulthood. All this about the kids of K.C., I learned from M'Deah. She heard these things from others that I had no contact with. Maybe by the "grapevine"? Hearing negative things about their welfare broke her heart. She really loved his children and was saddened that his family didn't.

I had no way to get in touch with any of them or with K.C.'s kids—my former siblings. His family had made clear that they now hated my mother. Emeal had done that too and I was surprised somewhat because he knew how his father had treated M'Deah and how well she had treated him personally—apparently, he was in agreement that this behavior was okay. I was sure those feelings included her kids too. So there would be no point in contacting them for a wellness check. Besides, we had no way to contact them at all. It was apparently forbidden by the system.

Billy just never mentioned Emeal after they were gone from us. But neither did I. It's as though he hadn't been a part of our lives for eight years. It was like a divorce from us—one we had no control over. K.C.'s family wanted nothing to do with us? So be it. It was understandable but not our fault.

M'Deah's knowledge of Linda's current whereabouts proved useful when I got married. I wanted no one but Linda to be my maid of honor and she quickly and happily agreed. We were in touch once again. In telephone talks with her, I learned of her hard life as a foster child in the system. It was very sad. I also

CHAPTER TWENTY-THREE

learned then that Linda was the most empathetic person I ever knew—before that time and since that time. She would truly "feel your pain". From this, she would do everything she could to ease your pain. Even to her own loss and hurt. Sometimes Linda shared with me some of her experiences in the system. In her foster world, there was always another foster child she knew that needed some kind of help. Linda would share anything she had to assist them in any way she could. I don't remember the circumstances, but once another foster teen girl needed financial help for something. I don't remember where Linda worked but she gave her all the money she had. That included her own food money. Linda said she had only lived on some potatoes she had. For a whole week! I was shocked and scolded her when she told me about it. You didn't take care of your own needs! She pooh-poohed it and said she had no problem surviving on potatoes for a week. It wasn't pleasant but it was doable, and she figured the other girl had the greater need. I didn't believe I could or would be so self-sacrificing in that situation—ever. I marveled at but didn't admire such sacrifice at that time in my life. It was only one of such sacrifices that Linda made on behalf of others. She certainly had grown up quickly. She did not have an easy teenage life in the foster care system. Few do. It was much harder than anything I had ever imagined. Indeed, I had no idea of its reality.

Life In Another Home

M'Deah chose to not get out of jail on bail. As juveniles, we weren't allowed to visit M'Deah in jail and she didn't have bail. But Auntie did visits. She didn't tell us at first that she was visiting M'Deah. Until maybe her second or third visit. Auntie could let M'Deah know that Billy and I were doing well and thus ease her mind. There weren't too many times to visit before the trial. On one such early trip, I insisted on sending something to M'Deah to cheer her up. It was a Bible, and a loving note of encouragement tucked inside which ended up with letting her know I/we loved her. I'm sure it helped her. It was all I could do but I could do no less. That and desperate prayer.

M'Deah chose not to get out of jail on bail. She would remain imprisoned until her trial. Billy and I missed her a lot.

My only worry was for M'Deah. I knew she'd go to trial. M'Deah was smart and resourceful—that's the way she had been raised. She hired one of the best defense attorneys in Minneapolis. I was happy Mr. Nemerov was defending her and I had a lot of confidence in him—the whole family did. His reputation was excellent. God gave us the best to defend M'Deah in court. Later, he asked me questions to know who I was. He asked about my school classes and activities. He asked about my memory of times M'Deah was abused. Oh, yes! He asked me to write them down for him and I did so as best I could. There were so many instances over a period of eight years. Then he told me I would be called by him as a witness in the trial. He told me what questions he would ask me. I was very nervous and somewhat anxious to be doing something so serious that I had never done before and that might affect M'Deah's future. He reassured me that I would be alright. Okay. Would the jurors get how much danger M'Deah was in, even as she stood holding a rifle? Did they understand how much danger she was in even before that? I just knew self-defense was her justifiable plea and prayed it would be her eventual judgment. Then I would worry and be concerned. I prayed a lot. As best I knew how. It certainly was desperate—and sincere.

Why Now?

I wondered why M'Deah had come to the point of her absolute end of being tormented and abused by K.C. Why did her challenge to him about divorce and the subsequent shooting take place on that particular morning? It would be many months later before I got the answer. Almost casually, M'Deah shared what happened the night before the shooting. K.C. had played Russian roulette with a pistol he held to her head! They were supposed to go to the Auto Show that night with his cousin and his cousin's wife—Curtis (pronounced "Sir-tis") and Voncille (pronounced "Von-seal") Taylor. Somehow that got canceled when K.C. suddenly decided not to go. And he tormented M'Deah instead, as they waited for them to arrive at our house and be told about the change of plans. (This was in the days before cellphones, so there was no way to notify them otherwise.) I'm sure M'Deah knew that she just couldn't take it anymore. And she thought about what seemed likely to happen to her, but also, she thought about what would happen to the children. She wanted—needed—a divorce.

Being Socially Stunted

I learned something about myself there during this time at Auntie and Uncle Robert's home. I was very smart academically. But I lacked "common sense". Interesting! I used logic and had NO "street smarts" either. How could I? I had led a closed life socially and was immature at 17. I had NO friends I went to parties with, NO real teen social life, etc. I always assumed that would NOT be my lot in any household with K.C. He disapproved of his brother who lived common-law with lots of their children and her daughter from a previous relationship. I think he was deathly afraid that I might bring such disgrace to his family. My fear ensured I was in no danger of that happening! Besides, our neighborhood and my school had NO other blacks to socialize with. They just weren't there!

I knew my social development was stunted—but it was something I had to accept as my lot in life.

CHAPTER TWENTY-THREE

Why make myself miserable by stressing about it? Just accept it as my reality. It wasn't totally stunted though. I had the outlet of radio and some TV. I had listened to the popular music artists of the day:

> Elvis Presley, Fats Domino, Chubby Checkers, Sam Cook, Paul Anka, Frankie Avalon, Harry Belafonte, Chuck Berry, Pat Boone, Glen Campbell, Ray Charles, Chubby Checker, Tennessee Ernie Ford, Buddy Holly, Frankie Lane, Peggy Lee, Johnny Mathis, Clyde McPhatter, Ricky Nelson, Patti Paige, Ike and Tina Turner, The Drifters, The Everly Brothers, The Impalas, Little Anthony and the Imperials, The Isley Brothers, Frankie Lymon and the Teenagers, The Osmonds, The Platters, The Righteous Brothers, etc. In addition, I listened to ole-time black artists: Bo Diddley, James Brown, Lightnin' Hopkins, Etta James, Little Richard, and Muddy Waters, etc.

I watched American Bandstand—as did nearly every teen of the 1950s. So, I didn't feel completely out of touch with others—I was up on things too! I danced with the columnar pole in the basement as I listened to the radio or jukebox music. Also, I wasn't above listening to older artists as well—those of M'Deah's generation: Gene Autry, Tony Bennett, Nat King Cole, Rosemary Clooney, Perry Como, Bing Crosby, Doris Day, Judy Garland, Dean Martin, Dinah Shore, Frank Sinatra, The Four Tops, Mills Brothers, etc.

And there's MORE—I had a variety of music inputs! Even Tennessee Ernie Ford was one of them. I really enjoyed him! The list could go on and on. But they all had an influence on me and formed my musical tastes. The only music I rejected was most country music. I saw it as the music of segregationists.

There were religious artists too. My favorite was Mahalia Jackson, of course! But I also liked James Cleveland. His "Peace, Be Still" was a favorite.

Years later, when I looked at birth dates of some of my favorite movie stars or musicians, I was surprised to see many were born in the 1890s—not even in the same century as I was! But the world didn't begin with my arrival. History should have taught me that!

I was surprised to learn late in life that many of my favorite Hollywood and other celebrities were my mother's contemporaries. I don't know why I thought of her as much older than them—she wasn't!

Common Sense Isn't Common

One day at Auntie's, we were lacking rolls for Sunday dinner. They were still in the freezer. So, I had the idea that because the clothes dryer was warm and could thaw the frozen rolls, why not put them in there until they thawed—and then bake them. Seemed reasonable to me. Apparently, others agreed too. So, that's what we did. Only to have the packaging come apart and the rolls disintegrate into broken pieces and crumbs. Bad idea! No common sense. I had to admit it.

I was smart in school and I knew God had made me this way—it was His gift to me. It helped me survive some very dark times. I knew I wasn't a fool, because I knew there was God. (Psalm 14:1 says only a fool doesn't believe in God!) But I was only smart. I wasn't always WISE! I thought I knew Psalm 111:10.

> ***Psalm 111:10a** The fear of the Lord is the beginning of wisdom*

But I didn't know this Truth:

> ***1 Corinthians 1:20** Where is the wise? Where is the scribe? Where is the disputer of this age? Has not God made foolish the wisdom of this world?*

I wanted to be known as an intellectual. Conclusion: I finally conceded that I was a PSEUDO intellectual—a wannabe! What false pride and vanity! It would be some years before the Lord showed me Truth so I could choose to throw away that attitude and belief. Thanks, Lord!

Back To School For Me

I never stopped going to school. It was a great value to me and a refuge for me. I knew I'd face embarrassing looks but I didn't care. I had done nothing wrong to be ashamed of. Neither had my mother. I knew I'd not get any nosey questions. That was against the Minnesota code of being 'nice'.

I don't remember that Billy went to school. I don't think he could, and he was not made to do so. For him that was someone's wise decision. When M'Deah came home after the trial, he asked her if he could change schools, and she agreed. That too was another wise decision. It greatly benefited him. (More on that later.)

It was a challenge going to school after the shooting. Physically, I now had to take a very long trip by public bus that took about two hours on dark cold mornings. It was difficult emotionally too. One teacher, a young Jewish woman, was very empathetic about me living in a household where there was domestic abuse. She got it and she was kind. My other teachers all ignored it. It was all business as usual. Maybe they thought that was best or they just didn't know what to say or how to act. Maybe it was just confounding that you never know what is going on in a student's home nor how it may affect them. Maybe they wondered how I'd done so well academically while having such a dysfunctional and violent home environment. I don't know. It was strange but I felt relief at the same time.

CHAPTER TWENTY-FOUR
The Trial

I had to testify at M'Deah's trial. Mr. Nemerov asked me to list some occasions when M'Deah had been beaten and suffered physical damage from K.C. There was NO shortage of such incidents! On the stand, I was unexplainably nervous. I wanted to say that I didn't believe M'Deah would ever have fired the rifle IF K.C. had not run towards her in a "charge". Certainly, I knew what her fate would be if he succeeded in getting the rifle from her! But I had seen enough Perry Mason episodes on TV to know that a witness is NOT to volunteer information—just answer the questions attorneys asked. OKAY. But would the jury understand this without being specifically told? I hoped so. I was not allowed in the courtroom to hear any other testimony. We just had to nervously wait for the outcome—and pray.

The Verdict

When the not guilty verdict was given, we were all so greatly relieved.

Thank God, all our prayers were answered! M'Deah was found not guilty by reason of self- defense and freed! And defense attorney Nemerov had done his job well. I was very grateful for that. It was years before I found out how costly this had been for M'Deah. She had to sign the house over to him as guarantee of payment. I have NO idea how she paid his fee—I think it was on the installment plan. That was "grown-folks business". I did learn later that she'd had to pledge her house as surety for his fees though. Until recently, I'd forgotten that she was charged with first degree manslaughter and faced several years in prison.

For a retainer, I learned that she borrowed $500 from her Uncle Lloyd who lived in Milwaukee—he was Big Mama's brother. I remember her having to pay him back later. She offered to pay in installments, but he demurred. He asked her to repay a loan in the same way she'd gotten it—in a lump sum. She could take her time to save up the $500 and then return it all at once. And that's what she did.

Kathy Carlson and Family

During this time, a classmate told her parents that the woman in the newspaper who was on trial was the mother of a classmate. I don't know everything she told them, but her family befriended us. I got encouraging phone calls from her mother and assurances that they were praying for us—with comforting words of Bible scripture. She often gave us, particularly to M'Deah, the phrase: "This too shall pass". I will never forget it. She was a stay-at-home

CHAPTER TWENTY-FOUR

mother—something many of my classmates had but which was slightly foreign to black families. Black mothers typically worked at jobs outside the home. The Carlsons (not their real name) were not wealthy by any means—living on a one-person income that was beginning to be contrary to the norm of the day. They even went further. I was invited to their home to have lunch with Kathy and to meet the rest of the family. Mrs. Carlson introduced me to an omelet for the first time in my life—a Spanish omelet. Later, I met Kathy's father, her older sister, and her younger sister. The father played the violin, and all the children played instruments too. They seemed like the family I had read about in books by Laura Ingalls Wilder! This was all new to me. Although Kathy and I knew and respected each other, we were nothing like best friends—just ongoing acquaintances. For her to even be interested enough in my life to share our family tragedy with her own family was a phenomenon—a real act of loving kindness. It was truly life changing. I felt closer to her family than I did to her. I had only known her as just a school acquaintance. I slowly knew the Carlsons to be sincere loving practitioners of the Christian faith—the best of any race I've ever known.

Over the years, I regretfully did not keep in touch with them. Thankfully, M'Deah did better. They were always so kind and encouraging to her. And she deeply appreciated their life-giving words and

THE TRIAL

actions. Later, I would learn from her of the father's death, the death of the younger daughter, and the death of the older daughter. All events were sudden and tragic.

Why didn't I keep in touch over the years? At some point, I was interested in reading to learn more about their religion. What did people believe that made them such "real Christians" that loved people like Jesus said? They were more than willing to speak about this love AND to show it in real action! I knew the church headquarters was on Mackinac Island in Michigan. The older sister mentioned going there some summers for church work and as an actress. They never tried to convert us to their religion but freely shared some things about it with us. Their actions spoke louder than their words of its true value. It was called Moral Re-Armament. The things I read later indicated it was NOT a true Christian religion. I was having none of that. At the time, I knew nothing about what a cult was, but was just a little leery. I knew the Carlson family to be good people, but I wasn't as sure about their religion After my "I know there is God" epiphany at eight years old, I was very easily doubtful. My family life experiences had already reinforced that for me—we were still alive. I had already questioned my Sunday School teacher about why God didn't talk to His people anymore. The answer I got was less than satisfactory. I was told God didn't need to talk to people anymore because

CHAPTER TWENTY-FOUR

we now had the Bible which revealed anything and everything, He wanted us to know. I only knew that WE needed to hear from Him! Thankfully, I slowed my roll though! The time wasn't yet right for me.

Back Home

After the trial, M'Deah was freed, and we all lived with Auntie and Uncle Robert for a while longer—maybe six months. Was it about returning to a house where there had been the shooting? I don't think so. Billy and I were fine, but maybe the family convinced M'Deah that we would be traumatized by returning there. At any rate, M'Deah told us one day that we were returning to "our own house". I learned years later that Billy had convinced her to do so. Living with other family can be a blessing. But it can also be difficult. Meeting unexpected expectations and demands among various differences can cause tension. Billy had questions for M'Deah. Why were we paying rent to someone else when we had a perfectly good house of our own in which to live? Why don't we simply return to our own home?

While we appreciated being able to stay with Auntie and Uncle Robert, it was time to go back home—no reason not to. Besides, their generosity meant a crowded home and complaints to him that he was using too much water to bathe daily. He was ready to go. M'Deah then knew we had no reluctance or trauma about going back to that house of bad memories. His logic persuaded my mother, and we happily moved back home—happy to be in a home of great peace.

Back home at Logan, life was so much different than when we had left there. We had so much peace and freedom in an atmosphere devoid of fear. No more domestic violence. No more death threats. No more tension and walking on eggshells. M'Deah worked hard so we still had a good lifestyle. It was all new and good. We were in need of nothing. I was 18 now and Billy was 16. We had a new life of no worries.

I felt freer after we moved back home. A very heavy weight was gone from my life: K.C. He had fulfilled some of the roles as a father figure, for sure. And I appreciated it. But it was meaningless because of the way he treated my mother. Sad to say, I was glad he was gone. No more moments, days, weeks months, years of that horrible tension of not knowing the next explosion. How bad would it be? Would it be our last and final? No more unknown terror.

I do remember a very few occasions when K.C. was protective of us children from outside forces. But mostly, he was the danger inside our home.

Thrifting Together

Over the ensuing years, M'Deah became closer to all her sisters. They developed a common hobby: thrift shopping. They attended rummage sales, estate sales, garage sales, etc. together and separately. Some

CHAPTER TWENTY-FOUR

were able to pursue this hobby more than others, but they all enjoyed it and enjoyed comparing bargains. They exchanged education of the value of various items. They became very good at it. And I was happy to see them bond this way. Later, M'Deah sold some items for income.

Fix It!

One lesson M'Deah had learned from her parents—particularly from Papa—was that when something is broken or needs repair, fix it. When? NOW! It could be a fence, a window, a screen door, a missing button, a fallen hickory nut tree, etc. It didn't matter what it was. If it was your property, you are to fix it. Can't hire it done? DIY! And she did, modeling for her children that this is how you properly do things.

Finances Now

During this time, M'Deah sold some possessions in order to make ends meet. That included the model T Ford and the jukebox. As I said before, she even sold Joe. It was very much necessary. Overall, I don't know how she managed financially at many different times in her life. But she did. She was always willing to work hard, doing whatever she could. God always made a way for her to survive and to even thrive. Thankfully, because her remaining daughter was usually sadly clueless—oblivious! I was not a clothes horse though and told M'Deah I'd be responsible for my own clothing needs. I still did babysit and had a part-time job with the public library. I was good. I could also still sew my skirts too.

One survival technique was to rent out the attic which had once been the boys' bedroom. The tenants would share our kitchen but had their own front room, bedroom, and bathroom. One such tenant was a husband and wife who had a cute young daughter around five years old. Her name was Marquita. I had never heard that name before and thought it was the most beautiful name for a girl I'd ever heard. Surely it was a possibility for my daughter's name whenever she came.

I don't know how other family before us made it either, when I look back. But we were NEVER victims nor taught to be so. Just trust God was the message for all. They did and He always came through for them! Always. If slaves and their descendants could do that in the WORST of circumstances, why can't we do so today? We'll have the SAME results too! We are NOT hindered by legal slavery and legal Jim Crow laws of segregation as they were. Do we believe Satan's LIE, popularized by current ignorant popular culture, that we are merely forever VICTIMS? "As a man thinks/believes in his heart, so is he" is what God has written in His Bible. (Proverbs 23:7) And He is ALWAYS right! BELIEVE you're a victim—and you are. But BELIEVE Him that you're His victorious overcomer of ALL odds—and you are. I choose to agree with our courageous and wise ancestors who agreed with God! Worked for them. Works for me.

Secrets Revealed

We learned more about K.C. after he was gone. For example, he had a mistress or girlfriends!

Also, he had an impressionable co-worker who admired him. They were employees of the same construction company. Our family knew their family. The wife had declining health and had stopped working outside the home. She was now a housewife taking care of their four kids. Both men had the same amount of education, but the coworker was a laborer rather than being the skilled professional brick and block mason that K.C. was. Whenever K.C. beat M'Deah, he would brag about it to this coworker. In turn, the co-worker would go home and beat his wife that night—so he could brag about it to K.C. at work the next day. He would provoke an argument upon some pretext. For these two men, domestic violence became a game about bragging rights. A very cruel game. Only after K.C. was gone did the two wives compare notes. Neither knew what the other was going through. Domestic violence is not something the victims ever talk about. It's the silent and shameful family secret. Fortunately, with K.C. gone, his coworker changed his own behavior of beating his wife. It seemed the sensible thing to do. Surprise.

This couple may have seen M'Deah and K.C. as happily married on the few times we saw them. Like M'Deah, she was a good cook. Cinnamon rolls were her specialty—delicious! It would be years before we knew this man didn't care for her son—his stepson. I now learned that he once hit his stepson in the face, causing him to lose a tooth—and to run away from home. But he was found and returned. I was sad to hear this is why he ran away. After high school graduation, this son joined the Navy to get away from home. By then, the couple had three children of their own—two daughters and a son. The mother taught them all the great value of education for themselves.

The Celebration

I graduated from high school in June 1959. I was happy to be in the top 10% of our class academically. We had started out with nearly 300 students in our class, but I do remember a very few dropped out before graduation. Mostly, I don't know why. The graduation event was on a happy sunny day, as we marched across the football field in our cap and gown attire with our watching families in the bleachers. M'Deah and Billy were there, of course. Maybe cousins Ruby and Juanita were there too. But I'm not sure who else.

I give thanks to all at Henry for giving me the great experience of a most wonderful six years of my life. And I appreciate having yearbooks for all my time there—1954-1959.

CHAPTER TWENTY-FOUR

My own extended family did no celebration for me that I remember. Rather, the family of a classmate did so! Kathy Carlsons' whole family had embraced us into theirs during the trial. They provided much-needed encouragement and love. I have lifetime memories of their goodness to us. They were rich in love, but not in goods. Even so, they unselfishly shared what they did have: unfeigned love and themselves. Unforgettable. I wondered what their secret was. I learned the Carlsons believed in God. Oh, good. Unselfishly, they gave me a graduation party at their home—guests were their household family and my immediate family. Small, intimate, loving, and deeply appreciated! Where was my mother's family? I don't know. But I was celebrated, and I was OKAY with that. This was even more important than I realized at the time. The entire Carlson family was more than kind to me. All this was from mere classroom association with Kathy—someone I barely knew and who actually cared about me. All this was from their living out their Christian faith in reality. This made a deep and lasting impression on me. I will never forget it.

The Age of Majority

This is what PolicyGenius says about that:

The age of majority is when a child becomes an adult in the eyes of the law. When a person reaches the age of majority, they can gain major legal responsibilities, like the right to vote, join the military, or sign a contract. The age of majority may sometimes grant other rights, like the ability to buy cigarettes, consent to medical treatment, or get insurance. Every state sets their own age of majority and the specific restrictions as to what the adult cannot do until they reach that age. The age of majority is 18 in most places, except three states. Alabama and Nebraska set the age of majority to 19 and Mississippi sets it at 21.

The 26th Amendment lowered the legal voting age in the United States **from 21 to 18** in **1971**.

So, I was still a minor after I graduated from high school. As such, I could not legally enter into a contract. I think it was a door-to-door salesman who told us of a set of books that I then learned I wanted very much to buy. Quote: *Great Books of the Western World is a series of books originally published in the United States in 1952 by Encyclopedia Britannica Inc. to present the western canon in a single package of 54 volumes.* The volumes came with its own bookcase too—a plus for me. M'Deah, after much sincere begging by me, signed the contract for me to purchase the set. I don't remember the cost—maybe $500. That was a fortune when I bought it in 1959! I promised M'Deah that I would make every monthly payment and that it wouldn't ever be an extra financial burden for her in any way. And I meant that. With my busy life, I had little extra time for reading. But

CHAPTER TWENTY-FOUR

I enjoyed the pleasure that their ownership gave me. For years. Later in my adult years, there came an urgent financial family need—so I sadly sold them. But I hope to buy them again someday.

CHAPTER TWENTY-FIVE
My View of M'Deah's Siblings

By high school graduation, I had formed my own opinion of M'Deah's siblings as I saw them. I can only do so through the filter of my eyes—how I knew them in my interactions with them, my impressions of them. Others saw them through their own particular filter. I briefly describe them and their lives as best I knew them and from my viewpoint. That's all I have, right or wrong. I do know they were taught not to look down upon any type of work. All the girls—except maybe Auntie—have done domestic work at some point in their lives, either as full-time work or as part-time work. They have served as house cleaners/maids or as cooks. I cannot say with great certainty the cause of each of the siblings' deaths. M'Deah offered to provide plane tickets for me at the deaths of each of my family members as they occurred. I didn't think it right for her to incur that expense on my behalf. So, I declined each offer except I did attend the funeral of the first one, Dan. Not for George in 1987. Not for Carrie in. Not for Eloyce in 2001.

Dan: He was the oldest boy and was married to schoolteacher Janie (Pace) from Coffeeville, Alabama.

CHAPTER TWENTY-FIVE

For clarity, we referred to her as Janie-Dan. When they moved to Minneapolis around 1958, she wanted to also teach there and did so as a beloved teacher for the rest of her career. In making the transition, she asked her 17-year-old niece (me) what would help her lose the Alabama speaking accent. I no longer had any hint of a Southern accent. She knew that wasn't the case when I came to Minneapolis years ago. I thought for a moment and came up with two things: speak the entire "i-n-g" ending to words and not just the "i-n" and pronounce the letter "r" as one syllable and not two—no "r-uh." I suddenly saw those as the two biggest immediate differences she could make. She later said just these two changes helped her tremendously to adapt to a Minnesota accent and was greatly useful in her ongoing teaching career here. I was glad to help her. I remember her as being a very kind Southern lady. Uninstructed, I called her Aunt Janie. She was a typical woman of her time, having a job outside the home with no neglect of her role as a wife and mother at home. I don't know how they did it! Dan and Janie had six children—three daughters and three sons. I didn't learn until recently that Dan's birth name was Houston, Lawrence, Jr! When and why the change took place to 'Dan', I don't know. I only ever knew him as Dan. At some point, I was told that he had been in the CCC (Civilian Conservation Corps) during the Great Depression. As such, he was once caught in a hurricane and a tree fell on him and left him with some permanent back damage—it seriously affected him all the rest of his life. He was very industrious though and liked working on cars. He was very quiet and even-tempered by nature.

Carrie: I've written about her previously. She was the oldest girl and was married to Tommy Bogan. Tommy was a cigarette smoker. They were childless. I saw a family photo taken of her as a teen and she was a very attractive young woman. She had health issues that began then, and I was told in my latter teens that she and another girl had liked the same young man in their youth. So her rival had worked "roots" on Carrie, which took her health and her appearance. I don't know what the ailment was, but she had weak eyes that often ran and a twisted mouth. Genteel Southern women didn't use Kleenex. They used beautiful cloth handkerchiefs and always had lots of them—dozens. When laundered they were also ironed as well. Carrie always had a handkerchief with her. To wipe her eyes that watered freely.

Carrie thought highly of herself as the oldest daughter. She saw herself as the family matriarch, especially after Big Mama died, and thought that her siblings should looked to her for advice on all things and that they should always take her advice! No. I wonder what she would have been like if "roots" hadn't otherwise affected her life so negatively. She definitely thought she had married beneath herself in marrying Tommy because her choices were now

CHAPTER TWENTY-FIVE

limited. So, in her mind, she settled. I assume they were childless because of her sickness.

Later, Aunt Carrie caused us great harm. It nearly cost us our lives—twice. Why did I not regard her as dangerous? I was a child, and I thought as a child for decades on this issue. It was inconceivable to me that anyone—especially an adult—could do something evil deliberately. It was unthinkable to even consider harming a family member. Surely it was unintentional or because someone did it ignorantly because they were sick. I chose to believe that. And I never mentioned that harm to M'Deah at all—never even once for the rest of her life. I know it would have pained her deeply. I couldn't do that to her. It was over 50 years before I truly realized that Carrie had nearly cost the lives of our entire family twice! She did it with her poison tongue via evil words spoken to Buster and to K.C. But for her, our lives would have been far different! But it took all that to make us the people we became. Except for this quirk, Carrie was always nice to her nieces and nephews.

George: This was the second and last son. He was married to Janie from Spartanburg, North Carolina. We referred to her as Janie-George to distinguish her from Janie-Dan. They were to have five children—four daughters and a son. They were very ambitious and also of great help to his family as they slowly migrated to Minneapolis—a real blessing. I don't know what later happened to George and his

MY VIEW OF M'DEAH'S SIBLINGS

family after they moved into the suburbs, far away from what they saw as an inferior neighborhood. They very rarely associated with his family. Maybe this attitude shift came with the Minneapolis 'urban renewal project' so popular nationwide in the 1950s black neighborhoods which caused them to move. It was just another face of racial discrimination. Almost suddenly, the cousins Billy and I knew on Glenwood Avenue were no more. As their family size grew with the addition of three more daughters that were strangers to us, their whole family became like strangers to us. And they remained so.

M'Deah was more than kind to them always. And in the end, I saw there was genuine love for and from them. It's only been in my latter years that I realize I really didn't know George or Janie-George personally at all.

It was Janie-George who chose Minneapolis to be their family's residence after WWII. I didn't learn this until I read her obituary in 20 Her family influence was very strong. At some point early in their marriage, her sister Polly joined the family as kind of a live-in nanny for the rest of their lives. I remember Polly as a very nice aunt to my cousins—like a second mother—and she was also an habitual smoker. She worked at a local hospital, as did Janie-George, I believe as a cook. Janie and Polly were both cigarette smokers. I don't know for sure, but I think George did the same or similar work he had done in the

CHAPTER TWENTY-FIVE

Army. My memory is that he had a clerical/desk job at the VA.

I don't remember that we ever had any interpersonal contact ever after that lifesaving event in 1950. I invited all the family to my wedding, of course, and he was there. Looking at miscellaneous photos taken, I saw him with a large group of people leaving the church. But I don't remember seeing him in person. I don't think he was at the reception. I was sorry when he passed away. M'Deah offered to pay for plane tickets if I wanted to attend his funeral. But I didn't want her to foot that bill, so I declined. I have always thought of George as my real-life hero: the one who saved my life and my family's life from certain death by a crazed Buster.

I remember Janie-George, coming to visit on one of my visits home. She was very friendly and brought her two grandchildren Rose's children to meet me. When Cousin Jimmy's stewardess wife, Margaret, died suddenly, M'Deah was there for the family. When he himself got very sick later, she was there for them again Janie had asked M'Deah's advice when doctors suggested they pull the plug on Jimmy. They all knew of M'Deah's past Godly wisdom and successful prayers in many situations. M'Deah prayed and advised that they NOT pull the plug because Jimmy would live. They later chose instead to follow the medical advice! When M'Deah called to let me know Jimmy had died, we were both very surprised

MY VIEW OF M'DEAH'S SIBLINGS

that her advice had been totally ignored. It was and was not puzzling. This is the only time I remember that anyone blatantly ignored M'Deah's advice after her salvation. She grieved with them. Over the years, she did other things for George's family, even after he was no longer here.

(**Drussie Juanita**—M'Deah—was next as the 2nd daughter. Of all the daughters, she most looked like Big Mama. Sometimes the sisters treated M'Deah more like a stepsister than the full-blooded sister that she was. Fact. Perhaps it was because of how she started out in the family: an occasional visitor with Aunt Daisy. Perhaps it was because she looked so much like Big Mama. Perhaps it was because she was a definite non-conformist whom their parents readily accepted and embraced into the family. I don't know. But M'Deah's love of family was undeniable. And I believe M'Deah was generally liked and respected by her nephews and nieces later after all.)

Arliece: This was the 3rd daughter, and she was married to Robert Grant, an orphan. We cousins all knew her as Auntie and that she was a private secretary—a big deal in black culture then. They were childless and lived in Meridian, Mississippi. Auntie was the subject of a big family scandal in her youth: she married a divorced man! What? The family finally got over it in time. Uncle Robert was an orphan who got adopted by a family that raised him well. I don't know anything about them, but they raised him to be a gentleman. He later joined the Masons. I don't remember what kind of work he did. Uncle Robert was a very cultured man, and they always enjoyed a robust social life. I never knew the scandal to be a problem for M'Deah. Auntie was genuinely liked by all of us cousins—and respected. I always remembered her and Uncle Robert's kindness to us when Billy and I had to live elsewhere during family emergencies. Twice, they had taken us in. Uncle Robert loved Auntie and often allowed her to call the shots! Or, rather, she took them anyway. Uncle Robert was also a cigarette smoker—common for the times.

Eloise: This was the youngest daughter and the baby. She was married to Sears ("Buster") Mitchell from Koenton, Alabama. He was my father's brother. They had one child, a son. At some point, she legally changed her name to **Eloyce**. After Buster, she married James Scarver. He was a cigarette smoker also. Together, they had three more children—a son and two daughters. She was always deeply interested in family wellbeing and very empathetic. As such, I always knew and trusted her to keep me posted about M'Deah's wellbeing after I married and left home. And she was faithful to do that. She was also an unofficial and important neighborhood watch.

Name Changes

Our branch of the Lawrence family believed in changing/selecting their own names! Houston,

Jr. became Dan. Eloise became Eloyce. Bobby Jean changed her name to Barbara. I later changed my name again, adding my middle name to my first name. I got tired of getting mail addressed to Mr. and of getting advertisements about my non-existing prostate!

Maybe all this name-changing was a carryover from the ending of slavery times when it was necessary. Slaves only had a first name, so after the Civil War they had to select a last name. About 20% of the time that was the name of their former master. Maybe they hoped that would make it easier to reunite with their slave family members sold off to others. Popular too was the name of a president or someone else famous or admired. Many times, their former first name was a nickname that they wanted to change to be more formal. For example, I think Drussie was the nickname for the more formal Drusilla. What did M'Deah do with her name? At some point, M'Deah began to use her middle name as her first name and her first name as her middle name. Drussie Juanita because Juanita Drussie. I believe she thought Drussie was too unusual a name for up North and that Juanita was easier to use. She was right.

CHAPTER TWENTY-SIX
Afterwards

Afterwards

After high school graduation, I read up on how to lose weight. I had always regarded myself as fat. M'Deah was overweight and so was I. It was due to stress eating. At a size 16/18, I thought I was humongous! I did comparisons. Most other girls I knew were never any bigger than size 12. I was huge—in my mind. But I took the advice of one author's view from the 1930s, applied myself to it, and lost 30 pounds! Yay! M'Deah was extremely helpful to that success. She always made sure I had whatever I needed to succeed. It wasn't a lot. But I had cabbage as my green vegetable most often, hot dogs for quick protein needed, red Delicious apples (my favorite) twice a day—one for lunch and one for after school snack before going to work—etc. Snacks weren't a big deal back then—just once daily between major activities. We had grown up having snacks of occasional popcorn—prepared in the cast-iron skillet with a lid as you shook the pan to prevent burning—roasted peanuts in the oven, pork skins/rinds dried in the oven, and occasional fried okra. I had my own Cheez-It crackers for homework emergencies on my term papers. M'Deah made sure dinner was always ready when I got off work. I was grateful for her caring ongoing efforts for my welfare and success.

The Golden Child

Every family has someone regarded as "The Golden Child", even if it's never spoken. I didn't think of myself that way. But a member of our extended family told me that's how I was seen. It was always assumed that I would go to college because I was an A student and learned easily/readily. Maybe I thought it could be a reward for M'Deah after all she'd gone through with K.C. But after the trial and the ordeal of being away from our home, and all that it entailed, I was tired. Emotionally. Psychologically. I wanted to take a year off before pursuing further education. I felt I deserved it and needed it. But that was way before the concept of a gap year between high school and college became a reality for some. I had gotten a small scholarship that had to be used immediately after high school—or I would lose it. I didn't know much about applying for scholarships and my guidance counselor, whom I trusted, didn't do the best job for me in that regard. Also, I had two preferences for the college I wanted to attend. One was Macalester College in Southern Minnesota. I had visited this liberal arts institution twice as a member of the Henry debate team. I had read much about it and was impressed. I thought it was also the alma mater

CHAPTER TWENTY-SIX

of a famous black graduate whom I admired: Patricia Harris. But I was wrong about her connection. And I wanted to be in the political/public service world as she was. When asked about my career choice, I told that to my school guidance counselor—that I wanted to pursue political science and not education, as my family had. He laughed in my face and said education would be a more likely reality because being Negro was somewhat limiting. It was very disheartening to hear that, although he was probably right and just being practical. I had thought that maybe I could serve in the diplomatic corps in Russia one day—I was curious enough to want to represent my country in that capacity. He strongly discouraged me from such an idea. I'm sure he thought it was for my good.

Another college choice was Lincoln University. I had never heard of it. I first learned of this historic black school when I did babysitting for a black couple who had graduated from there. I used to look through their yearbook and marvel to see black cheerleaders and blacks in all school functions. It was new to me and something I admired deeply. But my school choice for that kind of education would be Hampton University in Virginia. Needless to say, either of those options was completely out of the question for me. I simply didn't have the monies attendance there would require. And I would NOT expect M'Deah to fund any of that. She had already done so MUCH in raising her children. I refused to add any such burden to her. Government Student Loans were not an option then either. Thankfully!

The Beginning

So, the default was the University of Minnesota at the near-by St. Paul campus. No problem in getting admitted. I even tested as English-exempt for my freshman year. So, off I went. For transportation, I joined a small group of students who were transported there by another student who did this as a side job. They were all white and from various local high schools—no problem because that was what I had always been used to. I did well in whatever I applied myself to. I also joined the women's basketball team there—as just an average player. I wasn't an outstanding player by any means. I just wanted to do it for fun.

What were my dreams in college? My dream was to graduate with my degree in Political Science (with a minor in Education!) and join the Department of State in some capacity. Then I would work my way up to a position near ambassador rank and serve my country that way. Where? I hoped for an assignment to Russia one day. I would be living proof to refute their propaganda about how racist my country was. Opportunities existed for all in the USA. Only ability limits how far anyone can go in our society. That was not an ambition that couldn't be realized. I had truth about what my country is. And I had living examples in Ralph Bunche and Patricia Harris.

CHAPTER TWENTY-SIX

Did I achieve this ambition? Nope. But not because it was impossible. I got sidetracked by something called life. And I don't believe it was God's plan for me then. That was something I never took into consideration at all. Oops—big mistake! Not a minor detail at all. But I didn't know any better then.

But, mostly I was just tired of school. The desire left me. I stopped attending college and chose to work full-time at the Minneapolis Public Library main office as a Page in the Circulation Department. I checked books out and in with patrons, shelved books, etc. It wasn't hard work, my co-workers were pleasant, and I thoroughly enjoyed it. It was my first adult job, and it was in one of my happy places! It wasn't just baby-sitting or a summer job. I was making my own real money! (I took home a paycheck of $62 every two weeks.) So, I had a full class load at the U and then a part-time job after school. But I enjoyed it all for a while.

I voluntarily gave M'Deah the princely sum of $10 weekly from my $62 bi-weekly salary. M'Deah didn't require I do so, but it was common for employed recent high school graduates to pay rent at home. It was contributory adult behavior. I was determined not to be an exception! As usual, I was the only black in the department and only one of three blacks in the whole building. That was nothing new to me—it was my typical world.

Early in my employment, I purposed to buy M'Deah a stylish walking suit so popular at the time.

I saved up my money—it cost nearly two paychecks—and went to Lane Bryant. I chose one I thought she might like. It was lined, top and bottom, and of a very heavy-weight fabric. It was of very good quality and cost about $100. I liked the colors—a Fall-ish tweed. Mistakenly, it had a slim pencil skirt, which I overlooked. I forgot M'Deah only wore full skirts. When I gave it to her, she was overwhelmed with joy at having a walking suit. She knew why I bought it and that it was purely a love gift—a thank you of deep appreciation for her. She tried it on, but I don't remember that she ever wore it outside the home. It wasn't her proper style for a good fit. She kept it though—all her life.

My Social World

I lived in a white world. In all non-social settings. That included neighborhood, school, stores, movie theaters, restaurants, etc. None of those were black-owned. In social settings and the culture of the times, few people ate outside the home at restaurants. Very few fast-food places existed. Takeout food generally consisted of Little Tavern for small hamburgers or an occasional Rogers Chinese for chow mein. At A&W or Hires root beer stands; you could get a shake or a float. Dairy Queen locations were few. I knew of no McDonald's locations. And there were a few places that sold this new thing called pizza. It was an entirely different world from today! My

CHAPTER TWENTY-SIX

social settings consisted of church and—oh, church. I'd say it was somewhat limited. I went to church regularly. Other than that, it was to the public library. The Negro population in Minneapolis during my teen years was about 2% and maybe slightly over, for the entire city of half a million people! It was very easy to be the only black in your world among white people.

Still, although I was academically healthy in high school, it was socially that I was ignorant and awkward. I had accepted not having a normal teenage youth because of K.C. I was sure dating would be out of the question. I'd just grow up an asexual nerd. That's all I saw. I put pressure on myself to be as morally good as I could and to never anger K.C. with my behavior that would cause him to hurt M'Deah. I couldn't take being responsible for endangering her.

CHAPTER TWENTY-SEVEN
Life After K.C.

Help! My whole world changed. What was going to be like now? I had no idea. For sure, I had more options than I ever dreamed of. I could be fully me and not a repressed me. But what did that mean? Would I make the right choices for my life based on who I had been? Or would new options lead me to make unthinkable and unwise choices? I didn't know. It was a time open to great possibilities and also open to disastrous choices. It was life scary.

Again, never was counseling offered after the shooting or even mentioned as any kind of optional help for us. You're on your own, so do the best you can. Okay. That was true for everyone.

Without Linda, I sort of adopted my cousins Ruby and Juanita as my new sisters. I didn't know how to have two sisters, so I took turns. Ruby, Juanita, and then Ruby again. Ruby gravitated toward another cousin. She later got disappointed in that relationship. Her desire for them to have a better relationship was apparently somewhat one-sided. She mentioned gifting our cousin with an expensive cashmere sweater, only to see it hung up on a rusty

CHAPTER TWENTY-SEVEN

nail in their basement the next time she visited her. Ruby was greatly disappointed, feeling like that was the value and importance assigned to her too. As for me, I don't ever remember visiting their new house at all. Juanita gravitated toward Sametta (a friend from Zion church) and others, so I felt replaced. And rightly so. But I missed her.

Billy's Life Now

It was remarkably different—more so than mine. At some point, M'Deah shared with me that Billy had told her he was glad she shot K.C. Why? Because he himself had planned to kill him one day in the future. He was tired of his mother being mistreated. I just remember M'Deah was greatly surprised but also greatly relieved not to have had Billy do that on her account. It was really decades before I realized what a terrible burden of heart and mind this was for a 15-year old boy to carry. Wow. We can't know the impact hateful oppressive actions can have on someone else—even if those actions are inflicted on them to a seemingly lesser degree. Who knew that Billy had plans to kill K.C. one day? Who knew what he may have endured when the boys went hunting with K.C.? It had to altogether be torturous. And the only obvious way he saw out was the elimination of K.C. from the Earth and from our lives. Sadly.

(It makes me think of unjust wars. That's when one side acts with callous and heinous cruelty. Then they are surprised by the natural protective reactions of war that are the consequences of their own actions. They hypothetically cry "It's unfair what's happening to us!" But how can you start a war and then be surprised when it comes to your doorstep? Did you think you had a right to be hateful and harmful but not be hated or harmed in return? I have a right to hit you, but you have no right to hit me back? I learned later that people behave according to what they believe. People believe what they are taught. Some are taught to celebrate life. Others are taught to celebrate death. They could not be more different. Some people/ religions/cultures are taught to hate even when taking in their mother's milk. And it continues throughout childhood. They have no choice but to believe these hateful lies. They truly don't know what they do. It's just as Jesus said when on the Cross. For such we need to pray. Pray God's mercy upon them that they get to know Truth and be changed—saved through salvation in the Lord Jesus Christ. But their cruel actions are to be brought to an end. It profits no one for that to continue. They will continue to be blinded and bound by lies. As the Bible says in John 8:32, only knowing Truth makes one free. Jesus is Truth and He came to make us free. There's no other way.)

    Over the Summer vacation, after K.C. was gone, Billy's height changed dramatically. He had always been the shortest student in every one of his classes for quite a while. Suddenly that was no longer the

CHAPTER TWENTY-SEVEN

case! Billy grew and grew and grew—in height. I remember saying to M'Deah that he had grown nearly a foot and that it was probably because he was no longer living under the pressure of a life with K.C! His body was now free to grow, without all the previous stress. And it did! M'Deah was surprised by his growth and had to buy him a completely new wardrobe for the upcoming school year. And she was happy to do so. Billy had never grown like that before. That year, I was 18 and Billy was 16.

Learning To Drive

M'Deah taught me to drive. My approach to birds sitting in the road was to wait until they flew away. M'Deah soon corrected me of that! Sadly, when I took my license test I made a foolish decision. I had studied for the written portion of the test, but I decided that I was given trick questions—it's gotta be tricky because so many other students had failed it. Dumb thinking. As I tried to figure out the "tricks", I failed the test! It was shameful. No one else in my family had ever experienced that failure. I was a first! But I took it all in stride—oh, well. I remembered how afraid I had been after my childhood accident in Chatom. Driving was dangerous, after all. I was okay that I wasn't licensed to be on the roads with all the bad drivers out there.

M'Deah taught Billy to drive too. Of course, he passed with flying colors the first time he took the test. Now I was really embarrassed! My little brother was going to have his driver's license, and I didn't! So, I took the test again with a different mindset—and passed. Whew! Now I saw having it as a ticket to greater freedom. I could drive anywhere and go places otherwise restricted to me by public transportation. And this new form of ID also opened doors previously closed to me. I didn't know what I would do with this freedom, but I just enjoyed having it!

I don't remember much about our family cars during my childhood—only that we never had the usual cars for the time. We never had a Ford or Chevrolet. I do remember our last new car was a Pontiac. M'Deah never bought another new car after the death of K.C. but only bought used cars. She was content with them.

Back To School For Billy

Billy had asked M'Deah if he could change schools and transfer to Central High School which was in South Minneapolis. He didn't feel as comfortable at Henry as I did. Teachers expected much from him because he was my brother and that was hard. I'm sure that probably made it pretty uncomfortable for him. I had often wondered how his experience there was for him. He never mentioned it. Now I knew it hadn't been good—he was asking M'Deah for permission to leave! Central had a larger black student population and he preferred that environment.

CHAPTER TWENTY-SEVEN

M'Deah consented to the change. It meant a whole new life for him.

Billy found John Nichols there. John was a young classmate who became an instant best friend and near-brother to Billy. With John's help, Billy blossomed into the fine young man he would never have become without him. Billy's social growth had been stunted too. It was something I had never thought about. John and Billy needed each other to become who they were. John had the gift from God of caring and teaching. He taught Billy how to truly be a man—how to behave, shave, dress, date, etc. Who else in Billy's life would have done so? No one. Our uncles either didn't see that great need or didn't care. They did not step up at all. So God gave John to Billy. I don't know what John needed. Maybe it was just someone to draw this gift out of him and to really appreciate him—someone to love him besides his mother. John knew a lot of people, being as friendly as he was. But Billy was his only best friend and near-brother. They needed each other and fit so well together—as though it was meant to be from the time they were created by God. They were part of His Plan from the beginning! Where you saw one, you saw the other. John Nichols was a very unusually mature young man. He was the only child of a single mother and they were deeply devoted to each other. I don't know even know all the circumstances of his upbringing and life. But he was quite a remarkable young man. Emphasis on the word *man*. He wasn't childish in any way.

Billy really blossomed at Central. I know John was a big part of that growth for him. Billy joined the band at Central and became a very good trap drummer. I saw him march with the band in the Summer annual Minneapolis Aquatennial Parade. They did a great job, and he was really a good player and showman. I was so proud of him. And rightly so. Billy had a new physique and a new wardrobe. Best of all he had, for the first time ever, a new best friend! More than that, John Nichols was like a long-lost brother. Billy acquired other friends easily with John. Both were skilled swimmers and ice skaters. Billy was free for the first time to be Billy and not just someone's little brother. I was so surprised and happy for him.

Billy continued to do well at Central. His unknown innate athletic ability was able to be displayed as he shone in the water sports of swimming and hockey. Who knew? He had a real skill in his drafting class—a skill we never knew was there. I learned later that it was his favorite class. Drafting was something I knew nothing about but in which he excelled. It is a technical drawing skill vital for architecture or engineering. M'Deah saved his two main pieces of work: a drawing of a futuristic house and of a futuristic car. I kept them at some point in the 1990s but later lost one of them. Billy had a great imagination for what the future might look like. Not me.

CHAPTER TWENTY-SEVEN

The formal definition for drafting given by the CAD Academy is:

'Drafting is the detailed technical drawing or the graphical representation of structures, machines, or components. It is a key component of the design and manufacturing process and has a broad application across various industries such as architecture, engineering, and product design. Drafting can be done by hand, but it is more commonly performed using Computer Aided Design (CAD) tools.'

Of course, the latter part doesn't apply to what Billy did before we had computers. His work was all done by hand only! The 1950s was a strange decade for us. 1950 ended in December with our near-death experience. 1959 began in January with the death of K.C. and the end of eight years of daily fear of our possible death. But we survived and thrived!

PART FOUR
After Henry

CHAPTER TWENTY-EIGHT
M'Deah's Growth

I didn't know how hard these years were for M'Deah at the beginning. She had peace from the absence of K.C. in her life. Freed from that great bondage, she was free to mature and make better choices. She was far more relaxed, and I dare say she was happy. But unknown to me at the time were many financial struggles. I was oblivious. In my experience, M'Deah could successfully handle anything. So, of course, she knew how to handle the challenges unknown to me. I too had some growing up to do.

M'Deah's Re-marriage

One strange thing came about shortly after the trial. A stranger—a Jamaican man—had read of the shooting in the newspaper and seen there a picture of my mother as she was being arrested. He said the story's circumstances and her picture touched his heart. He contacted my mother, and they became friends. He also told her about the Lord Jesus Christ, which assisted later in my mother becoming a born-again Christian for the first time in her life. Eventually, they married in 19—another marriage trip to Iowa for

CHAPTER TWENTY-EIGHT

my mother! Iowa required no blood tests, no waiting period—it was the place to go for a quick marriage. These were all factors I was totally unaware of! Mr. Steele was a housing contractor and builder. He had a head for business and entrepreneurship. Actually, M'Deah did as well. She had gotten that from Papa. But Mr. Steele taught her how to develop and use it. They formed a construction business together, bought several houses that they rented out which paid more than their own mortgage and the mortgage of the houses, and they built houses to remodel and/or to sell. She became the business secretary—a totally new role for her. M'Deah was bold and courageous—even adventurous. She and Mr. Steele had both grown up in rural areas and were familiar with farming/gardening. They rented a vacant lot in St. Paul and always had a big flourishing garden there as well as in their own backyard. They were both generous in sharing garden produce with others.

They were wed by a Justice of the Peace in Iowa Come on down and get married quickly! I learned that's how M'Deah did all her three adult marriages. She never had a bridal shower, wedding, reception—none of the marriage trappings. None.

CHAPTER TWENTY-NINE
Forms Of Help

The U Of M

During one quarter at the U, we had a special guest speaker at the school. It was Martin Luther King, Jr. He was newly famous as the premiere civil rights leader in the black movement. I looked forward to hearing him speak. I remember it well too. It was a unique experience, but not in just what he said. He was a very riveting speaker! His audience was uniquely quiet as he spoke. No coughing, shuffling, any of the usual audience noises at a speaking event. It was awesomely inspiring. And I was very proud of this black man!

I attended the University of Minnesota Liberal Arts department for two quarters and stopped sometime during the third quarter. I was tired of school. It was no longer the great joy it once was. I didn't need a safe and happy place anymore. Somewhere during the 3rd and final quarter of the freshman year, I got a full-time Page job at the Minneapolis Public Library—and stopped attending classes. Before that, I did well academically. But I was just done with school.

CHAPTER TWENTY-NINE

My Help Comes

I've already said that I was socially-stunted in my development. I must have put out a silent cry for help that was heard. I really believe the Lord used Billy and John to rescue me. There was no one else to do it. They assigned themselves the task of making me into a normal teenager—something I had never been. I believe my weight loss after high school encouraged them to think it might be possible to achieve!

I saw anew now that God had blessed me with a wonderful brother. He knew of my lack. So he and John decided to help me. Where did they start? Step one: they taught me to dance. This was a teenage essential during the days of American Bandstand! And they were right. I became a very good dancer, to my surprise and theirs. I really enjoyed it so I learned quickly. Much else was still missing, but they got me started—mostly John. Step two: build up my self-esteem from the ground level. I think the most important thing they did was that John convinced me that I was attractive—something I'd never even dreamed of, much less heard. He told me that I was a fox. I didn't know what this new expression meant— I'd never heard it before. I learned it was black slang for a pretty woman—it was high praise indeed at that time! Billy said that he agreed with John—I was a fox. Wow. That was a status I had never dreamed of reaching. Step three: they taught me to socialize by giving a few small teen parties at home and then gradually taking me out to other teen home parties. Home parties were the only parties then. Where else would you go? There was nothing available generally.

Of course, Billy and John had a far more active social life than I did. They didn't always take me along with them. Who goes out with their sister? They continued to attend other teen parties in the homes of teens in Minneapolis and St. Paul. Homes were the only places for social life for teens. With one exception. There was a club for teens in South Minneapolis called Nacirema. It would be a long time before I learned that its name meant 'American' spelled backwards! I had never been there.

Billy and John's training of me did not include learning to smoke or drink—those were none of our values. They gave me confidence that I could handle social situations. That included conversations with others. What will I say? I remembered I had read somewhere that conversation was like playing tennis. You hit words back and forth between each other. So, untested, I thought I'd be able to hold a conversation with the opposite sex. And I did. Together, John and Billy made me the woman I became.

Fun times! Thanks to the work on me of Billy and John, I finally had a social life! I knew how to dance, did it well, and enjoyed it. One happy result was that I met some very nice young black men. One was Martin (not his real name), an intellectual from St. Paul. We eventually became boyfriend and girlfriend. Martin had good-looking intellectual friends too. I remember Ernest and Carlton. Another nice young man I met was a soldier from elsewhere—maybe Kansas—named Kenneth. We went out once to an adult jazz club downtown—a new one-time experience for me. But I had met someone else I liked a lot more. Martin was the winner. For a while.

My First Boyfriend

Martin (not his real name) was part of the St. Paul social group. Billy and John had invited a few of that group to a small house party we gave and that's how we met. I regarded him as an intellectual equal—something very important to me—and I was greatly flattered by his interest in me. He was 23 and still lived with and on his parents in his adulthood. His brother had died years earlier when they were children. So, Martin wanted to be a doctor. But he was afraid of blood and once fainted at the sight of it! I began to see that our values were not the same as I had initially thought. For one, he didn't work. Someone described him as being someone looking for a job in hopes that he didn't find one. After a while my family strongly urged me to break up with him, but I steadfastly regarded that as a decision I must make on my own—refusing to bow to pressure from anyone. And I made that choice in finally breaking up with him, returning his class ring to him. He was a very valuable part of my growth and development. Happily, I was a virgin when I met him, and I was a virgin when we broke up! I pin no roses on me for that. It was the norm for our generation—the fruit of how we were raised then. Many women of my generation could say the same thing. Later, Martin would marry and support his family as a city bus driver. Good.

Having a boyfriend was a good experience for me. I wasn't much of a partygoer. What would I talk to people about? Now, I can talk to anyone about anything. Okay, maybe I can learn from them if it's about something I don't know. I could be humbly teachable and remember that ALL have value and unique gifts. I could try to see the world from their viewpoint. It took time to develop that attitude. I was aware that I was socially awkward and immature and had been somewhat isolated in life.

A Strange Visit

I believe I made this visit at some point as Billy and John were helping me develop socially. There were two major department stores in downtown Minneapolis: Dayton's was regarded as more upscale and then there was Donaldson's for the middle class. I had somehow heard that Dayton's had a woman in their top floor restaurant who also read tea leaves as their employee or contractor. I had lots of questions about my future. It wouldn't necessarily be as limited as I had once perceived. K.C. was gone and my future was wide-open. But what lies ahead? I decided I needed to know. Not that I put much stock in such things, but it wouldn't hurt. Not knowing any of the protocol, except that you had to order something to eat with your cup of tea, I set off. When the lady came to read my tea leaves, I was fascinated and also on alert. What would she say? I wrote down what I remembered when I got home. Later, the notebook I used would become lost/stolen. What struck me most was that she said I would get married, and I would have three children—two boys and a girl, in that order. Of all she said, I remembered and understood that particular thing most of all. I was happy to hear this. I never went back for another reading. It was never something I ever intended to get dependent upon. It wasn't God, but I had just wanted to maybe have a clue about my future. If I would maybe make a decision to marry a man who'd become a wife-beater, I wanted to be warned beforehand! I had never done this before, so I didn't know all the protocol. She had told me nothing I understood to be devastating so I was content. One reading was enough for me.

My Favorite Christmas

In December 1959, I was blessed to be part of what can only be described as the best Christmas ever! Billy, John, Ruby, and I celebrated together. (Juanita was with another church teen, Sametta, and her family and friends.) It was as though the whole night was scripted for us! We sang Christmas carols together at the home of Auntie and Uncle Robert— who must have been out of town. Ruby played the piano for us. We had never done that before, but we sounded great as we harmonized beautifully. Again, I was reminded that I wanted to learn to play piano one day. Then we left to take Christmas presents to the homes of a few families and friends. They were small inexpensive gifts bought with our teen money, but they expressed our love to those we cherished. It was a clear cold snow-covered night. It was a long and happy time, lasting nearly all night. Who knew when we would all be gathered together like this with each other again? We thoroughly enjoyed this unique happy time—joyous, peaceful, and free. M'Deah had no problem with Billy and me being out so late at night. We were together and she knew what kind of kids she had raised—and that we were in good company. There was no danger of our being harmed by city crime either—not in idyllic Minneapolis! I think it ended with an early breakfast, around 5:00 a.m. None of us were tired though. We all knew this night had been special. It truly was a very special gift from God to us. I never forgot it—we all cherished its memory. For me, for a lifetime.

CHAPTER THIRTY

A New Guy

Perry

It was at another of these teen house parties in St. Paul that I met a handsome young man in Spring 1960. We met at the home of a teen girl whom Billy, John, and Martin all knew. I had not met her before. Also, part of our group was a mixed-race girl from our neighborhood who was a very casual friend of mine. I was wearing a red shirt-waist dress M'Deah had chosen and bought for me. I liked it but red wasn't my color—I didn't wear it much at all. This night, I wore that new dress for the first time. And I think it later got attention!

Our hostess was in the kitchen with Martin and a few others as they planned how to get enough money together to order a new treat called pizza for the gathering. I had never had any. As they went about this effort in the kitchen, I realized I was in a roomful of strangers, and no one had introduced us to each other.

I was shy at school for a long time. In my teens, I decided to address it and did some reading. I learned that shy equals selfish and self -centered. I didn't like that or want to be like that. I purposed not to be that way. So, at the party, I didn't think of my discomfort at not knowing others there. Rather, I thought of THEIR discomfort and wanted to change that. So I spoke up. And thank God that I did! It changed my life forever. It was a God -moment.

    I suddenly became very bold as we all sat silently looking at each other. I went beyond my normal timidity and boldly spoke up. "Hello, my name is Barb, and I don't believe I know everyone here—please tell me your names." It worked! Amazingly, people introduced themselves to the group in the living room. One of the last was a guy sitting in the corner with his eyes closed. He said he was "Perry". I liked that name. Someone began playing the phonograph again and dancing resumed. Perry got up and asked me to dance. Nice. At some point, he asked for my phone number. I hesitated briefly, deciding if I would do so or if I would give him a phony number. After all, I didn't know him. I decided that enough people at the party knew him and it would be okay to give him my actual number. Plus, I learned that he lived out of state, in Milwaukee, Wisconsin. It seemed pretty safe. So, I wrote it down. As the evening wore on, I learned that Perry was his last name—not his first. I also learned that he had been silent with his eyes closed, because he grieved for the loss of the basketball game that day. He and his team had come to St. Paul from the Milwaukee YMCA to play

CHAPTER THIRTY

a team there and they had lost. Oh. I wondered what would become of this encounter with a man I really liked on our first meeting. I had nurtured myself on historical fiction and the values of its characters. For the heroines, their ideal man was described as tall, dark, and handsome. That's what Perry was to me—I had finally met MY tall, dark, and handsome! As for my first taste of pizza, I remember it as very underwhelming and I wondered what all the fuss was about. That would drastically change later as I joined everyone else in the pizza craze!

Perry actually did call me just a couple of days later! He said he wanted to write to me and asked for my address. I saw no harm in giving it to him. A few days later, I got my first letter from him. These were the days before the Internet. Long-distance phone calls were still considered unnecessary expenses—usually for emergencies only. The common communication style for long-distance relationships of all types was letter-writing. So, we began corresponding regularly and phoning occasionally as we got better and better acquainted. Over the next few months, there would be many more phone calls and there would be lots of letters. Again, that's how you commonly communicated in those times. I learned from Perry that he greatly desired to be a police officer—that was his goal. He had applied to the force in Milwaukee, but he said they were prone NOT to hire blacks. So, that door didn't open for him. However, he had taken a test and also applied to the Metropolitan Police Department in Washington, D.C. They recruited nation-wide. He was just waiting to hear from them. I thought to myself that I had always wanted to visit D.C. It sounded exciting.

He Visits Me

Perry said he was planning another trip to St. Paul and was coming alone. He asked if he could visit me. I checked with M'Deah first and we agreed it was okay. He took the public bus from St. Paul to my house, we had a nice visit, he met M'Deah and Billy, and he took the bus back to his hotel in St. Paul. Both M'Deah and Billy liked Perry too. Better than they had Martin. Plus Perry had a job! M'Deah graciously regarded him as another son and Billy graciously regarded him as another brother. I was glad of that. He was soon to be 23 and I was 19.

As we grew to know each other, I learned he had attended Kentucky State on a basketball scholarship. Like me, he left before finishing to begin working full-time back home in Milwaukee. He also continued to take classes at the Technical College there. I later learned he had three very attractive sisters and that he was the youngest in his family.

I Visit Him

I also visited Milwaukee for the first time a few weeks later. I asked M'Deah if I could visit her Uncle Lloyd there and his second wife, Aunt Ella. He was

CHAPTER THIRTY

my great-uncle and Big Mama's brother. Uncle Lloyd had left Alabama as a young man. Why? One year, he planted crops on his land. Some white teen boys began to destroy his crops—for fun. When he objected, they said they would tell their fathers about his "uppity" treatment of them, and he would be taken care of. Uncle Lloyd knew what that meant: an unpleasant visit by the KKK with only bad results—for him and maybe for his family too. He was able to hide until dark, when he hopped onto a freight train headed North. And he never looked back. Now, he had found success in Milwaukee. But he never forgot his family. Nor did he ever stop loving them. Remember, he had helped M'Deah when she needed it most. So, M'Deah gave me the okay and I coordinated it with him by phone. I asked Ruby to go with me and we had a nice visit with this hospitable couple.

Perry's Family

But I also used this trip to visit Perry and meet his family. I wanted to visit Uncle Lloyd. But I REALLY wanted to visit Perry too. They were a lovely, hospitable friendly family and I liked them right away. I met his father, **Robert**. I also met his sisters. (I had learned during our courting days that Perry was the only son, and he was also the youngest child. That meant his sisters had pampered their baby brother a lot—whether he knew it or not!) The first sister was **Mary Ann**. She was married to **Theodore**, and they had four children: **Teddy, Kevin, Patricia,** and **Ronald**. All four of them were miracle babies. Mary Ann had been told at 16 that she would never be able to bear children. But Theodore loved her anyway, married her, and their miracle babies came! As the oldest child, Mary Ann always seemed to be what I regarded as the "responsible" one.

Next was his sister, **Helen**. She was married to **Raymond**, whom all called by his last name, Reed. They had two sons, **Kendall and Kraig**. Helen was always seemingly the most "considerate one". She saw the needs of others that may have been unseen by anyone else. It was she who sent small amounts of money to Perry regularly when he was in college at Kentucky State after high school graduation. That was an obvious blessing!

The youngest sister was **Bobbie**. Her name was the same as mine but spelled differently. That's the name spelling I had wanted at one time in my childhood. I bet she never got teased for having a boy's name! Bobbie had been married but was now divorced. They had no children, but she clearly loved her niece and nephews. I regarded her as the "caring" one. I also met a couple of cousins, **Paul** and **Gilbert**. I may be mixing the timing of when I met them all—first visit or second visit. They were all very nice and very hospitable and I liked them all! I watched, in particular, how Perry interacted with his one niece and five nephews. Ted was the oldest at 12

CHAPTER THIRTY

and played the trumpet—kindly giving me a demo. Ronald was still a baby in diapers. They all had a good relationship—Perry was good with kids! That was a good sign—and an important one, I thought, for our future children.

Perry's father was a great cook and family man. I don't know where this came from. But I remember once hearing from him or someone else that he had grown up having a rough childhood. It seems that at some point he was on his own as a teenager. He told me played the piano and was sometimes booked to play in local "juke-joints" of the time. Elsewhere they could be called saloons or bars or pubs. It wasn't considered the top of acceptable society, but it provided for your needs. When he got married to Perry's mother, Maria First, he settled down and did other work to provide for his growing family. I remember him being capable of doing anything around a home that needed doing. He would improvise or repair what was needed. A great skill to have in any home! He could cook anything and make it taste good. I remember particularly his homemade eggnog at Christmas time. It was smooth, creamy, custard-y with just a touch of liquor. Delicious! I don't think anyone in the family got and kept his recipe. I was interested in it but never pursued it—assuming someone else would surely have it. But they don't.

Actually, I had really wanted to visit Perry and his family. An old adage I'd heard was that if you want to know what someone's true character is like, meet their family. I did so and discovered that they were very nice people who'd moved there from Kentucky when Perry was eight. I was greatly encouraged about this man whom I was attracted to but didn't know that well.

    I had mostly a wonderful time with all Perry's family. There was one exception. We went to the home of a family member, and I was introduced to a family cousin and his wife. The wife subtly teased me about my youth. It was an ongoing put-down that I didn't enjoy. I couldn't help it that I was only 19 years old. Finally tired of it, I did something unexpected. I asked her how old she was. She paused and said she was 32. The conversation continued but I don't remember it. I was remembering the old rubric that you never ask a woman her age. Not only had I done so, but I did it in public! I had committed a real social blunder. Maybe my youth was a problem after all. I did apologize to her at the end of the little get-together. I told her that I shouldn't have asked her age. (It had seemed to me to be appropriate at the time because of the way she had treated me. At least her behavior towards me changed after that awful question.) She left me alone and sort of ignored me. I was okay with that and realized I had offended her. Thus the apology was necessary. I don't remember seeing her again in the ensuing years and I was okay with that.

CHAPTER THIRTY

I learned later that the Perry family had relocated from Russellville, Kentucky to Milwaukee in 1943. They were migrants too.

One More Time

During the summer of 1960, I had a sudden strong desire that I wanted to go South to visit my paternal grandmother, Miss Janie. I had a strange urge to see her one more time. I hadn't seen her since my father's funeral. M'Deah always maintained good relations with her and with his sisters. She would send annual after-Christmas boxes South with treats of Spam, Vienna sausage, candies, etc. I called them her "Care" packages, after the United Nations program then. (In those days, I was a big fan of the UN. They've changed so much since then as to make that impossible now.) They always appreciated her thoughtfulness. So, M'Deah was in agreement that I go for the visit. But I knew so very little about the South now. It was still a dangerous place, and I didn't want to make any social missteps there that would be risky. I remembered what happened to Emmett Till. Who could go with me as a guide? Maybe my cousin, Ruby. Ruby was the oldest daughter of my mother's brother, Dan. They had moved to Minneapolis when she was 16—we were the same age. We—our families—lived together for a while with Auntie and Uncle Robert during M'Deah's trial. That's when Ruby and I also became friends. I regarded her as a sister. I asked and Ruby agreed to go with me. We could stay in Coffeeville, Alabama where her mother's family lived. It was nearby to my destination of Koenton. Ruby was working full-time too, having just graduated from high school. Miss Janie and I had no phone calls, only a very few letters, and no time together. I reasoned that Ruby had lived in the South since I had and knew all the Jim Crow customs and laws which I might inadvertently cross or offend. We would save money and a hotel where Negroes could stay was not likely anywhere nearby anyhow. Ruby knew who could possibly take us to make the visit to Miss Janie's home—she could make the arrangements with them. We saved our money for the train tickets, packed a small lunch, and left in August. The train trip went to Chicago first, with a stop in Milwaukee.

A Pit Stop

Enroute South, we stopped in Milwaukee to visit Big Mama's brother and his wife, Uncle Lloyd and Aunt Ella. By now I knew how helpful he had been to M'Deah in her time of need. She had asked him for a $500 loan for an attorney retainer fee, which he'd given her. She offered to pay it back in installments. He declined, telling her to just save her money and repay it in a lump sum when she was able, just as he'd loaned it to her in a lump sum. No deadline was involved—she was to take as long as she needed. That took a lot of pressure off her. She repaid the

CHAPTER THIRTY

loan in one lump sum just as he taught her. Ruby and I had a layover of a day or two.

Perry took me to the Wisconsin State Fair. I rode the Ferris wheel for the first—and last—time in my life. My carnival choice of ride has always been the merry-go-round. That's my speed and my idea of fun! I've ridden other rides but prefer the merry-go-round pace and horses. Why was this my last time on the Ferris wheel? It got stuck when Perry and I were sitting at the topmost point! It took a while for them to get us down too. Whew! Never again!

Onwards

After our Milwaukee visit, Ruby and I continued our trip. We ran out of food in our carry-on lunches. But my pivotal memory is when we got to a rail stop where passengers could disembark to get something to eat from the railside café. We were really hungry by now. White passengers entered the front door. We went around back through the "colored" entrance. However once inside, we could hear and see white patrons were waited on first. We had to wait our turn—last. When it came time to take our orders, it was also time for the train to depart to keep its schedule! So, we left hungry. No other choice. I found an apple still left in my purse and happily and gratefully ate it. Ruby had declined sharing my apple but she was hungry too. The injustice hit me hard: As "colored", we were

NO less hungry than the whites. But it was their justice system that required us to leave still hungry. It was the lowest point in the whole trip—for me. Ruby knew it to be the norm for the South. This was the only food I remember for the trip from Chicago Illinois to Coffeeville Alabama—a distance of some 700 miles.

Courtship and More

Perry visited me once more and I visited him once more. But there were lots of letters and phone calls along the way. I think we had seen each other only four times before he popped the question. I gave a resounding "Yes!" Wow!

It was my intent to be engaged for a couple of years, so we could get to know each other better. It had only been a few months since we first met. But then Perry received his Army draft letter, and he wanted us to marry before he left. His departure date was in October. After some discussion, I agreed to his preference and we set our wedding date for October 22nd. Not much time to prepare! On one of my trips to Milwaukee, he took me to a jewelry store and had me select my engagement ring. I chose a yellow gold band holding my favorite jewel—a pearl. I did NOT want a diamond ring and thought them "too cold". Perry was surprised.

CHAPTER THIRTY-ONE
A Wedding Comes

I was still somewhat socially awkward and knew little about what a wedding required. So, I did what I always do in such circumstances. I read books about it. I foolishly thought I could get all the "expert" advice that I needed. But only later did I find out it wasn't advice for ME! I had only known one other person in my high school class who had gotten married. Carolyn, a white classmate, did it very smoothly and all went well. I was invited to her wedding but didn't attend. Somehow in my reading, I foolishly and wrongly got it into my head that wedding invitations were to be hand-written—personalized, instead of using printed invitations like any party invitations. I don't have the prettiest handwriting and it took a long time doing them all.

I didn't really discuss my wedding plans with anyone other than Ruby. I made my own decisions, right or wrong. My wedding colors weren't really my own though. Something called "Hot pink" was popularized then by Jackie Kennedy. It looked great on her and just about every woman had something in their wardrobe that was hot pink. I didn't. But I chose that color anyhow!

The big question others of my family had was who would give me away? Having no father, extended family insisted it had to be an uncle. Would it be George, Dan, Robert, Tommy? NO! I only wanted ONE person to give me away and I was strangely very insistent. It would be my brother, Billy. Against all opposition, I stuck firmly to that decision. Billy was the CLOSEST/DEAREST male relative to me. M'Deah left all my wishes regarding attendants to me. She never inserted herself into any of my wedding decisions. What a wise and generous woman! M'Deah told me some of my aunts thought it ridiculous that I wanted Billy to give me away. They suggested it was more appropriate that I select one of my uncles for the role—the nearest male relative of my father's generation. It should be someone to represent a father -figure in my life. None of them were ever a consideration by me. It was only to be Billy—my truly nearest and dearest male relative.

For some unknown reason, I decided to make my own wedding dress! That wasn't hard when I shopped for wedding dresses and realized how expensive they were. I was only working from my personal budget, I thought. I didn't want to add expenses onto M'Deah. So, I made my dress on our in-home treadle sewing machine with just the skills I got in one semester of sewing instruction in 7th grade Home Ec class. It was my first dress and my last dress—the ONLY dress I ever made! Why did I do it? It was just a sudden

CHAPTER THIRTY-ONE

desire I had to make my own wedding dress. I didn't know where that desire came from and still don't. Maybe it was from the pioneering spirit I picked up from the books I read. But I was determined. This time, I even got an upscale Dior-style pattern for it—not just a Simplicity pattern. The material I got was white brocade—a thick forgiving material. And I did it. I still have that dress now—kept it for all these years. And I still have that old treadle sewing machine.

Everyone let me have my way regarding the wedding choices and didn't present suggestions or opposition of any kind. M'Deah thought I was underestimating the amount of work and tasks needed doing. I assured her I was okay—I'd done things I read about in a wedding book from the library. I was wrong on so many levels!

My Wedding Party

Who was in my wedding party? It was small—only four people. I only wanted two girls with me—my cousin Ruby was my maid of honor, and my stepsister Linda was my bridesmaid. If I added another it would be my cousin Juanita whom I'd also gotten really close to when we stayed with Auntie and Uncle Robert. She was Ruby's younger sister and like another sister to me. But my chosen color for attendant's dresses was a color I knew Juanita didn't like—Hot pink was NOT her favorite color but maybe was her LEAST favorite color! I wasn't going to change that and I'm happy that I didn't even try. That would have been very selfish of me. And it meant I would need another male in the wedding party—I had no one in mind. When I told Juanita I would not be using her in my wedding party, she said she understood and was OKAY. I was forever sorry that I didn't choose her anyway. It never occurred to me that I could have included John in my wedding party too. I wrongly thought I had to have an even number though and a wedding party of three women and three men didn't fit that wrong concept. And, because they both sewed, Ruby and Linda would make their own dresses—I just had to buy the dress pattern and pay for the fabric. So that's what I did. Maybe Ruby could have made her sister's wedding dress, but I wouldn't put that burden on her. I really regretted that Juanita wasn't part of my wedding party. She was as dear to me as Linda and Ruby were.

What about the males in my wedding party? I knew very few black males in my life and was close to none of them. Except for family. So, I chose my two cousins, Melvin and Jimmy, to be groomsman/ushers. I really didn't want to slight them. It was only later that I realized John would have been a good choice if I had added Juanita to the party. It was because of him and his efforts to update me socially that I was even seen as worthy to be anyone's bride! And I loved him like a cousin—or like a brother. Sigh.

CHAPTER THIRTY-ONE

Perry only needed his best man, childhood friend, Maurice Beckley.

Eloyce took charge of everything related to my flower girl. It was her daughter, Sheila. She did it well. I was happy with the great job Sheila did in her beautiful white outfit.

A Last Visit

I went to Milwaukee the weekend before my wedding. Maybe to make sure I was doing the right thing in marrying him—someone I had known less than six months and had seen only four times. What was I thinking? Ruby would go with me. M'Deah was shocked and asked if I knew how much work still needed to be done for wedding prep. I tried to assure her that I did and that it would all get done. What else needed to be done? I was clueless. I had already arranged for wedding veil rental, had bought my shoes, had spoken to a professional photographer at church, had my two wedding party girls working on their dresses, finished the invitations, etc. I couldn't think of anything else and wondered what M'Deah was talking about. I took my wedding dress on the trip with me. It wasn't finished yet. I remember hemming it by hand on the train but I didn't get as much done as I'd hoped. Was I right in telling M'Deah all would get done for the wedding? I had my first but not least doubts. But the trip assured me that I was truly in love with handsome Perry. Yeah, he was a good guy. I loved him and I wanted to marry him. Okay to proceed!

Thanks, M'Deah!

Thank God for M'Deah! She really did know what remained to be done! And she did it. She arranged rental for the punch bowl and cups. She arranged to tie a bow on the knife for cutting the wedding cake, etc. Most of all, the reception was to be at our home. Strangely, her sisters had all decided they would do NOTHING to help M'Deah with this wedding and told her so. I knew nothing of that then. M'Deah wondered about housing Perry's family when they came to Minneapolis for the wedding. Thankfully, her sisters volunteered their homes at the last minute. M'Deah later said she thought they would be embarrassed at having Perry's family wonder what kind of family I had that was so inhospitable. She had purposed to pay for their hotel rooms somehow. Thankfully, that wasn't necessary. I was only grateful that it all worked out in the end. They were hospitable and really enjoyed getting to know his family. Most of all, M'Deah had to do ALL the cooking for the reception! Her sisters gave her NO help. She cooked everything. It was, of course, delicious—but it was also a lot of work. I was no help, because I had to work daily at my job—I took no time off before the wedding. Besides, I didn't comprehend all that M'Deah had to do. I was blissfully ignorant about the

CHAPTER THIRTY-ONE

reception at my home, etc. I'm not sure if I made the dinner rolls but I think I did. If so, that was my only contribution though!

The Wedding

How did it all turn out? Well—in the end. Ruby spent the night with me on the eve of my wedding. I was nervous about getting married, yet calm and sure at the same time. It would be my last night as a single woman. We talked a lot, and I slept very little. I needed Ruby also to do my hair for the wedding. I didn't regard myself as good enough for the task. She really did a great job of making it look neat and natural, something I wouldn't regret looking at years later in my wedding photos! I had gotten my hair done for the wedding. It had become part of my routine and it relieved M'Deah of this lifelong chore. But I looked to Ruby to style it for me—I knew that was not my forte.

Our wedding began with Mr. Steele forgetting to pick up M'Deah for the ride to the church! When I found out M'Deah wasn't there, I REFUSED to go on with the 1:00 p.m. wedding. "I am NOT getting married without my mother!" So, we had a half hour delay while he went back and got her.

I had not met with my photographer beforehand and just assumed he knew what photos to take. He was a professional photographer who I knew as a member in my church. He didn't do a very professional job. I didn't think I would need to direct him on what photos to take—he was a professional. Wrong. He took none of the classic shots. I have no photos of M'Deah, of the wedding party, of our families, etc. They were just missing. I didn't find this out until later and I was disappointed—but too late. When he sent his bill I was reluctant to pay him. I think M'Deah finally settled it—maybe it was for about $25. I do have two or three good photos though that I cherish. And I'm glad that wedding attendees took casual photos that I still have.

    I didn't socialize with my Henry classmates, really. I remember that only three of them ever invited me to their homes—Carolyn, Judith, Kathy. I invited no one to my home. Selfish, I know. For some reason, I didn't think they'd be comfortable. Maybe because of K.C. I pretty much knew nothing of their struggles and home life. And they knew nothing of mine. We were just school acquaintances with a common school life. Sadly, I didn't invite any of my classmates to my wedding. Whites and blacks were of different social classes and didn't really mingle socially. I did invite to my reception the one who had invited me to her wedding: Carolyn. And, of course, I invited the Carlson family to wedding and reception.

The Reception

    Unbeknownst to me M'Deah's sisters had told her they would assist her in no way with regards

CHAPTER THIRTY-ONE

to the wedding. They would do none of the cooking. When she requested their housing assistance for Perry's family, they refused. M'Deah prepared to pay the hotel expenses instead. But the sisters changed their minds at the last minute, not wanting to seem inhospitable and rude to the Perrys. Clueless, I just thought what a wonderful family I have!

I don't remember the whole reception menu—just that M'Deah outdid herself in providing delicious homemade food. There was roast turkey, baked ham, fried chicken, lots of fresh vegetables from her garden, and desserts besides wedding cake. We had champagne to toast the newlyweds and lots of punch and pop. Yum!

M'Deah had to be utterly exhausted from all the work she'd done to make her daughter's wedding such a success. Her daughter was grateful but mostly oblivious. For a long time.

The food was plentiful and delicious, of course. M'Deah was a great cook. And she had done it all by herself, with zero assistance from her sisters. She was a magnificent one-woman catering service. When I realized all, she had done, I could only say "Thank you". Gratefully. The reception crowd was huge. The house had never held so many people before—150 at least. Additionally, I was an excited and exhausted bride. I certainly don't remember all who were there. Some of them I haven't seen since then. Sadly.

The Honeymoon

This was likewise frugal. We spent our first night at an inexpensive hotel in St. Paul. We had a bottle of champagne that we put in the window to chill overnight. I had never been so tired in all my life. So, we waited for the morning. I knew I was lacking in some social graces and looked forward to my husband teaching me certain social skills—how to drink alcohol, bowl, play cards, ride a horse, play tennis, etc. I trusted him to do so eventually. By my background, I later preferred to drink a sweet cocktail. Someone recommended the Daiquiri to me and it became my favorite. I've had one maybe half a dozen times in my lifetime. Did I learn all these other things? No. But that's another story.

I always knew from my mother that I was welcome home whenever I had a need. Perry told me now of something M'Deah had told him on our wedding day. She told Perry to never abuse me but, anytime he no longer wanted me, to just instead return me home where he had gotten me from. She meant it. Neither Perry nor I ever forgot that.

From St. Paul, we went to Milwaukee where we stayed for a few days and waited for Perry to report for the draft. It was bittersweet and concluded with his departure and my return to Minneapolis. We didn't know when we would see each other again or where he might end up being stationed after basic training.

CHAPTER THIRTY-ONE

At 19 I thought I was all grown up. I had graduated from high school. I had a job. I mostly made my own decisions. I had a driver's license. I now even had a social life. I paid "rent". And now I had a husband too. Shoot, I was hot stuff! Hah! I didn't know what questions to ask, because I didn't even know what I didn't know! There was so much more that I could have learned from M'Deah—so much more that I didn't know I needed. Time would reveal my shortage of knowledge and my abundance of ignorance! Too late to avoid a bunch of mistakes though.

Wedding Cost

Certainly, the total cost of my wedding was well under $500. I was pleased that it was not more. I hadn't planned for it to be even near that amount. Another fault of mine: I gave no gifts to my wedding party. They were all family and would understand. Plus, I had no extra money nor any idea what to gift them. I hadn't realized M'Deah would incur extra expenses unknown to me in carrying off a successful wedding reception. I was blissfully ignorant that all the rent money I'd paid her likely went to the cost of the wedding—she had no profit or benefit from me at all! For me, I had a wedding for less than $500 in total cost to me and I was content with that. I never believed in having a lavish expensive wedding and had little regard for marriage expenses. I'd rather have a down payment for a house and for the new couple to begin building a new life together! I'm sure M'Deah probably paid nearly that same amount for my wedding—$500. And she did it with grace—never mentioning to me the cost to her. The honeymoon costs were all Perry's—M'Deah and I didn't have to worry about that!

Another Wedding

This took place shortly after Perry and I married. This couple I knew had some controversy told about them while they were engaged. He had told all and sundry that there would be no wedding if there were no pre-marital sex. That was not commonly a deal-breaker at that time. Many women were virgins at marriage. However, he was adamant to "try before you buy". I thought it was so disrespectful to make that publicly known. A week before the wedding, they went away on a weekend trip together. Unknown to the bride when they did marry, all knew she had complied with his requirement. What a way for a marriage to begin! And it didn't last very long. Divorce ended it all a few short years and two children later. That had to be painful.

Every Family

Over the years, I've heard some others talk about their families and I learned something. I learned EVERY family has pain and trauma. It differs only by amount, kind, and intensity. We can all relate to

CHAPTER THIRTY-ONE

one another on that. Again, enemy satan hates us all and inflicts as much misery in our lives as he can. Through whosoever he can use. Our Good God is FOR us and does all for us as we look to Him for His help. That's surely been my experience!

PART FIVE
The Denver Years

PART FIVE

The Denver Years

CHAPTER THIRTY-TWO
Now, The Marriage

Our First Christmas

As newlyweds, Perry got a furlough to come home for Christmas. Oh, joy! I don't remember what I got him, but he bought me a beautiful large wooden jewelry box. I still have it. We split the time between Minneapolis and Milwaukee, so as to spend it with both our families. And we really enjoyed this brief time together before he had to return to the Army.

Together At Last

After completion of basic training at Fort Leonard Wood in Missouri, Perry was sent to Fitzsimons Army Hospital in Aurora, Colorado—a suburb of Denver. He was a medic there. A few months later, he sent for me to join him, and I did. I packed everything I thought our new home together would need: a household in a foot locker. Our first apartment was small: one bedroom, a shared kitchen and bathroom with another Army couple. But it was ours. And it was by no means our final home.

CHAPTER THIRTY-TWO

Our Marriage Overview

Who were my role models for marriage? M'Deah? I definitely didn't want that kind of marriage! TV's June Cleaver, etc.? I knew that wasn't real. Those from the fairy tales and fiction that I read about? That's sort of the one I chose by default! My choice was not made from a position of being whole. I knew I was damaged and broken, but I didn't know what to do about it or know how it could affect our marriage. As the Bible says in I **Timothy 1:13**, "I did it ignorantly and in unbelief". Even so, God was Good to me and the marriage lasted.

Just imagine two people with at least 100 differences being put together and told to live happily ever after. For two people who lived about 350 miles apart, knew each other six months, and saw each other only four times before marrying, I think we did very well to stay married for 38 years. That's a miracle! It was unique as all marriages are. Perhaps our biggest uniqueness was in how quickly we had married without getting to know each other in many ways. We therefore had our own ups and downs. We had our own sureties about each other and our own doubts. We didn't really know each other. All we had going for us was our love for each other. Thank God that love plus our character was enough!

Does everyone enter marriage with the expectation of living together "happily ever after" as I did? That's how all the fairy tales I read ended and that was my unrealistic expectation. Of course, it doesn't always happen. Differences bring about arguments! That can be a good thing. Your spouse will point out faults they see which you may be totally unaware of. If you admit them to yourself, that provides an opportunity for you to change and grow. Perry had a few faults too, of course, but none that were a deal breaker. I discovered that I had a few more faults than I had known about before marriage. Thankfully, they weren't a deal breaker for him either! Altogether I was a very blessed woman to have Robert Perry as my husband. His best man, Beckley, used to tell us often the slogan of the day for marriages: "togetherness—just be sure to have togetherness". We would promise him that we would. And we did. For nearly 38 years. In spite of all our combined differences and faults, we loved each other. The greatest thing we had in common was that we loved each other. That is nothing to take lightly. We had both love and "togetherness". That was the glue that held us together in solid commitment for 38 years. We had learned what that meant.

Perry had learned to play poker as a gambling game and event as a teenager. He enjoyed it as a pleasant recreation. He was a gambler, but nowhere near irresponsible as my father had been! He didn't have the interest and skills of his father as a handyman. But he had pretty much the same values I'd been raised with. He was a responsible man. He also

CHAPTER THIRTY-TWO

had necessary "street smarts " that I totally lacked. That gave me a sense of safety under his guidance.

No marriage is perfect. It can't be when it involves two fallen people in a fallen world. They begin with innumerable differences between them. Some may get addressed and discussed in pre-marital counseling. That didn't happen for us though. That was still a mostly new concept, and my church didn't offer it. Besides, how could we do it, living so far apart? Like others, we mostly (not always!) did the best we could. And that worked! Really, it was our genuine love for each other that ultimately worked and got us through all the challenges that arose.

I believe we had another advantage in marriage. I was a virgin when I met Perry, and he was the only man I ever knew in the Biblical sense. Nothing else was ever necessary. Thus, Perry and I had a good marriage. It can't be described as a great marriage, but it was a good marriage of nearly 38 years. And for that, I thank God, and I thank Perry. Not everyone has that. In later generations, virginity was not only seen as unnecessary and unimportant but was even seen as a disadvantage and an impossibility! What a change from what my and M'Deah's generations knew as the norm! It actually is of great value in many ways, including trust. Even if all didn't have this before marriage, it was still regarded as the achievable norm. That was a solid cultural foundation.

Another marriage blessing I had was that one of Perry's Godly gifts/talents was in giving gifts and in giving awesome greeting cards. He was so expressive in the appropriate cards he gave, and he put a lot of thought into the gifts he gave. It said a lot that words didn't and maybe couldn't say. Our children are so gifted that way too. And I've always been thankful and appreciative of that.

Misunderstanding

I discovered early on that falling in love had opened up my emotions. I didn't think of myself as hardened, but I wasn't a cry-er. I didn't know when I had last cried about something not drastically dramatic. But now? I seemed to cry at the drop of a hat. It was new to me. And, apparently, Perry didn't like it. I would cry when we argued—I was emotionally touched then. One day during an argument he told me my tears wouldn't move him so I might as well stop them. I was shocked. Somewhere in his experience he saw a woman's tears as merely a manipulative tool. Angrily I said my tears were for me and not for him so just ignore them. Later, I tried to explain my emotional awakening as the reason for my tears. He didn't budge from his thinking. After that, I tried to staunch my tears during any arguments we had—but I still argued, intent on not being the weak little woman.

CHAPTER THIRTY-TWO

Denver Life

I don't remember the amount of my monthly Army allotment check as an Army wife. But it was comparable to my library paycheck. I couldn't understand how Army couples made it without the wife working too. Even so, we were kinda poor. But we were able to buy a used car—that was a necessity. Trips to the really inexpensive movies at the base theater were rare—even at the cost of 25 cents each. I shopped at the PX but it was difficult to make sure we had food left until the end of the month. (On one such trip I discovered I was missing the $20 bill I'd put in the deep outside pocket of my purse. I knew I hadn't lost it, so I concluded I'd been the victim of a pickpocket. A loss that big was devastating! But we made it.) We had wanted to tour the nearby Colorado mountains, but that required extra gas money. We were kinda stuck at home!

My childhood experience on the importance of the telephone was something we also gave up. No telephone bill. We wrote letters to the family back home.

I had read the book, "Ben Hur" as a teenager and really liked it. Wikipedia's summary of the book says:

> "Ben-Hur is a story of a fictional hero named Judah Ben-Hur, a Jewish nobleman who was falsely accused and convicted of an attempted assassination of the Roman governor of Judaea and consequently enslaved

by the Romans. He becomes a successful charioteer (and a Christian). The story's revenge plot becomes a story of compassion and forgiveness."

MGM made it into an award-winning movie and I convinced Perry that we should go see it. He was reluctant because of its 3 ½ hour length, but I persisted. I knew he liked action movies and I assured him there would be enough action to hold his attention. So, we went. Reluctantly, Perry said he did like the movie.

One reason, I looked forward to the movie was that its star was Charlton Heston. I had really enjoyed his appearance as Moses in The Ten Commandments movie. One of the lines I never forgot was when actor Yul Brynner as pharaoh said, "Their God IS God!" I came to agree with Him after many years.

I'm not sure at what point Perry heard from D.C. that he had been accepted to be a police officer there. But they knew he was in the Army and would hold the job for him until after his discharge. Good!

A New Job

I wanted and needed to work, So, I took a 6-week course at Central Business School to better prepare myself for a good clerical job by improving my typing and to take a PBX class—to make myself more marketable in a new city. Then I was sent on to the job search and did interviews the business college had set

CHAPTER THIRTY-TWO

up for me. One place was a black insurance company I'd never heard of. Apparently, it was well-known to other Negroes—just not to me. They were slow to get back to me. I felt like Perry Mason's secretary, Della Street, when going on interviews. Another comparison was Lena Horne. Whoever thought I would be compared to someone like that? It's what I'd always thought of as a Negro woman in the secretarial field. Another interview was at the University of Denver Admissions Department. I was offered both jobs. But the one I accepted was the offer I received first—as an auto-typist at the University of Denver. I didn't know what an auto-typist was but got on-the-job training. It involved setting up a machine to automatically type scripted reply letters for college admissions. It was sufficiently challenging, I liked it and did it well. My only regret was in not getting to use the skill I'd acquired as a PBX telephone switchboard operator. You know, the old plug and talk boards in the old movies! That technology was on the way out—not found in modern offices. Again, I was the only black in the department. I didn't mind—my co-workers couldn't have been nicer, and it was for me a familiar circumstance.

I'm pregnant!

I became pregnant—quickly! Perry was on the Fitzsimons basketball team and would sometimes travel with them for games on the road. After one such trip in March or April of 1961, we happily reunited. And I found out a few weeks later that I was pregnant. My pregnancy experience began after Perry and I went on base one evening. I had there one of my few mixed drinks, a daiquiri. When we got home, I was nauseous. I finally had to go down the hall to the bathroom where I threw up violently and repeatedly. I also had diarrhea! So, I was sitting on the toilet with fluids coming out of both ends of my body! Perry stayed with me to try to help however he could. What is wrong with me? This can't be the flu—I have no other flu symptoms! Was it the daiquiri I had drunk? I had so little experience with alcohol. We didn't know. So, the next day I went to the base doctor. Oh, oh. I got the happy but surprising news. I was pregnant with a delivery date of early December—the 11th.

But wait! I wasn't mentally ready for this. Now that I'm pregnant, I don't feel like an adult at all. I'm a child having a baby! That's a lot of grown-up responsibility! I had hoped Perry and I would have two years together before this happened. But we'd done nothing to prevent the possibility. We were so happy and so were all the rest of the family when we told them. M'Deah was happy at hearing the news and so was Billy. So was the Milwaukee family. Absolutely everyone of our families. Billy was really looking forward to being an uncle. He and John planned to visit us in the Summer and we all looked forward to that. He wrote to me about it in the only letter I have from

CHAPTER THIRTY-TWO

him—we had never lived apart before. This was all so new to me, of course. I felt totally unprepared and thus did what was totally normal for me. I read books about it. And I talked to others about their experiences. I was blessed to have no great morning sickness—hardly any at all. I can't say that I craved any particular foods either.

CHAPTER THIRTY-THREE

Great Loss

I had experienced trauma in my young life before. But this was different. It truly was a tragedy—my first. No other word fits.

Bad News

One day after arriving home from work in Summer 1961, I was surprised to see a Western Union telegram advising me to call Auntie immediately. (Perry and I had been trying to be frugal, so we chose not to have our own phone in order to save money.) But why was I to call Auntie and not M'Deah? Was M'Deah alright? I went to the nearest phone booth about a block away and called. Auntie answered and gave me the shock of my life. Was M'Deah OKAY? Yes. But Billy wasn't. What? She filled me in, saying Billy and John had drowned the evening before and their bodies had been recovered. Billy was dead? He had drowned? NO! Billy swims like a fish! He's a lifeguard! That's impossible! No. It wasn't impossible. Auntie told me His best friend, John, had also drowned. Billy had drowned while trying to rescue John whose foot had gotten entangled by the rope

CHAPTER THIRTY-THREE

on the anchor he threw from the boat where they'd been fishing on big Lake Minnetonka. They had gone there with John's mother, Viola, who had bought beer for them all to drink. It's thought that the beer was a factor in their drowning. I was in shock. Some more words were said about me flying home to be with my mother and for the funeral. I assured her I'd be flying home ASAP.

Somehow, I got home to our apartment in my state of stupor. I couldn't help thinking, "How could this be? Billy was like a fish in water. He was at home in on the water (he played hockey). It was he who knew how to swim and I didn't. He knew how to approach someone drowning." I just couldn't comprehend it all. Did the beer cloud Billy's judgment when he swam to rescue John? Probably. His lifeguard training and experience knew better. But the emotion of being fearful for the life of your best friend surely overtook him. Maybe. Or a panicked John grabbed the first thing he could and that happened to be Billy. Although they were teen males, I had never seen either of them drink beer or any alcohol! Either way, both drowned. In less than a few minutes.

When I got home, I sat on the stairs in the rear stairwell between our basement apartment and the first-floor apartment. I could go no further. And I cried. I cried like I never had before. I cried my eyes out. Uncontrollably. My stomach even felt the pain of it all. Finally, the first-floor neighbor, who

I didn't know very well, came out and asked if I was okay. Obviously, I wasn't. I explained the reason for my sorrow and she said some few words of comfort. I was crying so hard; she offered me a glass of water to catch my breath and I took it. Drinking it, I couldn't also cry at the same time, and I began to settle down. It may not seem like much, but she knew it was all she could do to add this consoling offering to her kind words of sympathy. It helped me a lot and was just the human compassion I needed at that moment. I was always thankful for that kindness from her. I finally went downstairs to my Denver home. Inconsolable is all I can describe of my state.

But strangely, I remembered a newspaper article I'd read the day before. The details are fuzzy now, but it was about someone losing a best friend in a boat drowning that weekend. But this person was an only child, and I remember how sorry I felt for them not having a brother. Now, all of a sudden, I felt great gratitude toward God that He had given me a brother—a wonderful loving brother. I'd had something many didn't have: a brother I treasured for his loving concern for his socially backward sister. And this thanksgiving gave me comfort somewhat. An everlasting comfort.

When Perry arrived home, I told him the bad news. He was equally shocked. He comforted me as best he could.

CHAPTER THIRTY-THREE

Go Home

I wanted to get home to Minneapolis as quickly as I could. I knew the pain that must be gripping M'Deah. Hadn't I heard her say to Mary Jane how much she loved her children? Now, her baby who was her only son was gone. What could I do to help? I have no idea. But I've gotta be there. To do the best I can. I don't remember when or how, but I booked a flight home for the next morning. It was my very first flight ever. Perry had never flown at this time and was reluctant to start now. We agreed he'd come by train as soon as possible, after getting permission for a leave from the Army.

(Home is the term I use for where we lived in Denver. But home is also wherever we grow up in and come from. Home for me was still also wherever M'Deah was.)

I left and went straight to M'Deah after I was picked up from the airport. She was being as stoic as she could, but I knew the great pain she felt. Mr. Steele was with M'Deah. A few families and friends had come to offer condolences. I heard some of them complaining about Mr. Steele, saying that he wouldn't allow them to hug M'Deah. He tried to explain it would make her feel worse. To them it was just his strange behavior at the time. But I understood what he was doing and why. It still brought painful memories of that childhood snake incident, and she didn't like being hugged. That was no comfort at all, and he knew that and was trying to protect her—maybe not tactfully but effectively. I don't remember what M'Deah and I said to each other. I thought she was handling everything very well. Everything else was just a blur. I tried to be stoic too, for her sake. I had wondered, but it was decades before I learned that she had taken Valium in order to get through it all. It was the only way she could make it through this horrific time.

I got more details now. As said, Billy and John went on a fishing trip with John's mother. Viola had bought beer for them all to drink. At some point, John threw the anchor into the water from the boat. The anchor rope caught his ankle and pulled John into the water. He began to drown. Billy, safe in the boat but an experienced lifeguard, jumped in the lake to save him. Somehow, he must have reached John from a bad angle and John grabbed him in desperation. I don't believe Billy would have forgotten how he was to approach a drowning man from the rear. When he reached him, John grabbed fast ahold of Billy and they both began to drown. Viola saw what happened from the shore but could do nothing. Fishermen in another boat saw what happened and rowed quickly toward them. Sadly, John and Billy both drowned before they could be rescued.

The police/sheriff investigation revealed that this group of three had consumed one 6-pack of beer. Then Mrs. Nichols had bought them another one.

CHAPTER THIRTY-THREE

M'Deah was devastated, of course. She was angry with Viola for buying beer for them all to drink—something M'Deah would never have done and knew nothing about. I do know that M'Deah held Viola responsible for the drownings. Two young men had their judgment impaired by alcohol in a dangerous situation. But for that beer, they would have lived. Viola chose that day to be what she thought was their friend, and not their mother. To their great harm.

It all happened two weeks after their high school graduation and two weeks before Billy's 18th birthday. What must Mrs. Nichols have felt as she watched helplessly from shore? Even through the hours it took for their bodies to be recovered late that night? That consideration didn't penetrate our grief.

M'Deah made alone all the funeral arrangements for Billy. Considerately, she didn't involve me at all. I would have been of no help to her. I'm sure Mr. Steele was a help and a comfort to her.

Great Sorrow

The next day was the viewing at the funeral home. I went but thought I'd be okay and said so when others questioned me. I'd been to funerals before. I'd been fine at my father's funeral and only cried when I saw M'Deah crying graveside. But I think that was it. I would be okay because I had to be strong for M'Deah. And I had already cried tons of tears in Denver. How could I have any more tears left? Ruby stayed with me constantly and was of great comfort. At the funeral home, M'Deah and Mr. Steele stayed in an adjacent room. Several of the large group of teens were crying—and the adults. It was touching but not unexpected. The funeral home was very crowded as I prepared to enter the room that held the casket. I had never seen so many teenagers before—from Minneapolis and from St. Paul. I knew very few of them and thought how well-liked Billy had been. Ruby was with me, thankfully. She had mercifully assigned herself to watch over me. Juanita was there too. But when I entered the viewing room and saw my beloved Billy lying so still in the casket, I totally lost it. I cried tears I didn't even know I had. I heard wailing come from me that I didn't know existed. I nearly collapsed. I don't know what I would have done if Ruby hadn't been with me. For now, she was my strength. I had cried unbelievably deep tears on the steps at home after Auntie told me of Billy's drowning. But this was that and more. There were more deep tears now than in all my life.

All stoicism vanished, as I wept uncontrollably for a long time. Others tried to console me as best they could, being mindful that I was halfway through my pregnancy, but it only ended when I was just too exhausted to cry anymore. I do remember that M'Deah did not try to comfort me at all. She had her own deep grief to contend with. We cried separately. It was a very hard trial for us both. I couldn't imagine what she was going through.

CHAPTER THIRTY-THREE

I thought of the things Billy would never be able to do. I thought of his many loving kindnesses to me over his lifetime. I thought of the dear friends we had become as he lovingly rescued me from my geek-dom and from my non-existent social status. I thought of him never meeting the child I now carried—his expected niece or nephew. I thought of me never having a brother for the rest of my life. I thought of the senseless loss on so many levels.

Billy: I think the funeral was the next day. But I don't remember it, nor do I remember going to the cemetery for Billy's burial. It's a vivid blur in my memory that I only saw the very long cortege of cars in line for the drive to the cemetery. Billy was truly shown much honor and much love. And rightly so. But Billy and John were so much together in life that it didn't seem right that they were now separated at death.

(Decades later I learned that Emeal Jackson had been one of his stepbrother's pallbearers. I was surprised but glad he still had some regard for us. There wasn't as much hate there as the enemy wanted him to have.)

John: John was Catholic, so their funerals were separate. Someone made the decision that I shouldn't go to another viewing or funeral and that it was too much for me in my pregnancy. I wanted to go but couldn't. I was just out of it. John was like my brother too. But I didn't go. Neither did M'Deah. I know we both loved John. But there would be no way we could avoid an encounter at his funeral with the one person we wanted to avoid: Viola Nichols. She was a very emotional person. I don't think either of us knew how we would handle that. We each said our own private farewells to John. He knows. But, more than that, we just couldn't take any more grief. It was all so overwhelming. While we knew Viola's loss was great, we just had no comfort to give her. I don't think any of our family attended John's funeral because they never spoke of it.

I don't know what became of John's mother, Viola. She had bought them lots of beer to drink on this fishing trip. That impaired their judgment, no doubt. Viola was a twin, but I don't think she and her sister were close. Viola was also thought to be emotionally fragile. I don't remember that she survived well without John. He was her only child. They were inseparable. Handling the guilt of it all could not have been easy for her. She loved them both. M'Deah told me that she passed a few years later. Sadly, and alone, I think.

And More

I do know Billy and John had some of the largest funerals in the Minneapolis/St. Paul area. Nearly every black teen was in attendance at both funerals. Billy and John were inseparable—with their families. Again, the corteges to the cemeteries were very long.

CHAPTER THIRTY-THREE

I truly believed I would see Billy and John again—in Heaven. But for now, all I had was profound grief at missing them, especially Billy. It was a grief that would last for years, every time I spoke of what had happened to him. Until God removed the pain when I met Him in salvation.

Again, I had wondered for a long time but learned years later how M'Deah had been able to hold up through this whole ordeal. She said she took sedatives given her by hospital medical staff. She knew she needed help to be able to get through all that lay ahead of her. She had meds and the help of her God. Job well done.

M'Deah told me later that on the day of the drowning, Billy had cleaned the house and done absolutely every chore she needed done around the house. He asked if there was anything else before he had to leave for the fishing trip. Nothing. As he drove around the corner from the house, he looked back and waved good-bye to her. The last good-bye. Of course, her thought later was "If only I could have thought of something else that needed doing..."

M'Deah also told me later that Billy had been contemplating joining the Catholic Church shortly before the accident. We didn't know how far he had progressed in the process, but we didn't think it was completed. I prayed that I would see both Billy and John again in Heaven. And I believe that I will. Thank You, Lord.

M'Deah said Billy had also signed up to join the Marines after graduating from high school two weeks earlier. He even had a photo taken by them of him being in uniform. I have it and I'm so Godly-proud of him.

M'Deah was 43 years old when Billy went Home. She would be without him for another 43 years or so. I was 20 years old.

My brother, Billy, and his best friend (John Nichols) brought me out of my shell of VERY low social self-esteem—it was a part of my life that had been stunted. I am incredibly grateful for Billy and John in my life as blessed gifts of God. I knew I was a socially inept nerd of sorts. They gave me hope to be better—and an opportunity. They rescued me from that condition, somewhat. I don't know how I would have been without them. They made it possible for me to truly be the woman I became and to realize who I was as a woman. It was impossible without them. I, for one, can answer the current question in our culture of "What is a woman?" So can most of my and M'Deah's generation. Billy and John have no mark or monument in history for feats of invention or discovery. But what they did for me was crucial—part of God's Plan. Who I became affected my children and lineage. Thanks, guys—I thank God for you. And I remember my favorite Christmas—fondly celebrated with you both.

When they were gone, I had "no man to put me in the pool" so I could be further healed. (John 5:7)

CHAPTER THIRTY-THREE

GOD wanted to be that Man for me, but I didn't know that then nor did I know how to let Him do so. My concept of fairy tales came to an end. Billy and John had made me a princess, but I never went to the ball.

Perry had taken the train to Minneapolis and missed both funerals. I remember wishing he'd been there to comfort me at this most devastating time of my life. But fear is fear. I didn't need him with me if he was gripped by fear. That's no help at all. And I remembered I had never met HIS mother—she died in his last year of high school. Understandably, funerals were hard for him. So, I understood. He had never flown before, and he hadn't yet dealt with his fear of flying. That he would do later. His fear turned into loving to fly. But not yet. My example and words of assurance helped him a lot though, I believe. At the end of our time in Minneapolis, we flew back to Denver together. Perry never feared flying again and did it many times later.

When we left for Denver, I was glad M'Deah had Mr. Steele and would not be alone now with Billy gone. She had a husband to rebuild her life with.

Some months later, M'Deah had a visit from Billy's last girlfriend. She said she'd had his baby, a daughter, and wanted her to know. When M'Deah shared this news with me, I thought she would have been happy about it. Maybe she was. But she seemed strangely calm and nonplussed about it. I think she had a wait-and-see attitude, wondering what requests might follow. And because she wasn't excited, I was calm about it too. Though I asked M'Deah, I don't even remember the baby's name. And I've forgotten the girlfriend's name too.

A Look Back

As I enjoyed the loving relationship of a new marriage, I sometimes wondered more about M'Deah's marriage to K.C. How could she possibly have had any joy at all being a domestic violence victim who could deliberately and viciously be given pain at any moment for no reason by someone who is supposedly a loved one? That would be torment and not pleasure! How could the abuser expect any pleasure by the one they beat to enjoy the act of married love? How does that compute? I don't get it at all. It makes zero sense. Sex not about love is sex with violence. That's the only way I can see it. What kind of married life is that? I can't comprehend marriage without love. I know that's the reality of some, even where domestic violence is not involved at all. But I can't comprehend living that kind of life voluntarily. It would be impossible for many—including me. Impossible to have any real affection, attraction, or enjoyment of married intimacy from an abuser. What should have been married pleasure becomes merely a chore or duty with no real joy. For years. Intolerable. Sigh.

In Denver, Perry and I got a phone and service immediately. We were NEVER without a phone after

CHAPTER THIRTY-THREE

that. Pretty much everyone—then and now—knows how important they are. As evidence, cellphones have exploded in popularity and commonality—all over the world. They are not a luxury but a necessity. Especially now that our little immediate family of three had suddenly now become a family of two: M'Deah and me.

CHAPTER THIRTY-FOUR

My Life Goes On

Yes, Perry and I got a phone and service immediately. And I trusted that I had left M'Deah safely and happily in her still-new marriage to Mr. Steele.

Back in Denver, I re-read a recent letter that Billy had written me about two weeks earlier. He told me that he and John were planning a trip to visit me in Denver that Summer and that he was really looking forward to becoming an uncle. Because we had been together our whole lives, this was my first letter from my brother. And my last—my only. I was happy to get it. But I remember also my inner unspoken criticism that his English grammar skills weren't as good as mine. How petty! It was a loving and precious letter that I still have and will always keep.

I continued to have lots of questions, of course. The most common one was, "Why?". Why did Billy drown, being so much at home in and on the water? Why was the best of the two of us now gone? I was smart, yes. But that had limitations. Billy was so much more than that. He had an amazing future before him. And so on and so on. My brother provoked me to be a better person overall—and a better daughter to our mother.

CHAPTER THIRTY-FOUR

I wish I'd had more time to get to know this wonderful person who I was blessed to have as my brother. And to know John better too. John was more than just another teenager Billy met in high school. He was his best friend/mentor/brother. And my friend and mentor too. He rescued us both in many ways. We both needed John in our lives—very badly. And God sent him to us. Thanks, Lord!

As a newly married couple, I've told you our first home was a Denver small apartment. It was one of two units on the top floor of an older small house. It was really just a bedroom with a shared bathroom and a shared kitchen. That's all. It fit our Army income though. The other couple there on the top floor was also a black newlywed Fitzsimons Army couple in an apartment the same size as ours. They were from California. They were there first and she had an established routine for cooking, etc. So, I adjusted my kitchen time to not interfere with hers. It was our first home together for both couples and we were happy there. Being small, it didn't require a lot of house-cleaning! Both wives got pregnant around the same time, and she gave birth about a week before I did. But by then, we had moved.

Unforgettable here it was that I lost my wedding ring! I had been told by my Army doctors that I was not allowed to gain more than 20 pounds during my pregnancy—or I would be assigned to complete bed rest. I didn't want that, so I complied. Somehow my fingers changed in size though. Washing my hands one day in the shared bathroom, my wedding ring simply slipped off my finger. Not landing on the floor, it fell into the floor grate that led to the furnace room in the basement. Devastated, I told Perry, and we called the landlord to ask if he could have a plumber look into the furnace before it burned up my ring. No. Oh. We had to accept the permanent loss of my ring. I was saddened and foolishly wondered if it were some omen about our marriage. When would Perry be able to get me another one? It would be no time soon. I also didn't like being pregnant in public without a wedding ring! What would people think?

When I told M'Deah what had happened, she did something totally unexpected. In her shopping at rummage sales/garage sales/thrift stores/etc. she sometimes bought old jewelry she admired that was very inexpensive. She had bought a couple of old gold wedding bands. She sent them to me through the mail. One had someone's initials engraved inside but I didn't care. I once again had a wedding ring and quickly began to wear it for the rest of our marriage. That was M'Deah—utterly kind, loving, and considerate.

Our Second Home

Pregnancy meant we needed someplace bigger though. Perry was able to find another furnished

CHAPTER THIRTY-FOUR

place where we had our own bathroom and kitchen in a basement apartment. It was here that our neighbor was so kind to me at Billy's death. But it was still too small for a baby. We didn't remain there long after the tragedy.

Our Third Home

Next, Perry got another better furnished basement apartment. It was luxurious compared to our other apartments! It had two bedrooms, a living room, an eat-in kitchen, and our own bathroom with space for a wringer washing machine—which I bought used. It was perfect for us then! We had good neighbors again too. She went to church, and I accepted her invitation to attend one Sunday when they had baby christening. We were still trying to decide on a baby name, so this interested me greatly. One of the babies was christened Ezekiel Hezekiah. No! That was not the name I was looking for! (And all these moves happened in the space of 21 months in Denver!)

Our First Anniversary

I had fantasized earlier and briefly about what a special occasion this would be. And it was. But it couldn't be marked by any huge celebration. We were too poor, and I was too pregnant for that! But we certainly did rejoice at being together with our new baby on the way. Grab happiness where you can!

A New Post?

A few months later, (in the Fall) Perry got notice that the Army was sending him to South Korea in a few weeks. I had to quit my job and prepare to go home to Minneapolis. Before I left, the office gave me a baby shower and many gifts. Just before his departure date, it was all canceled: he would NOT be sent to South Korea but was to remain at Fitzsimons! Thankfully, I was able to cancel my job resignation and stay there longer! Whew!

Our Second Thanksgiving

For the first one, Perry and I were separated by Army Boot Camp training. This was a holiday that had always meant a lot to me growing up. But this one was to be quite different! We didn't have the money to buy all the usual holiday fixins' and I was 8 months pregnant. We were away from home and family. What to do? We chose to eat our Thanksgiving dinner at the local Woolworth's five-and-dime store. It wasn't much but we were happy with it. It still met the description of a Thanksgiving dinner: turkey, dressing, and mashed potatoes with a green vegetable, cranberry sauce, and a roll. It was still a special occasion, and we had much to be thankful for. I don't remember the cost, but we could afford this dining out on our limited income. We were happy. The birth of our first child was just a few short weeks away.

CHAPTER THIRTY-FOUR

Farewell

I did finally quit my job about a week before my due date of December 11. I told them I would not be returning to the job afterwards. I had no one to provide childcare and would be caring for my own child. How long? I thought it would be long-term. No parting baby shower was needed—I'd already had that!

CHAPTER THIRTY-FIVE
Childbirth #1

I thought nine months would go by fast—and it did. Meanwhile, I kept working. I soon needed to buy maternity clothes. Remember those? There was planning to do, doctor's appointments to keep, nursery room preparation, etc. Again, Army doctors then allowed a weight gain of 20 pounds. When I reached that point, I was told I couldn't gain any more or I would be ordered on bed rest. We couldn't afford that loss of income! We still had baby things to buy! I don't know how it happened, but I gained no more weight than was allowed.

My thinking about preparation was so different from Perry's. I thought "get ready now". He thought "'there's plenty of time". I couldn't change his mind. So, I did the preparatory things. Spending money on Todd was my only vital concession. I got the best baby crib and crib bedding that we could afford. I bought a used chest for Todd's clothes. Etc. Scrimp where you can. Because you must. Much later, Perry helped me put the crib together, I bought an outfit to bring the baby home in, I bought a baby-carrier (fragile things we think them to be now), I bought a

CHAPTER THIRTY-FIVE

gentle detergent for washing the baby's diapers and clothes, I bought a high chair for feedings, I bought glass bottles and cleaning brushes, I bought teething rings, I bought a potty-chair, I bought a toddler stepping stool, etc. (One thing I did NOT buy: a baby pacifier. I didn't believe in them and thought them cruel—teasing a baby with the promise of milk you knew wasn't coming to them!) Now, I was ready!
I did wonder for a while if I'd have twins though. M'Deah had twin aunts, she was a twin, and she had stillborn twins early in her marriage to K.C. There was a definite possibility! But as the months went by, doctors continued to hear only one heartbeat—it didn't happen.

The one huge decision we had to make was the baby's name! We wrestled with that, and Perry finally suggested "Todd". That was the name of one TV character on a show we enjoyed, "Route 66". I liked it too and we were in agreement! But what about a middle name? That took longer. I suggested it be something in Billy's name, to honor him. Maybe "Mitchell"? Perry was opposed to that. Finally, we settled on something mild/plain: Alan. There's another reason for the final choices we made. I had initially wanted the first name to be "Scott", a name I liked. But I had a picture of our son being a successful businessman with a briefcase bearing the initials SAP. We couldn't have that! Yes, "TAP" would be better!

CHILDBIRTH #1

The baby was due early-to-mid December 1961. Early that Monday morning around 4:00 a.m., I was awakened by feeling something wet in the bed. I somehow knew my water had broken and woke Perry to let him know it's time to go to the hospital. We got dressed and left just before sunrise. The weather was dry and cold, with snow covering the ground. I walked gingerly. At some point before Todd was born, we were able to buy a used car that worked well. I was glad to have it now. At the hospital, I was placed and got settled in my room. Occasionally, I would hear a woman scream in pain. I had none. I thought, "Surely, it can't be that bad and I won't scream like that!" I didn't know that my labor had not started. And it didn't. The next day went by and my blood pressure occasionally spiked, so it was monitored regularly. I also had regular exams to see if I had made any progress. Nope. At one such exam, I flinched when a doctor put his stethoscope on my abdomen. He yelled at me that he knew that didn't hurt me. My reply? "I agree—but I can still feel hot and cold and that's COLD—you've obviously just come in from outside!" He looked sheepish as he admitted he had just come inside, warmed the stethoscope between his fingers, and apologized before beginning the exam again. Just think, people! I had occasional minor pains but only a little cervix opening. The decision was made to induce my labor—and my hard labor began. I heard someone

CHAPTER THIRTY-FIVE

screaming loudly and realized it was me! Repeatedly! It was awful. (When I had asked a pregnant co-worker who gave birth a couple of months before me about her experience, she described it as like passing a watermelon-sized bowel movement! It was something big coming out of a hole much too small for it. I had never heard anything like that and didn't believe her then, but now I understood.) Induction gets the process going, but it's not a fun process.

    The Army had begun something new with childbirth at that time: an epidural. I had read a few things about it in the news—good and bad. It was a fairly new technique. I knew there was a risk of paralysis, excess bleeding, etc. When they asked if I wanted one and described it to me, I agreed. It was then my labor was induced. Why did I agree to an epidural? Because I thought I would not only have a pain-free delivery, but I would be conscious—fully awake to be sure the baby that came out of me was the same baby brought to me later. In childhood, I had read too many news stories of women being given the wrong baby to take home and I didn't want that to happen to me! I had to be the conscious one, because fathers weren't allowed in delivery rooms then and Perry wouldn't have the opportunity to know this about the baby. Besides, Perry was on duty and at work elsewhere in the hospital while I was in labor. I had no problems with the epidural and don't regret it. I finally had a beautiful baby boy. As he grew, he

CHILDBIRTH #1

reminded me of Billy: a handsome fastidious fashion plate and a genuinely good person.

There was something else newly available for mothers to be informed of. It was a contraceptive pill that never existed before. Military families were offered it first. My take? Because it's new and much is still unknown about it, I'll wait. Though we didn't like it, I'll stick with the cumbersome heavy plastic diaphragm that was offered for now. I remembered the recent thalidomide debacle. A drug given to alleviate morning sickness had produced many deformed babies. Women were flying all over the world to get abortions before these babies could be born. And the drug had first been given to military wives. So, this new drug? No, thank you. I'll wait. There were some later issues with it and I never regretted my decision.

Knowing no one I trusted to babysit Todd, I kept him myself. Our time in the Army was somewhat strange. The main thing I remember about it was feeling poor for the first time in my life! You had to be careful not to have any month left over after the money was gone. We lived near the mountains of Colorado, and I would love to have traveled there. But gas cost money—which we never seemed to have enough of. Going to a movie on base was 25 cents each but usually unaffordable when you factored in costs for gas, popcorn, babysitter—out of the question for our tiny budget. And I did my own hair for the first time in my life. Hairdresser trips cost money—money

CHAPTER THIRTY-FIVE

that I didn't have. Army spousal allotment checks only go so far. Sadly. I read accounts now that it's only gotten worse. Many military families need food stamps to survive. That's a shame for our nation.

Another thing happened to me then. I began to very slowly gain weight. Why? In my teens it was due to stress in a dysfunctional family environment. Add to that was that M'Deah was a great cook and we had lots of food available at home to enjoy but not to waste. Now I began to think that maybe I was lonely! My school friends were only in that setting. I went shopping or to the movies with none of them. My neighborhood friends were back in my Minneapolis neighborhood. My cousin-friends were likewise back in Minneapolis. My Denver work friends were white, and we didn't socialize. Basically, I had no Denver friends—just acquaintances. I was away from home for the first time in my life and I was homesick. Food was again a comfort. We didn't have a lot, but I could cook from scratch and looked up recipes for old favorites. They were too often for sweets—oatmeal or chocolate chip cookies with raisins or nuts, etc. They were indeed a comfort—except for the added pounds! Thankfully, there weren't a lot, though noticeable.

Of course, I chose Ruby to be Todd's Godmother. We didn't make it official in any church service. Ruby was very much a nonfunctioning Godmother though. There were no gifts, no advice, etc. I hope she prayed for him though. Todd survived all the

CHILDBIRTH #1

neglect—no problem. He got lots of prayers from his grandmother, for which I am forever grateful. They are still being answered. (Sadly, I later became a non-functioning Godmother to other children.)

CHAPTER THIRTY-SIX

Our Interim Life

U OF NM

Perry was drafted just before we got married in October 1960. He served only 21 months in the Army, rather than the normal two years—or 24 months. Why? He got a 3-month early-out Army discharge because he had gotten a basketball scholarship to attend the University of New Mexico in Albuquerque. Perry really wanted this opportunity to see where his considerable basketball skills and his love for the sport could take him. So, we sold all the furniture we had bought—it was mostly things for the baby. I packed our remaining household goods and shipped them to D.C. via REA—the famous Railway Express Agency that was commonly used then by the Army. Don't worry if you haven't heard of it. REA was a national package delivery service that operated in the United States from 1918 to 1975. The Army had already booked Perry's flight to New Mexico. Then I booked a one-way flight from Denver to Minneapolis for Todd and me.

Back To Minneapolis

I moved back home to work and to save money for our next move in life. Todd and I went to live with M'Deah and Mr. Steele in the neighborhood of Four Corners where they now lived. It was an old neighborhood they'd moved after selling the house on Logan. And while the freeway duplex house they'd bought was being moved and set up on its new foundation. (Family thought M'Deah was being foolish in this decision, but she was being wise and bold—unafraid of the future.) Their plan was to invest in other properties, and they did so successfully. For me, there was never any doubt where I would go to live. I always knew I could always go back home—M'Deah had made it clear without spoken words. I quickly got my old job back as a Page with the Minneapolis Public Library Circulation Department, where I had worked after high school graduation—and begun in the Camden branch during high school. I think I now gave M'Deah $20 weekly for room and board for the two of us. I was still making the princely take-home pay of $62 every two weeks.

(From the beginning of my work life to the end, I regarded my coworkers as another family—maybe to an only slighter lesser degree. I was very genuinely interested in them and their lives. I cared about them. As I did my school classmates.)

I often walked to and from work. It was only about a mile away. My walking to and from Henry

CHAPTER THIRTY-SIX

had prepared me for this little walk. Enroute there was a potato chip plant. I had seen it only a few times before in my teens when I rode past it on the public bus. There was a big, long window where you could stand on the sidewalk and watch the process. I certainly didn't understand it all, but it was fun watching the potato chips ride down the conveyor belt. A coworker lived nearby named Vivian. This was not an affluent neighborhood but an older poorer one with a bad reputation. It was totally safe though. Minneapolis was not crime infested back then. Vivian was a middle-aged single American Indian woman who had come to Minneapolis with her family from the reservation in northern Minnesota. I didn't learn much if anything about her time and culture there. Most Indians were still looked down upon even then and were pretty private. She was one of the nicest and sharpest coworkers I ever knew.

I was blessed that M'Deah kept Todd while I worked, even though she worked too. She knew how to handle things to get them done! Once, Todd was not his usual pleasant self. He became cranky, played less, drank less from his bottle, and sometimes pulled at his ear. His clueless mother thought he was just teething. M'Deah had to tell me that I needed to take him to the doctor. I did and was told he had a serious throat and ear infection! I cried at the needless suffering he'd gone through. I promised myself I would never play doctor with my child's health again. And I didn't.

OUR INTERIM LIFE

Perry and I were looking at a temporary long-term separation while he completed work to get his degree. But we were okay with that—it was for our future benefit and he would come to be with me as often as he could. But that's not how it turned out! Perry didn't like being one of the very few black students there and he missed his family. He left after just a few months—dropped out and gave up his scholarship. He wanted to start his preferred career as a police officer and get his family settled down instead. I was surprised and yet not surprised. I had gotten my old job back but gave it up for our future together.

CHAPTER THIRTY-SEVEN

What's Going On With M'Deah?

I didn't know how hard these years were for M'Deah at the beginning. She had peace from the absence of K.C. in her life. Freed from that great bondage, she was free to mature and make better choices. She was far more relaxed, and I dare say she was happy. But unknown to me at the time there were many financial struggles before she remarried. I was oblivious and had more growing up to do. In my experience, M'Deah could successfully handle anything. So, of course, she knew how to handle the challenges unknown to me. Thankfully, all this changed for her.

She had married Mr. Steele. They were wed by a Justice of the Peace in Iowa—where there was no waiting period for blood tests that some states required. Come on down and get married quickly! (I learned that's how M'Deah did all her three adult marriages. She never had a bridal shower, wedding, reception, honeymoon—none of the usual marriage trappings. None.) They had both grown up in rural areas and were familiar with farming/gardening. They rented a vacant lot in St. Paul and always had a big flourishing garden there as well as in their own backyard. They were both generous in sharing garden produce with others.

M'Deah took on a small project for herself after Billy was gone. She did photo albums separately of her two kids. I always enjoyed looking at them on my home visits. Later, she gave them to me. I consider them valuable family heirlooms.

And she continued thrift shopping as well. Sometimes it was with her sisters. Sometimes it was done alone. I have many of the crystal pieces and other things she bought.

M'Deah's Moves

M'Deah continued being a saved M'Deah. Once an alcoholic tenant of my mother's and Mr. Steele's had death in his family of someone who lived in the South. He had no means of being able to have funds to travel there or even for personal clean-up and new clothes for the occasion. M'Deah prayed for funds to become available, contributing some of her own funds, and prayed for his alcoholic condition to end. Both prayers were answered. And he also got saved— life-changing! There were prayers for restored relationships. There were prayers for healing. She prayed a lot of prayers for people, and they were ALL miraculously answered. She would share some of these experiences with me and I was greatly encouraged to know this Amazing God of hers.

CHAPTER THIRTY-SEVEN

M'Deah never saw people as merely tenants or as lesser vessels. She saw them as people created by God, just as she was, and thus of great value. That is rare for anyone at any period of time. May their tribe increase!

I once thought myself an intellectual superior and judged others by their intellectual prowess. Thank God that He didn't leave me helpless in this great ignorance! M'Deah knew and modeled for me the value of ALL people. Even the lowliest drunk had value in her eyes. This became a Truth that was never absent from my mind and life. Marvelous. Actually, this reality had been lived before her by her parents. They would always feed the destitute who came to their home during the Great Depression... and before and afterwards. Descendants of slaves often valued others as their ancestors had NOT been honored for being humans too.

Gratefully, M'Deah and Mr. Steele prospered greatly with all their hard work and investments. I was so grateful that she experienced prosperity without domestic violence.

What Else?

As I said, M'Deah became a born-again Christian sometime in the early 1970s when she was in her 50's. She accepted Jesus into her life as her personal Lord and Savior. It was as a result of her own desire to know God, influenced by some few Christian acquaintances. By this time, I had married and was living in Denver with my new husband. I didn't know all that led up to this life-changing conversion. She was married to Edgar Steele now and he had some background and interest in Christianity. But I think it was mostly cultural rather than personal. A friend of hers also had gotten saved, was praying for her salvation, and was witnessing to her of Jesus. (This friend, Mary, would later become a precious daily prayer partner with M'Deah.) What God used to draw M'Deah to Him, I don't know. Maybe it was her life history experiences. Maybe it was a desire for something better—a hunger for Him. Definitely it was from prayers—from those who knew her personally and from those who just saw the news story. I don't know who all the former were. Maybe it was coworkers or some church members. And Mr. Steele had some influence in this regard too. So did the Carlsons.

M'Deah also wrote/told me of someone named "Sister Goode". She was a traveling evangelist. M'Deah invited her to stay in her home while Sister Goode was on a mission trip to M'Deah's church in Minneapolis. I have no idea how that came about. I only know the fruit of all these seeds planted was salvation for M'Deah. In His perfect timing. She and M'Deah talked lots about the Lord. M'Deah saw prayers answered, and miracles performed. It all led to salvation for her and her new husband. M'Deah would speak to me of her but it was all new and

CHAPTER THIRTY-SEVEN

strange to me. M'Deah wrote me of this new change too, and I could sense her happiness about her new decision.

My attitude? I thought it was probably a good thing so that she would have some peace in her old age (based on her being older than I was!), knowing that she would go to Heaven when she died. She would see Billy again there. And if it gave her peace and comfort along the way, that was fine. And maybe she wouldn't be lonely in the absence of her children. But I really didn't yet know what the terms salvation or born-again meant. I was just glad on her behalf. I only remember thinking, "How good for her—she's getting old, and this will be a comfort to her after all she's been through!" How condescending and how little did I know!

M'Deah's life changed significantly after her conversion. The Lord used her naturally bold nature to behave as someone with what another saved friend, Sister Mullins, called "reckless faith". The two of them became prayer partners and were very effective in the Kingdom of God. They saw MANY answers to prayer.

The Effect

But this new life of hers affected me too. A lot. Her faith was remarkable. It seemed her prayers were ALWAYS answered! I could confidently ask her to pray about anything of concern to me. And the

Lord would come through on my behalf! Remarkable. Once, I asked for prayer for some issue regarding the children—probably their health. They were plagued every winter with colds, sore throats, and infected ears. When she finished praying on the phone, she asked me if I believed the prayer would be answered. My reply was, "I hope so". She quickly corrected me. "If you're gonna pray, don't worry. If you're gonna worry, don't pray. The two do NOT go together!" Oh. It seems so simple! My mind was changed, and I didn't do that again! What M'Deah's prayers taught me was that God cares for us, hears and answers our prayers. We are blessed to have such a God Who is for us and not against us.

Not only that, but her prayers on behalf of herself and of others were answered as well. Impressive. She would pray for jobs to come through for people—and they would manifest. One such prayer was on behalf of McCary, that same double-cousin I had rescued from drowning in childhood. He wanted to become a firefighter but was concerned his light weight wouldn't qualify him, etc. But he got the job which eventually led to him making history by becoming the first black fire chief in Minneapolis! There were myriads of such instances of answered prayer. All to the glory of God.

M'Deah and I had always communicated by letters and by phone calls. Her generation wrote letters. I learned that from her, as a practice. Her handwriting

CHAPTER THIRTY-SEVEN

was beautiful. Her letters to me began to include Bible verses. I would generally read them once only. I don't remember them, but she was planting seeds that would bear fruit later.

Negative Family

During this time, M'Deah learned of the harm caused by tobacco smoking—including the dangers of second-hand smoke. She posted a sign near the entry of her duplex home, denying it was OKAY to smoke in her house. Formerly, she had always customarily gifted smokers in the family with a carton of cigarettes at Christmas or birthdays. My Uncle Tommy was a regular recipient. So was Uncle Robert and James. And I remember growing up that we always had ash trays in our home for guests to use. It was the cultural norm. Now all of that has changed. Some people were understanding, as more and more information came out publicly about this danger. But other close family members saw M'Deah's new behavior as extremely discourteous—and loudly told her and told each other so. They meanly tried to give her a bad reputation and were very critical of her. M'Deah didn't fit THEIR definition of what it meant to be a Christian. It wasn't easy for M'Deah either. They judged her in other ways too. But she didn't budge from her beliefs. I admired her brave and kind stance!

Miracles

Once, M'Deah and her prayer partner, Sis. Mullins, learned that their pastor was in great need. He and all of his immediate family (wife and three kids) had come down with very bad cases of flu. They were all bed-ridden, unable to care for themselves, and had no one to help them. Learning of this, M'Deah and Sister Mullins went to visit them to assess the situation. Things were bad. There was NO food in the house, no one to cook it if they'd had any. So, M'Deah and Sis. Mullins prayed and were told by the Lord to get groceries for the family—it was a priority. So, they set off to the supermarket to provide for them out of their own finances. But, between the two of them they didn't have much money on hand. But M'Deah said the Lord led them to shop as though they did and to get everything they thought the family needed to recover and more. They ended up with three grocery carts of food and other resources the family needed. Confident that God would help them, M'Deah spoke to the store manager. She explained the nature of their shopping trip and she asked to use the store announcement system to request other willing shoppers to help in their cause. Surprisingly, he agreed! M'Deah made the announcement on the store P.A. system and other shoppers gladly and generously flooded them with donations. They had enough money to complete their missionary task! Needless to say, the pastor and his family were extremely grateful for this act of love. They now had plenty of food and other provisions to aid in their complete recovery. But M'Deah and Sis. Mullins didn't just deliver the food and leave. They cooked meals enough to last the week, cleaned the house, gave them bedside baths, and prayed for their healing from sickness, etc. Sister Mullins told M'Deah, "Steele, you have strong faith—reckless faith!" It was because M'Deah had prayed before they shopped, telling the Lord she'd serve Him no more if He didn't undertake for this family—and He sure did! God is Faithful to His Word. I found it all very impressive as M'Deah told me about it later. And I never forgot it. They were Godly people who served in words AND in deeds. Was this what it meant to live a real Christian life? It certainly seemed like it to me.

The Dream

Once M'Deah had a dream she shared with me. She was in a casket and visitors passed by to view the body. I came with my family too. Todd asked me, "Who is that?" I had to explain who she was. Shocked after waking, M'Deah purposed in her heart that she did NOT want Todd to grow up and to not know his grandmother! It wasn't always possible for my whole family to go back home to visit. But I always made a way for Todd to visit his grandmother every Summer. Todd loved these visits where his grandmother lavished him with love and whatever else he needed. She was happy to have this time with her only grandchild who was such a great kid. For transport, I used Northwest Airlines which was based in Minneapolis. The airlines were remarkably efficient and responsible at that time to assist children flying alone. He was always cared for by the kind hospitable stewardesses and it was a safe way for children to travel alone. He always got a set of "pilot's wings" each time. I was grateful and confident in doing this—it was never a problem to comfortably rely on this method of travel for Todd. And because I was at ease with it, he was too. Sadly, that is not the case today. It now involves great risks for children to fly unaccompanied. I usually came to Minneapolis at the end of the Summer to get Todd and bring him back home.

(M'Deah had other dreams too. One was about seeing Closed signs on many banks—reminiscent of the Great Depression days. Or the later crashing of the entire Savings and Loan industry. Another one was about seeing Closed signs on many schools. That puzzled her until I later explained that perhaps abortion would likely decrease the number of children alive to even attend school. Both of these dreams seemed prophetic, but neither of us could have imagined the later reality they foretold.)

My Visits Home

Whenever I visited Minneapolis I looked forward to being with M'Deah, of course. But I also looked forward to seeing others of my family too. I assumed

CHAPTER THIRTY-SEVEN

I would go visit them. But M'Deah had a certain outlook about out-of-town visitors that I assumed she got from her Southern upbringing. She expected family to come see me and my kids when we were in town visiting her from wherever we lived. Why? She said we had done the major travel of hundreds of miles. M'Deah said I shouldn't have to travel all the way from out of town and then go traipsing around Minnesota. She thought it rude that they not come see me in a single location known to all. Her part was not to be my taxi driver but to let them know when I was coming and how long I would be staying. Surely family in town could drive the few miles necessary to come see us. Not all saw that the same way she did. Results? Some very few came. Most didn't. So there are families I didn't see for many, many years, even though I was often in Minneapolis near where they were. It was disappointing.

Miracle Healings

After salvation, M'Deah experienced many healings. They're part of God's Plan and Provision for His people too. First, the migraines left. Were the doctors wrong to say they were caused by strands of her hair having been left in her brain as it was stitched together? Nothing was done physically to remove them. The headaches were no more.

M'Deah had damaged her back when lifting a patient onto the bed. She was told she had slipped discs in her back. The back pain she experienced was no more. This healing came uniquely through a one-time visit she had desired to make to Miracle Valley, the A.A. Allen ministry location. Her back was healed after prayer there in Arizona. Ironically, M'Deah had paid the cost for this trip of a busload of church members signed up to go. The church couldn't afford the cost, and she paid it with the understanding that she would be reimbursed. She never was fully. But she counted her healing worth it all. Although she had never stopped the gardening that she enjoyed so much, now she could do it comfortably. More to come.

Over the years, I learned that church envy and jealousy is a very real thing. Sadly. I believe M'Deah learned this sad lesson too—she learned it first before I did. I once expressed to her my deep admiration for an engaged couple who decided to dedicate their wedding to Jesus. I said, isn't that nice? M'Deah warned me to not judge only by peoples' words. Because we don't know what's in their hearts—their deep motivation for what they do. It could be pride. I knew she was right. We only see the outward, but God sees their heart. What looks pure to us may or may not be so. That's wisdom to realize the distinction.

A New Church

How new was it? So brand-new—it had never existed before! M'Deah and Mr. Steele used one of

CHAPTER THIRTY-SEVEN

the small commercial buildings they bought to begin a new church. It was called "Bread of Life Church." It was a non-denominational/independent Pentecostal church. I was surprised. M'Deah had previously joined another Pentecostal church that was very regimented in their traditions. During one recent service, the Lord had her observing the men on the church platform dressed in their regalia finery. He said, **"Dressed-up devils"**. That confirmed M'Deah's doubts about that particular church that had so much form and very little Godly function. When she shared this with Mr. Steele, he told her it had been a lifelong ambition of his to pastor a church. So, he became pastor and M'Deah was the assistant pastor. The church grew quickly. Its calling card was many miraculous signs and wonders—healings, prayers answered, dynamic praise and worship, etc. I was happy for them. When M'Deah told her mentor, Sis. Goode, she said that the correct order told her by the Lord is that M'Deah was to be pastor and Mr. Steele was to be her assistant—according to their depth of spiritual maturity and calling from God. Both had been taught that church tradition dictated that the man be in charge—and not the woman. So, they left it as it was begun. M'Deah also spoke at the church as assistant pastor and was very influential and effective.

My Other New Son

M'Deah and Mr. Steele had become pastors of their own church. When he came home at the end of the summer, Todd would tell me of his enjoyable times at church. Perry's sister, Helen, would allow their son, Kraig, to visit Minneapolis too. So, first-cousins Todd and Kraig were company for each other during their summer vacations and Helen too got a much-needed break. The two were the same age and became close.

I was not surprised in one sense, when 12-year old Todd came home to tell me he had gotten saved at Grandma's during the summer. In another sense, I was very surprised—my child knew God and I didn't! But I purposed to change that. And I knew M'Deah and Todd would be praying for me. About 25 years ago that M'Deah gave me life twice—once when I was born and once when I was born-again. Both were labors of love. Thank you, M'Deah! She encouraged Todd's help on the latter. I am eternally grateful to them both.

Todd's conversion prompted me to begin my own faith journey. I was on a mission to find God! It would take me two years.

There's More

I came to learn later that Mr. Steele had several children by many wives and women. Some were back in his home country of Jamaica. Some were in Kansas

CHAPTER THIRTY-SEVEN

City (I think) and some were in St. Paul where he had lived previously before meeting M'Deah. How many? I don't really know but I had the impression that it was about a dozen altogether. Though an absentee father, he knew the circumstances of all his children and was quick to give them a helping hand if asked. In fact, one of his sons, Gerald, lived with him and M'Deah for a while. It was to get armed for success as he attended school as an adult and worked. Gerald had practical skills too, like his dad. He once restored a vintage chest beautifully and meticulously

Linda

During this time, other things were happening too. Linda loved fashion in her teens and designed clothes and sewed them. She was a beautiful young lady and also did some rare minimal modeling. She even had a full-page spread in the Minneapolis Star-Tribune for a major downtown department store. M'Deah always dearly loved Linda and sent me the newspaper page of the ad

The Family Reunion

Once around the early 1990s, the Lawrence siblings had a family reunion gathering. But M'Deah was not invited! It hurt her deeply. And that treatment of my mother hurt me too. There was no justification for it at all, but they were all apparently in agreement for this behavior. Sadly. And that's family? Yes, it can be. There were times when all the women behaved as loving sisters. But it was mostly inconsistent until their later years.

I don't know how she did it. But M'Deah never responded to mistreating others as they mistreated her. And because she didn't, neither did I. It worked to her advantage. In the end, they loved her as she loved them. Only Auntie and Eloyce were sad to see her go when she later left Minneapolis for good in 2000. After 53 years being there. This kind of love M'Deah had was deep and genuine but not blind.

I don't know why M'Deah's sisters regarded her as the family football to be kicked around at will. But that often seemed to be their attitude. I never knew her to be anything but kind and loving towards them. Maybe that's why M'Deah was truly a good friend to a few women who were very good friends to her too. Years later, I heard an expression that described such friends: "ride or die" friends. She was blessed to have such and to be such. They included Mary, Connie, Sis Goode, Voncile, Hilda, Sister Wilson, Sister Mullins, Cynthia, and others I've forgotten.

I believe M'Deah lived this scripture below—long before I understood it.

> **1 Peter 2:1-3** 1 Therefore, **laying aside** *all malice, all deceit, hypocrisy, envy, and all evil speaking,* 2 *as newborn babes, desire the pure milk of the word, that you may grow thereby,* 3 *if indeed* **you have tasted that the Lord is gracious.**

CHAPTER THIRTY-SEVEN

An Unexpected Divorce

Sometime during this decade, an unexpected divorce happened in our family. M'Deah called one day to tell me that Carrie and Tommy had divorced. I was shocked. For one, our family didn't do that. For another, this couple seemed unlikely candidates for divorce! At least, that was my thinking. I don't pretend to know all the details. But it appears Tommy had waited until he retired, and both were of age to collect Social Security. They sold their house and split the proceeds evenly, although Tommy had made all the mortgage payments. He didn't want to leave Carrie destitute and still looked out for her. But he wanted his freedom. I remembered how he had endured Carrie's unending corrections and criticism for years and I couldn't blame him for wanting out. After the divorce was filed, he left Minneapolis and moved to California, surprisingly. That's where his sister lived. That was the end of his relationship with our family. As far as I know, none ever heard from him again.

Carrie was able to get a nice but modest apartment and lived comfortably and enjoyably the rest of her life. Not long after the divorce—maybe a couple of years—Carrie was diagnosed with terminal cancer. The sisters worked together for a plan for her care. M'Deah hired a young lady she knew to be a daily home aide for Carrie. She cooked all her meals, did housework, gave medications, etc. I don't know what the financial arrangements were. Certainly, Medicare didn't cover the cost. But M'Deah made sure the aide was always paid. And yet the other sisters gave constant complaints and criticism. There was no pleasing them. How M'Deah handled it all, I will never know. But Carrie left her inheritance to another one of her nieces—Eloyce's oldest daughter. Life happens. In very unexpected ways.

CHAPTER THIRTY-EIGHT

Onward and Upward!

Obviously, a lot more happened in our lives. And I may have to save its telling for another time. I can say, however, that Perry and I did indeed have two more children—a son (Scott) in 1971 and a daughter (Drunita) in 1974. So, just as my tea leaves read when I was 18, I gave birth to two sons and a daughter! Also, M'Deah moved to live with me and my family in D.C. in 2000. But the most significant thing in my life happened in 1976. It was after what I thought was a long journey. The journey began when our 12-year old son, Todd, came home from a Summer with Grandma as a born-again Christian. I couldn't have my child know God and I didn't! It was a challenge that I just had to overcome.

My Explorations

I wasn't alone in my explorations for God. M'Deah and I regularly exchanged letters and sometimes phone calls too. In every letter, she would include scripture for me—but she never flooded me or overwhelmed me with Bible verses. I always read it, of course—even if I didn't always understand it. I hadn't yet become a new believer. Along with the prayers of her and Todd, they eventually bore fruit though.

But before that a co-worker at Sears—my first DC job—invited me to join a group she belonged to. OKAY. She gave me information and I was impressed by two things: it was for special intellectuals and didn't require a belief in God. That was left up to you. As long as it didn't forbid belief in God, I was OKAY because I knew where I stood on that. And I thought I was a special intellectual—God had made me so. I joined, got the materials, and began this journey—this strange journey. I was introduced to learn of someone named Edgar Cayce and read his book. I knew the group believed in reincarnation. I didn't oppose that. It seemed reasonable that we'd have to go around more than once to become better people. I knew of the Hindu belief in reincarnation that forbade them mistreating any animal, in case it was your relative going through a reincarnation phase. If you did, you would pay for it in your own next phase. But it allowed people to even starve before eating one of these animals—which I thought utterly foolish. They didn't rightly value human life! But then the Rosicrucian teaching mentioned going through multiple phases of life on multiple planets—nine in all—and getting better each time, as you progressed toward perfection. Well, I knew of NO humans who were anywhere near perfection, so I rejected that! Otherwise, I thought I was OKAY to be a member.

CHAPTER THIRTY-EIGHT

There were regular Rosicrucian tasks to do. Fortunately, I had little time for them. I found it to be too much and tired of all the secrecy involved. No one else, even immediate family members, were to see any of the materials—they weren't Rosicrucian members. You were to leave instructions for the materials destruction after you died. And your family were still not to see them even then. I began to understand that I wasn't the special intellectual I once thought I'd been! Life experiences took care of that. I quit. I simply stopped paying the monthly dues and threw all the material away. I don't remember that I ever heard back from them.

I visited a few churches during my search period too. One was a Pentecostal church nearby. I knew of them because they had a choir that was somewhat famous. They had produced a song and album ("God Gave Me A Song") that I liked a lot, which was led by their choir director, Myrna Summers. So, I visited them one Sunday by myself. They were very legalistic. I was strangely offered what they said was a lap cloth at the door when I entered. I had no idea what it was for—it made no sense to me. I observed others and learned its purpose was to cover my lap and legs for when I sat down in my dress. Also, I habitually wore just a touch of a very light shade of lipstick at that time—nothing bold. I unmistakably felt the unfriendly stares because of that. As a visitor, I didn't feel welcome and loved at all! And I thought, if that's how you treat visitors who might want to join your church, did you treat your members any better? I never went back.

Another church I visited was because of an invitation from a co-worker. It was Baptist. The sermon was good, I thought. But the congregation was silent. There were few/no "amens" throughout the whole service. They were NOT encouraged to say anymore! This was mostly an older congregation. I decided that a church where even the old people didn't say "amen" was too cold for me. I never went back there either.

Another co-worker invited me to an event her church was having that wasn't just a regular service. It was a bunch of choirs that would be singing separately. I liked music, so it sounded like fun. Besides, it being a Pentecostal church, the choirs were sure to be good quality. I bought a ticket from her and so did several other co-workers. We decided to make it a group event. As we entered the church, a member was exiting and spoke to us. Her greeting was, "Praise the Lord!" I responded in the coldest, most formal voice I could muster and said, "Good evening". It would be rude of me to say nothing, but I also didn't want her to feel comfortable enough to say anything further. But I couldn't help but wonder, "WHY did she say that and why would anyone say that?" Her behavior struck me. It was weird but it was also real. It provoked me to continue my search. Inside, the music was good, the atmosphere was show-offy, and it lasted for more than four hours. Enough already.

Christian TV

I also had Christian TV to accompany me on my journey of searching for God. I had just recently begun to watch Christian TV in 1974, and I continued to do so. It was all new to me. I regularly watched TV so God wisely used that, as I watched certain programs. Surely, I could find God too, even though I wasn't at my mother's church—or any church. My TV watching was mainly the Christian Broadcasting Network (CBN's) The 700 Club with hosts Pat Robertson and Ben Kinchlow. I remember Jim Bakker was host for a short while. I also watched Oral Roberts, Rex Humbard, Jerry Falwell, etc. The last two were "new guys" to me. I included a few Billy Graham crusades in the mix.

Being logical (and quasi/pseudo intellectual), I also watched a program by a professor at the American University. He had a panel weekly of Christians from various Catholic and Protestant denominations—men and women. He ended every program on Sunday with a prayer for the viewing audience: "May God guide you in your search for His Truth". That's what I needed and what I wanted! I was in agreement with that prayer and saw it as my journey guide. It was a specific prayer that would protect me for what was real, I believed.

Leaning on my own intellect, it took me TWO YEARS to "find God!" Someone on a program explained once that we didn't need to "find God" because He wasn't lost! We were lost and He was doing all He could to lead us to Him! I accepted that as Truth and my search finally ended. Thankfully.

During my searching time, I heard a radio announcement that a pastor from elsewhere was visiting a church in D.C. I had heard this pastor on the radio enough to be familiar with his name: Fred Price. The church he was visiting was near where I worked. I thought I could go there one evening after work. And I did. It was a fairly new church that was located in an old neighborhood movie theater. Okay. I remember that I enjoyed the service. Afterwards, those seeking to know the Lord were invited to remain for their questions to be answered in personal ministry to them. I decided to stay and to ask the one question that stymied me. How could I honestly say the sinner's prayer seeing that I was morally good? The woman who ministered to me was very patient with my foolishness. She showed me in her Bible and had me read for myself:

> ***Romans 3:23*** *for all have sinned and fall short of the glory of God,*
> ***I John 1: 8-10*** *If we say that we have no sin, we deceive ourselves, and the truth is not in us. 9 If we confess our sins, He is faithful and just to forgive us our sins and to*

CHAPTER THIRTY-EIGHT

cleanse us from all unrighteousness. 10 If we say that we have not sinned, we make Him a liar, and His word is not in us.

Wow. That certainly seemed to include me. And I was certainly too polite to call God a liar! So, He must be right. I was a sinner. But I still couldn't quite say the sinner's prayer! So I took a few more days to think about it. I tried to think of things I'd done to identify me as a sinner. I went over the list of the 10 Commandments. I was morally good because I was so inclined and taught. And I didn't ever want to do anything that M'Deah might be punished for by K.C. Oh, oh. I did find one I might be guilty of committing. Lying. But did those small childhood lies count? They were necessary lies—to keep me from getting in trouble! I decided that they did count. So, I concluded that I was a sinner. The only out for me was to say the sinner's prayer. To agree with God.

Journey Over!

So, after two years of searching for Him, God found ME! One day in my living room in Spring 1976, I decided "That's it!". I said the "sinner's prayer" with Pat Robertson on The 700 Club. What is that? It's a simple prayer you sincerely mean that basically says you AGREE with God about your current state (lost without Him) and ID (sinner) and that you accept His remedy for that: salvation by belief in His

Son Jesus Christ Who died and rose again to forgive ALL your sins forever and to make you a member of God's Family. That's Redemption. Oh. And you request to be filled with Holy Spirit, as the 120 believers were on the Day of Pentecost in Acts 2. Some question if this latter is needed, but why would you refuse any Gift from God? Plus, Jesus said we needed this. (Luke 24:49) I was 35 years old when I made this decision to believe in salvation through Jesus and to have a personal relationship with God—I KNEW it was the right decision. I was convinced that God was greater and smarter than I was. I could believe in Someone like that! I made the choice. I decided to agree with God that I was indeed a sinner. I chose to disagree with the enemy liar that I was morally good and that was good enough. No. It was years before I learned that faith and believing are simply to agree with God. It reminds me that God told us millennia ago what to choose in Deuteronomy 30:19-20: Choose LIFE! Simple Truth.

I said something else to the Lord too from somewhere deep inside me, something new came out. "God, I want ALL You have for me—whatever it is!" I had never had such a hunger and desire before. Later, I read a verse that sorta explained it to me. I would understand it later. (Matthew 5:6)

One instruction for those accepting salvation and being born-again was to TELL someone about it as soon as you could. I called and told M'Deah. She was

CHAPTER THIRTY-EIGHT

so happy for me that I was now finally saved! Now, we both were and we had more in common than ever before in life. About 25 years ago, the Lord had me realize that she had given birth to me TWICE: once in the natural via childbirth and again in the spiritual via re-birth to become a new creation! I also had Todd's help on the latter. I am eternally grateful to them both. Wonderful.

Before salvation, I thought God was harsh and Jesus was nice. Who was this God I'm giving my life to? God seems to be the Big One in charge and Jesus is His Subordinate to do God's will on Earth. It was confusing. Yes, God COULD be Good. He had Noah build the Ark, opened the Red Sea to rescue His people, sent manna in the wilderness to feed them, closed the lion's mouths to save Daniel, helped David kill Goliath, kept Joseph safe, and so many other things. Best of all, He sent us Jesus. But God could be harsh too. He sent 10 plagues to Egypt, He drowned pharaoh's army in the Red Sea, He wiped out whole enemy armies, He drowned all outside the Ark, and so much more. And Good Jesus healed people, died for all sinners on the Cross, fed multitudes, etc. The Holy Spirit was mostly Good, but caused Ananias and Sapphira to die for lying to Him. It wasn't at all clear Who God was. I learned I was to give my life to Jesus though and that was okay with me. And like Him, I would submit to God Who is the Big Boss. His Holy Spirit would help me in life. And the reward would be NO hell for me in eternity. It was surely a Good choice—the right choice. Once I learned that to make NO choice was to choose hell by default, I could reasonably make no other choice! And over the years I learned more about God: that He IS Good and that He IS Love! More than that, He is FOR me and not against me! (Romans 8:31-32, 1 John 4:7-8)

I had thought there were measures of sinners—some were bad and some not so bad. I didn't know we sinners were all equally dead. That's the same condition for all without God.

Do you question/criticize/mock/challenge/mock God as YOUR Creator?! You don't know God—you have NO idea of Who He really is. How then can you walk together?! You don't even agree on the basic reality: Who God is. Thus it's impossible to know who you are—no matter how long and how much you search. It's all in vain. You deny yourself any way to have the Abundant Life that Jesus SAID He came to give us (which I chose fully years later). I concluded rightly that HE is God and I am NOT! (John 10:10)

John 3:16 was one of the obvious scriptures I devoured. I once thought the world was Creation—Earth, trees, animals, etc.—not man himself. When I learned that to God 'world' meant those created in His image and likeness, I saw this verse personally. "For God so loved ME that He gave His only begotten Son so that if I would believe on Him I would have everlasting life." It was a life changer. After 35 years on Earth, I finally had a personal relationship with God Almighty. Wow. It only gets better from here!

Holy Spirit Baptism

A few weeks after my salvation experience in my living room, I heard a radio announcement that Fred Price was coming again for another speaking engagement at the same theater church I had attended before. I purposed to go. For one thing, I wanted the woman who had ministered to me to know that I had indeed come around to realizing that I was a sinner and had accepted the Lord as my Savior. Plus, I wanted whatever else the Lord had for me there. Listening to The 700 Club and other Christian radio, I knew there was something called the "baptism of the Holy Spirit". I had heard explanations on Christian radio programs that Holy Spirit inhabits us at salvation—we have Him. But baptism in Holy Spirit is when He has US. It involved a deeper relationship with God and included His gift of speaking in tongues—a Heavenly language between you and your God that builds you up as His Family member. I knew M'Deah believed it and spoke in tongues. Jesus recommended it (Acts 1:4-9) and I wanted it. Remember, I had told God I wanted ALL He had for me! And I meant it. I don't recall the sermon Pastor Price preached. But afterwards, an invitation was made for all those wanting to receive this baptism to remain behind and we were sent to another room. There were about half a dozen of us. Someone taught us briefly about this Gift from God. There was also an organ and organist there and we sang a worship song. Then we were told not to focus on speaking in English because it's impossible to speak in two languages at once. Then we proceeded and received this new baptism! I was surprised to hear words coming from me that I had not thought or learned. I don't remember all that was said but I do remember suddenly speaking in tongues slowly and then rapidly with a rush of unknown words! It wasn't just a few syllables as sometimes happens, but with a whole language! It was voluminous—a waterfall outpouring that went on for about 15 minutes. I was happy and talking and crying at the same time. It felt great— as though a dam had been broken and I was saying to God a lifetime of words that had been formerly blocked up. Now they were coming out from my very most inner being—from the new and real saved me. It was very refreshing and freeing! It opened up a whole new wonderful world to me!

Now?

What is my life attitude? I'm happy to be alive! That has been my belief and attitude ever since my survival of the murder attack from Buster which I knew was only a miracle of God. After Buster it took a lot to annoy me. I now put petty grievances into

CHAPTER THIRTY-EIGHT

perspective. Compared to nearly being murdered, it ain't no big thing. I was far less selfish than before. That new attitude has lasted a lifetime. It only solidified when I realized God had protected me from death at the hands of K.C. too! Like every life, I have had great joys and great hurts and disappointments, pleasure and pain. But nothing has shaken me off my life attitude: I'm happy and thankful to be alive. That has helped me to face and handle any circumstances and any times of pain. I thank my God for giving me that attitude. Before I reached my 40s, a LOT had happened to me in life. I could have blamed all that for who it caused me to be. It was easy to do. And sometimes I did. Or I could be thankful for all I'd survived! Most times, that was my attitude. I thank God for that! Gradually, that became my total life attitude. It truly makes a difference to how you approach and handle life's challenges. I recognize that I've not had a lucky life. But I have had a very blessed life. That only comes from God. It began with him giving me M'Deah. And I'm very thankful to Him for all my many added blessings.

And for M'Deah and me? Our journey continues! But the telling of it is for another time.

THE END

M'Deah and me and my Godmother, Aunt Mary Jane. 1941

Billy and me in Minneapolis. 1947.

My high school graduation photo. 1959

Billy's high school graduation photo. 1961

Billy walking me down the aisle. 1960

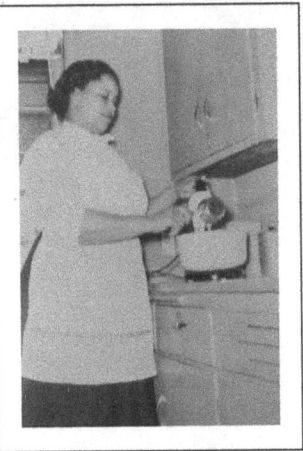

M'Deah in her happy time the Christmas K.C. went to Mississippi alone.

The famous Lawrence family photo with Big Mama and her kids 1947—M'Deah is second from the right.

Perry and me in the car on our wedding day. 1960

Perry and me at the wedding reception in M'Deah's house on Logan. 1960

www.ingramcontent.com/pod-product-compliance
Lightning Source LLC
Chambersburg PA
CBHW011955150426
43200CB00016B/2910